DETROIT PUBLIC LIBRARY
3 5674 00642734 9
W9-BWR-875

THE STATE OF THE EARTH ATLAS

DETROIT PUBLIC LIBRARY

Business, Science & Technology

DATE DUE

AUG - 7 1993

FEB 1 8 1997

BST

THE STATE OF THE EARTH ATLAS

Edited by Joni Seager

A Pluto Project

A Touchstone Book
Published by Simon & Schuster Inc.
New York London Toronto Sydney Tokyo Singapore

333.70223
S797

AUG 20 1990 '91 C.3

TOUCHSTONE/SIMON AND SCHUSTER
Simon & Schuster Building
Rockefeller Center
1230 Avenue of the Americas
New York, New York 10020

Text copyright © 1990 by Joni Seager
Maps and graphics © 1990 by Swanston Publishing Ltd., Derby

All rights reserved
including the right of reproduction
in whole or in part in any form.

TOUCHSTONE, SIMON AND SCHUSTER and colophon
are registered trademarks of Simon & Schuster Inc.

Simultaneously published in Great Britain
by Unwin Hyman Limited,
15–17 Broadwick Street, London W1V 1FP

Edited and coordinated by Anne Benewick

Design by Grundy & Northedge, London
Artwork by James Mills-Hicks, Andrea Fairbrass, Jacqueline Land
and Jeanne Radford for Swanston Graphics Ltd., Derby

Printed and bound in Hong Kong
by Mandarin Offset International (HK) Ltd.

This book is printed on paper made from pulp from Finland and
Sweden. It comes from managed forest, where the rate of replanting
means that timber stocks are rising.

10 9 8 7 6 5 4 3 2 1
10 9 8 7 6 5 4 3 2 Pbk.

Library of Congress Cataloging in Publication Data

The state of the earth atlas.

"Simultaneously published in Great Britain by Unwin Hyman Limited"—
Verso t.p.
"A Pluto Project."
Includes bibliographical references and index.
Contents: Habitat earth—Food and water—Shelter—Energy—Industry—
Defence—Consuming tastes—Green politics.
1. Man—Influence on nature—Maps. 2. Natural resources—Maps.
I. Seager, Joni.

G1046.G3S4 1990 333.7'0223 90-675120

ISBN 0-671-70523-7

ISBN 0-671-70524-5 (A Touchstone Book: pbk.)

CONTENTS

INTRODUCTION 11

1 A GLOBAL GREENHOUSE 16

HABITAT EARTH

2 A POPULAR PLANET 18
3 A SHRINKING WORLD 20
4 CUTTING OUR ROOTS 22
5 RAINFOREST 24

FOOD AND WATER

6 DRINKING WATER 26
7 HUNGER AND PLENTY 28
8 LIVING OFF THE LAND 30
9 THE CHEMICAL FIX 32
10 SHRINKING GENES 34
11 LOSING GROUND 36
12 FISHING FOR FOOD 38

SHELTER

13 CITY SPRAWL 40
14 COASTAL CRISIS 42
15 WASTE 44
16 SEWAGE 46
17 AIR QUALITY 48

ENERGY

18 ENERGY BUDGETS 50
19 THE NUCLEAR FAMILY 52
20 HYDRO POWER 54
21 FIREWOOD 56
22 OIL POLLUTION 58
23 FOSSIL FUEL POLLUTION 60
24 ACID RAIN 62

INDUSTRY

25 INDUSTRIAL WASTE 64
26 DEADLY INDUSTRY 66
27 TOXIC TRADE 68
28 HOLES IN THE SKY 70

DEFENCE

29 WAR-WASTED LANDS 72
30 NUCLEAR BLIGHT 74

CONSUMING TASTES

31 AUTO CULTURE 76
32 TOURIST TRAPS 78
33 THE WILD TRADE 80
34 HUNTING 82
35 THE TIMBER TRADE 84
36 PAYING THE PRICE 86

GREEN POLITICS

37 A CLASH OF INTERESTS 88
INTERNATIONAL TABLE 90

COMMENTARY 99

INDEX 125

EDITOR

JONI SEAGER is a Canadian geographer, currently living in the United States. She is a lecturer at the Massachusetts Institute of Technology and a member of the New Words feminist book collective. She is the co-author of *Women in the World: An International Atlas* and author of *Earth Follies: Making Feminist Sense of the Global Environment* (forthcoming).

ACKNOWLEDGEMENTS

For their assistance in providing information for individual maps, we would like to thank the following:

Hayward R. Alker, Jr., Massachusetts Institute of Technology, Cambridge, Mass.; Carl Bartone, World Bank, Washington DC; Margaret Bluman, London; Steven Broad, World Conservation Monitoring Centre, Cambridge, UK; Marva Coates, Food and Agriculture Organization, Washington DC; Peter Cebon, Massachusetts Institute of Technology, Cambridge, Mass.; Mark Davis, London; Stephen Davis, World Conservation Monitoring Centre, Surrey, UK; Cynthia Enloe, Clark University, Worcester, Mass.; Environmental Project on Central America (EPOCA); Joe Farman, British Antarctic Survey, Cambridge, UK; Paula Ferguson, Massachusetts Institute of Technology, Cambridge, Mass.; Hilary French, Worldwatch Institute, Washington DC; John Gille, National Center for Atmospheric Research, Colorado; Rupert Hastings, Royal Botanic Gardens, Surrey, UK; Norbert Henninger, World Resources Institute, Washington DC; Richard Hosier, University of Pennsylvania; Carol Inskipp, Worldwide Fund for Nature, Surrey, UK; Jodi Jacobson, Worldwatch Institute, Washington DC; Judy Johnson, Environmental Protection Agency, Washington DC; Peter Kearns, Department of the Environment, UK; Victoria Lane, Somerville, Mass.; Nick Lenssen, Worldwatch Institute, Washington DC; Christine Leon, World Conservation Monitoring Centre, Surrey, UK; Robert Mason, Temple University, Philadelphia; Alison McCusker, International Board for Plant Genetic Resources, Rome; Christine McGowan, Advisory Committee on Genetic Manipulation, UK; Arthur McKenzie, Tanker Advisory Center, New York City; Maldives Services Ltd, London; Norman Myers; Nature Conservancy Council, Data Support for Education Service, Peterborough, UK; Sam Ozolins, World Health Organization, Geneva; Steve Parcels, Natural Resources Defense Council, New York City; Bonnie Ram, Washington DC; Scott Saleska, Institute for Energy and Environmental Research, Takoma Park, Maryland; Cindy Pollock Shea, Worldwatch Institute, Washington DC; Seth Shulman, Science for the People, Cambridge, Mass.; Teresa Squires, American Cancer Society; Koy Thompson, Friends of the Earth, UK; World Action on Recycling Materials for Energy from Rubbish (WARMER), Tunbridge Wells, UK; Worldwide Fund for Nature, Data Support for Education Service, Surrey, UK; Worldwide Fund for Nature International, Switzerland.

INTRODUCTION

Concern is the catalyst that shapes this atlas. We share with many the belief that habitat earth, in the late 20th century, is in growing trouble. This is not really news; as the media, advertisers and even industry take up the 'green' cause, this unsettling assessment can scarcely have escaped the attention of many.

And yet much information about environmental matters remains confined to the privileged domain of specialists. Our purpose in undertaking this atlas is to translate specialist information into a form that can be more widely appreciated. As environmental consciousness grows to a popular groundswell, we need to be able to make sense of the mass of facts bombarding us from our newspapers and television screens. The need for a coherent overview of the state of the earth has never been greater, particularly so for information presented in an accessible and engaging manner.

In this atlas, we use the fact of environmental crisis not as an endpoint, but as the place from which to begin further enquiry. Not all parts of the global environment and not all places in the world are in the same state of distress. We ask where threats exist to a greater or lesser degree, and why they are so distributed. Most of the deterioration in our environment is the direct or indirect consequence of particular human arrangements of economic and political power, superimposed on vulnerable ecological systems. Not all economies nor all cultures, however, impose the same burdens on the environmental equilibrium. This atlas seeks to identify where such threats originate and why, indeed, they do so.

We encompass the state of the earth as broadly as possible. Thus, we offer information on issues that may already be familiar to many, such as ozone depletion, tropical rainforest destruction, and the plague of oil spills. But we also extend our reach to include topics that have received less popular attention, such as tourism, car culture, wetlands loss, and the international trade in tropical timber and in wildlife.

A primary truth of environmentalism is that everything is connected. The web of life is seamless, and the consequences of disruption to one part of the ecosystem ripple throughout the whole: soil erosion in the Himalayas contributes to massive flooding in Bangladesh, the deforestation of the Amazon may alter the atmospheric balance over the whole globe, and chemicals and gases produced in the richer industrial countries are destroying the ozone layer that protects everyone, rich and poor alike.

This interconnectedness makes it an excercise of frustration to arrange environmental topics in a clearly demarcated, apparently logical sequence. It should be understood that both sections and subject sequence in this atlas are largely artificial. The topics we have chosen are essentially part of a synergistic whole, wherein as much information can be gleaned from drawing comparisons and contrasts between maps as from studying them individually. The use of maps does, at least, facilitate such cross-referencing; continuities and contrasts become visible patterns on the page; threads of similarity and difference weave their way through the book.

It is a startling fact, which this atlas makes clear, that much environmental degradation transcends traditional economic and political boundaries. Environmental problems are much the same in centrally-controlled Communist states and 'free market' capitalist ones, in people's republics and diehard monarchies. The residents of Beijing and Paris suffer much the same levels of sulphur dioxide poisoning in the air they breathe; the impact of soil erosion is much the same whether in Jamaica or the USA; per head of population, Saudi Arabia, the UK and the USSR emit similar levels of carbon dioxide into the world's atmosphere; both the Aral Sea and the North Sea are dying because of the misplaced priorities of governments and industries, East and West.

When trying to make sense of environmental issues, the conventional way of conceptualizing world divisions by political boundaries seems inadequate. Dividing the world into communist and capitalist states, or free market and state-controlled economies, is of limited value in explaining the environmental state of the earth. More useful connections can be made between those countries that are fossil-fuel dependent and those that are hydro-dependent; or between those with and without tropical rainforest; or between those that produce CFCs and those that do not. By creating new links and categories of explanation in this atlas, we enable alliances to be reconceptualized: the USA and USSR have more in common than not, and the biggest blocs of environmental alliance are among rich and industrial nations and among poor and non-industrial ones.

New alliances based on environmental affinities and commonalities are already forming and will shape environmental politics into the next century. In 1989, the Maldives government hosted the first 'Small States Conference on Sea Level Rise', bringing together oceanic states that will be the first affected by global warming; in the late 1980s, a number of caucuses of poorer countries, including meetings of the Non-Aligned States, the Economic Community of West African States, and the Organization of African Unity, passed resolutions calling on industrialized countries to halt toxic waste dumping; and the '30 percent Club' has brought together those countries of Western Europe committed to cooperate in reducing sulphur dioxide emissions, the major cause of acid rain.

Certainly the weight of evidence underscores the responsibility of rich states for many of the global environmental problems we now face: the loss of animal, bird and plant species, fossil fuel pollution, the production and use of ozone-depleting chemicals, the ocean pollution that comes with oil dependency, the sulphur dioxide emissions that destroy forests and lakes, the stripping of tropical forests for timber and cattle-ranch farming - to name but a few. The catalogue of problems caused by the voracious resource appetites of the rich is almost overwhelming and the by-products are fouling our environment. The rich industrial world is stripping the earth of resources and in the course of so doing is generating enormous quantities of effluent and pollution that burden global ecosystems.

Rich countries continue to enhance their wealth by expanding their resource reach beyond their own borders while frequently exporting their problems. Having stripped their own forests, they are turning to timber-plundering in former colonies; choking on a glut of municipal, household and industrial garbage, they seek to ship away their waste to small Pacific islands or debt-strapped countries in Africa. But this is a small planet: there are limited resource frontiers to exploit - and there is no 'away'. There is no safe place to store carcinogenic chemicals, nuclear waste or the toxic by-products of industry. There is no safe way of dispersing CFCs or many of the other harmful gases being vented into the atmosphere. There are limits to global tolerance.

The global scale of this atlas makes powerful generalizations about the responsibilities of the rich world. It is less able to expose the local examples of environmental degradation that are all around us. Yet the destruction of wildlife habitat, the pollution of waterways and fuelwood scarcity – to name but a few issues – are often at their most serious at a regional or site-specific level.

On this smaller scale, it is important to recognize that the role of individuals in influencing environmental fates is mediated by, among other factors, gender, class, ethnicity and religion. Men and women, for example, have different relationships to the large institutions – governments, militaries, industrial corporations – that hold the balance of power on environmental issues. Similarly, the implications and experience of environmental decay are often different for men and women, rich and poor, elites and disenfranchized. Within a country, region or city, environmental degradation will be experienced differently, and more direly, by poor people living in slums with limited access to safe water, food and health care, than wealthier people insulated from environmental problems by their privilege.

The maps in this atlas inevitably focus on the physical form of environmental problems. With this in mind, in the Commentary to the maps (see page 99*ff*) we have tried wherever possible to discuss social, political and gender issues.

There are important environmental issues that, for one reason or another, do not appear in this atlas. Mining, perhaps because it includes a wide range of activities, defied our concept of global mapping even though it is a universally destructive enterprise, causing land degradation, pollution from tailings, chemical leaching, deforestation and landscape scarring. Although car culture and its concomitant air pollution are both included, the increasing density of road networks is omitted, for lack of appropriate global statistics. For similar reasons we do not map the spread of industrialization, the displacement of subsistence agriculture by cash cropping and luxury foods, the increasing numbers of environmental refugees, or grassroots mobilization to confront environmental problems.

Global information-gathering technology is proliferating. At the same time, access to and control of information is becoming more privatized. Full disclosure of environmental problems does not necessarily serve the purposes of the industries and governments that gather most environmental data. Without the untiring work of independent environmental groups such as the World Resources Institute, Greenpeace, Friends of the Earth and other international, national and community-based groups, we would know even less than we do about the state of the earth. We would like to think that this atlas will support and contribute to their efforts. An informed citizenry is the world's best hope.

The creation of this atlas drew on the goodwill and good sense of many dozens of individuals. I extend elsewhere our collective thanks to those who provided assistance with particular maps. I wish to single out for appreciation here a few brave souls who gave encouragement, criticism and invaluable support through every stage of this project. My greatest debt is to Anne Benewick, whose keen eye and wit shaped this project from its very beginning, and who shepherded it through all the editorial and production stages from mere doodles on paper to finished artwork and text. David Pratt made a valuable contribution in the formative stages of the project and Grundy & Northedge added their fine and distinctive design style. Swanston Graphics proved stellar, true to form, and an editor could not ask for a more competent and pleasant production and support team. Two project advisers, John Baines in the UK and Jeanne Kasperson of the Center for Technology, Environment & Development at Clark University, assisted in the early conceptualization of the project and, in particular, helped to assemble our research team.

Cynthia Enloe's unwavering support sustained me throughout the year-and-a-half that this atlas took over my life, and I have drawn heavily on her analytical acuity to steer a course through the intellectual maze of trying to make sense of the state of the earth. My colleagues in the New Words collective – Gilda Bruckman, Mary Lowry, Doris Reisig, Kate Rushin and Laura Zimmerman – tolerated my more-than-usual eccentricities and accommodated my absences with good humour.

The compilation of the research for this atlas was a collaborative effort in which I was aided by an able team of contributors who each provided not only specialist knowledge and timely insight, but a sense of camaraderie and shared purpose. The strength of this atlas rests on the firm research foundation which they built, map by map. For any errors that slipped into the presentation of their research, or for the liberties that I may have taken in its interpretation, I take sole responsibility.

Joni Seager
Somerville, Massachusetts
April 1990

Copyright © Swanston Publishing Limited

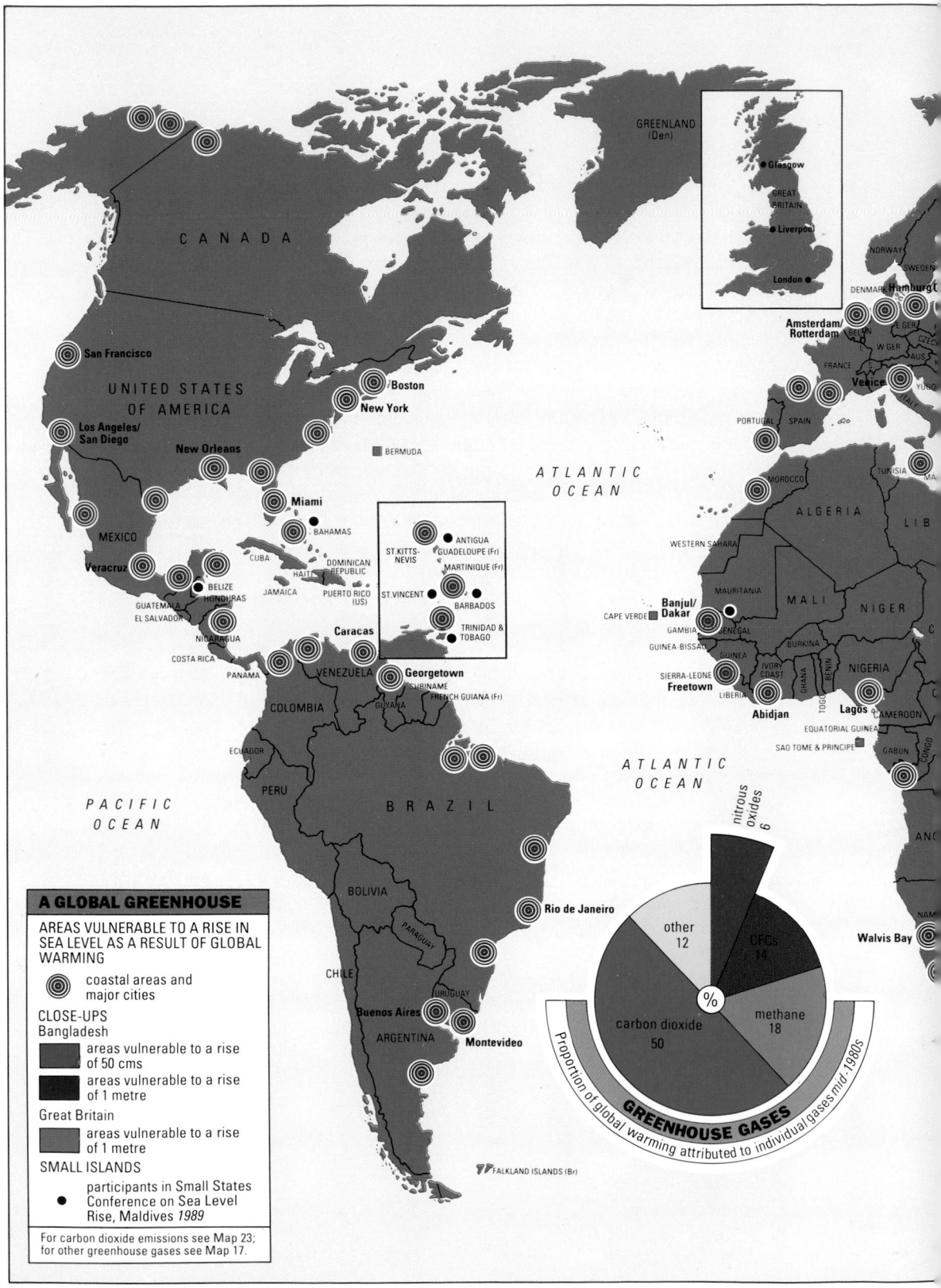

Data compiled by Nigel Dudley Main sources: National Center for Atmospheric Research/National Science Foundation; World Resources Institute (1988); Hansen (1988).

Present evidence of global warming is controversial, but the implications could be so severe that the threat must be taken seriously.

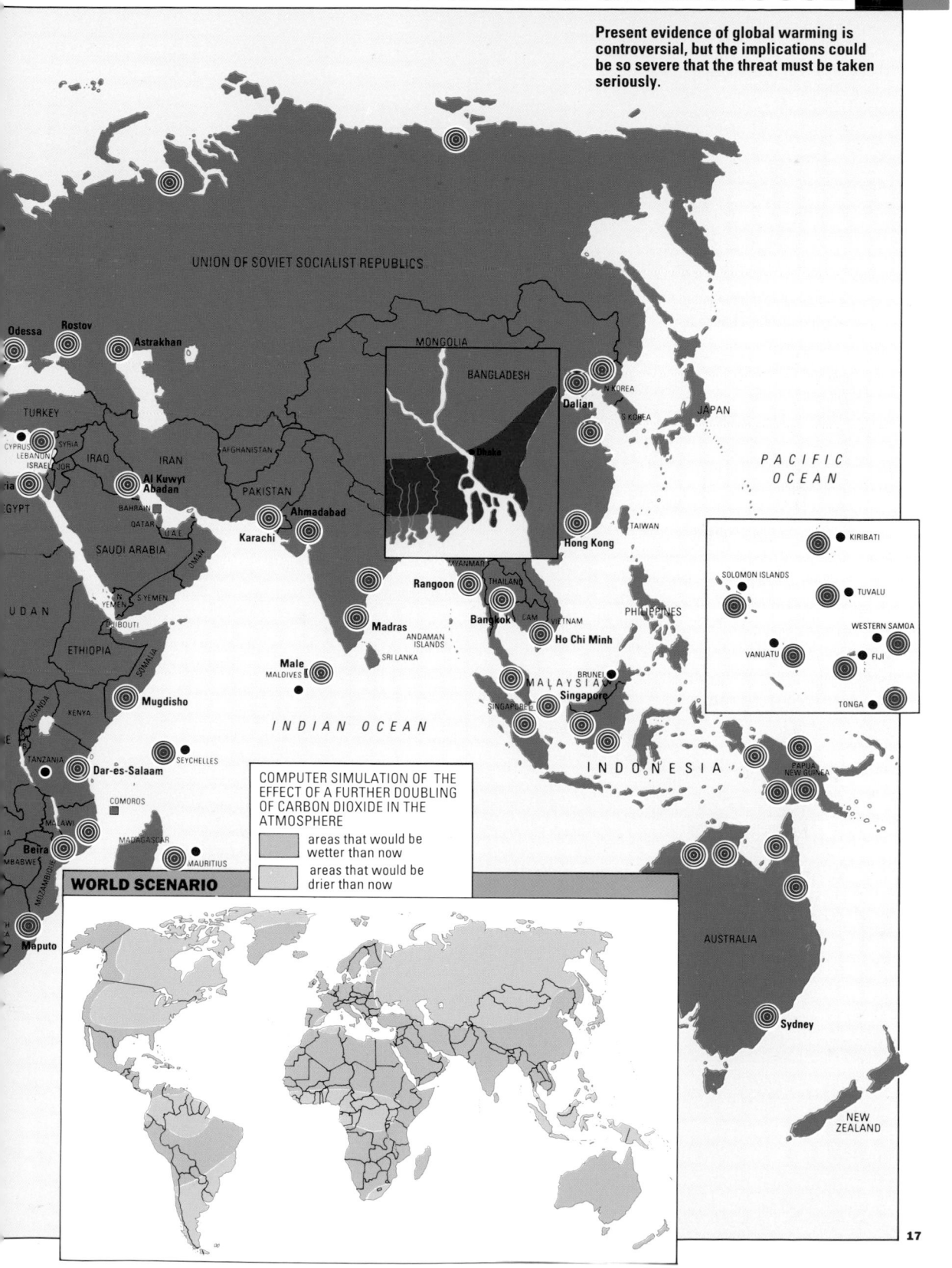

Copyright © Swanston Publishing Limited

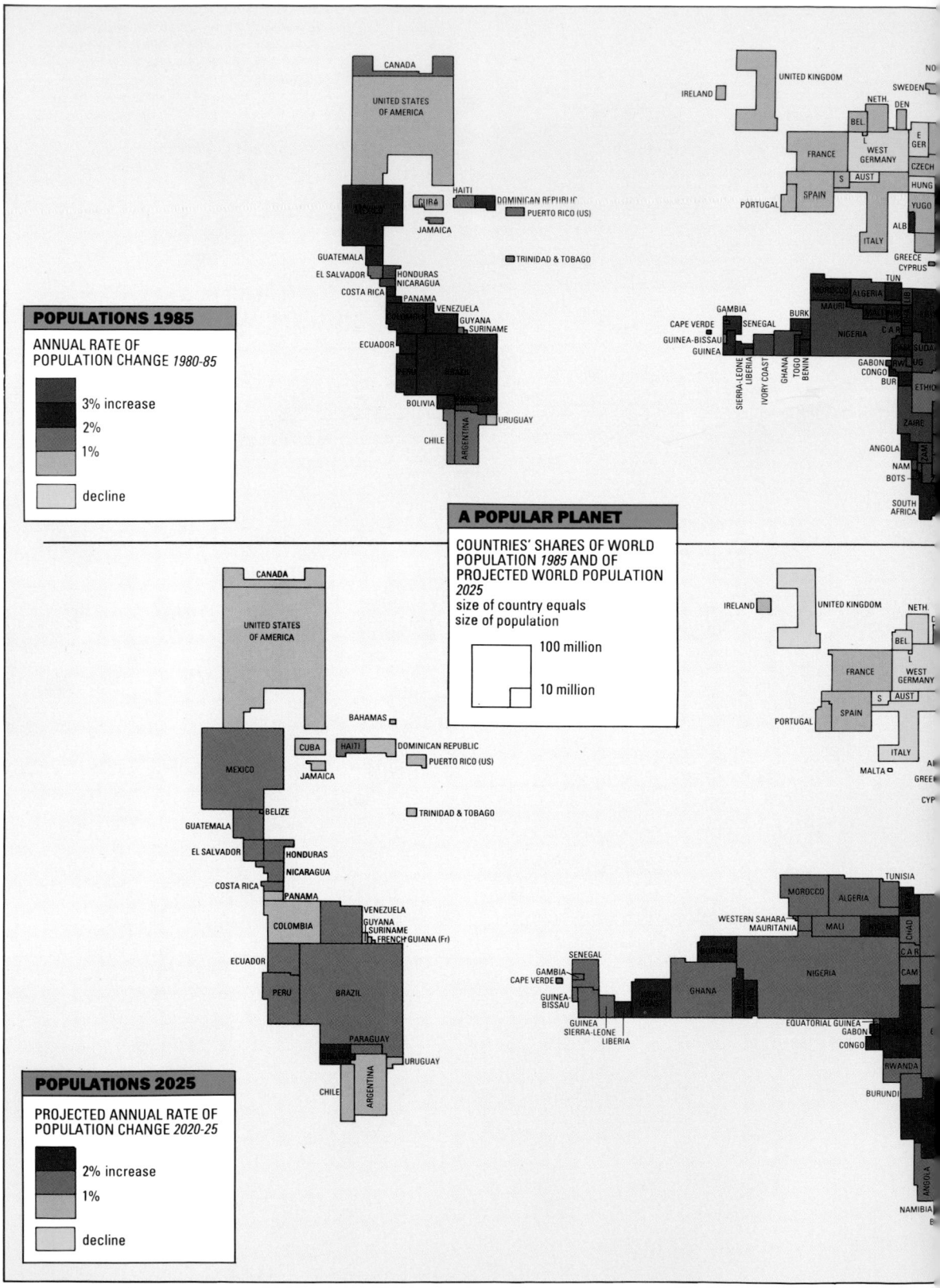

Data compiled by Michael Steinitz Main sources: UN *World Population Prospects* (1988).

The average person in the 'developed' world consumes 10 times as much energy and one-and-a-half times as much food – and produces 16 times as much air pollution – as the average person in the 'developing' world. The deterioration of the global environment has less to do with population growth than with industrial economies and priorities.

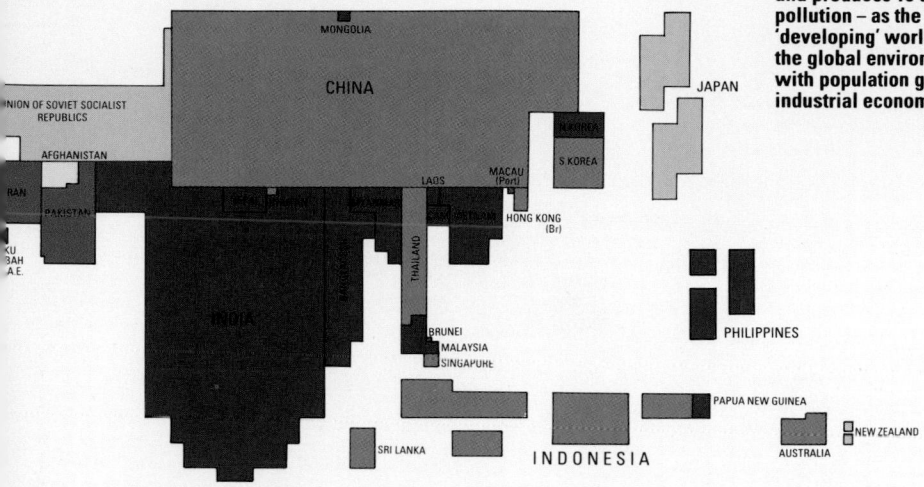

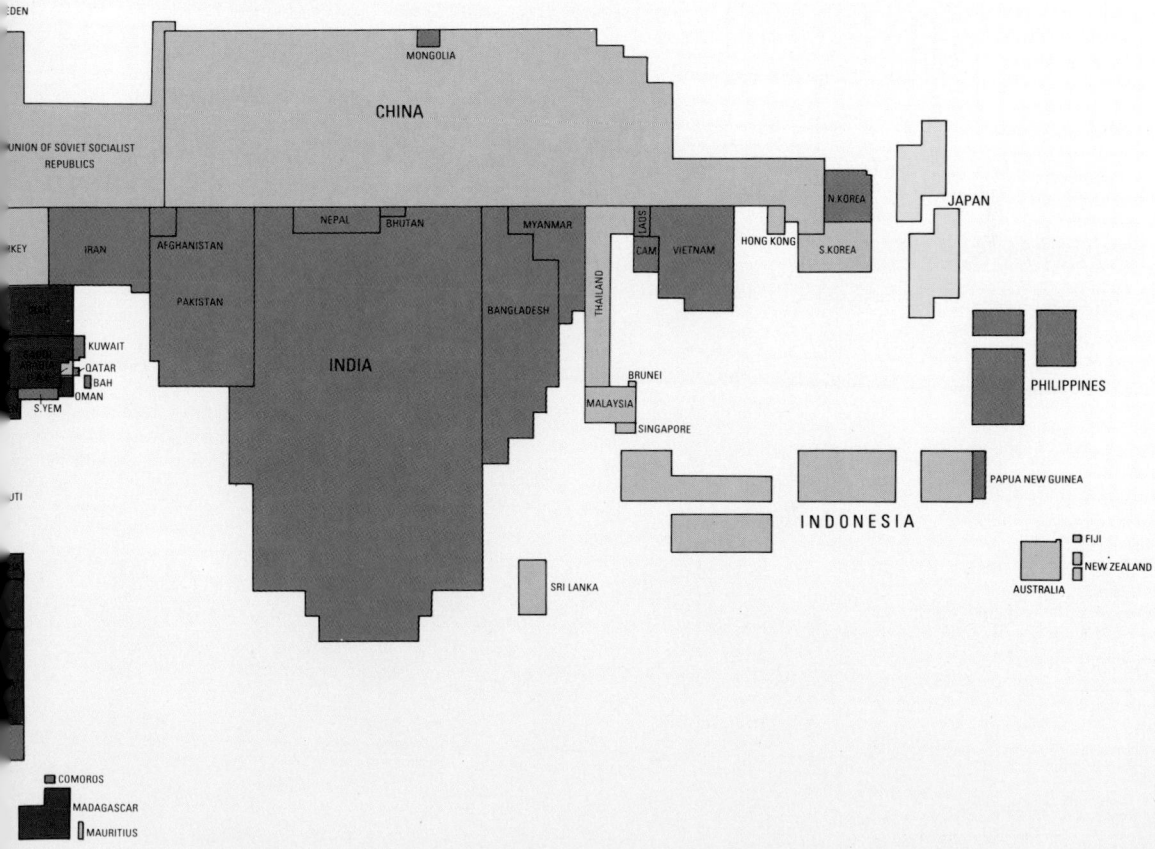

Copyright © Swanston Publishing Limited

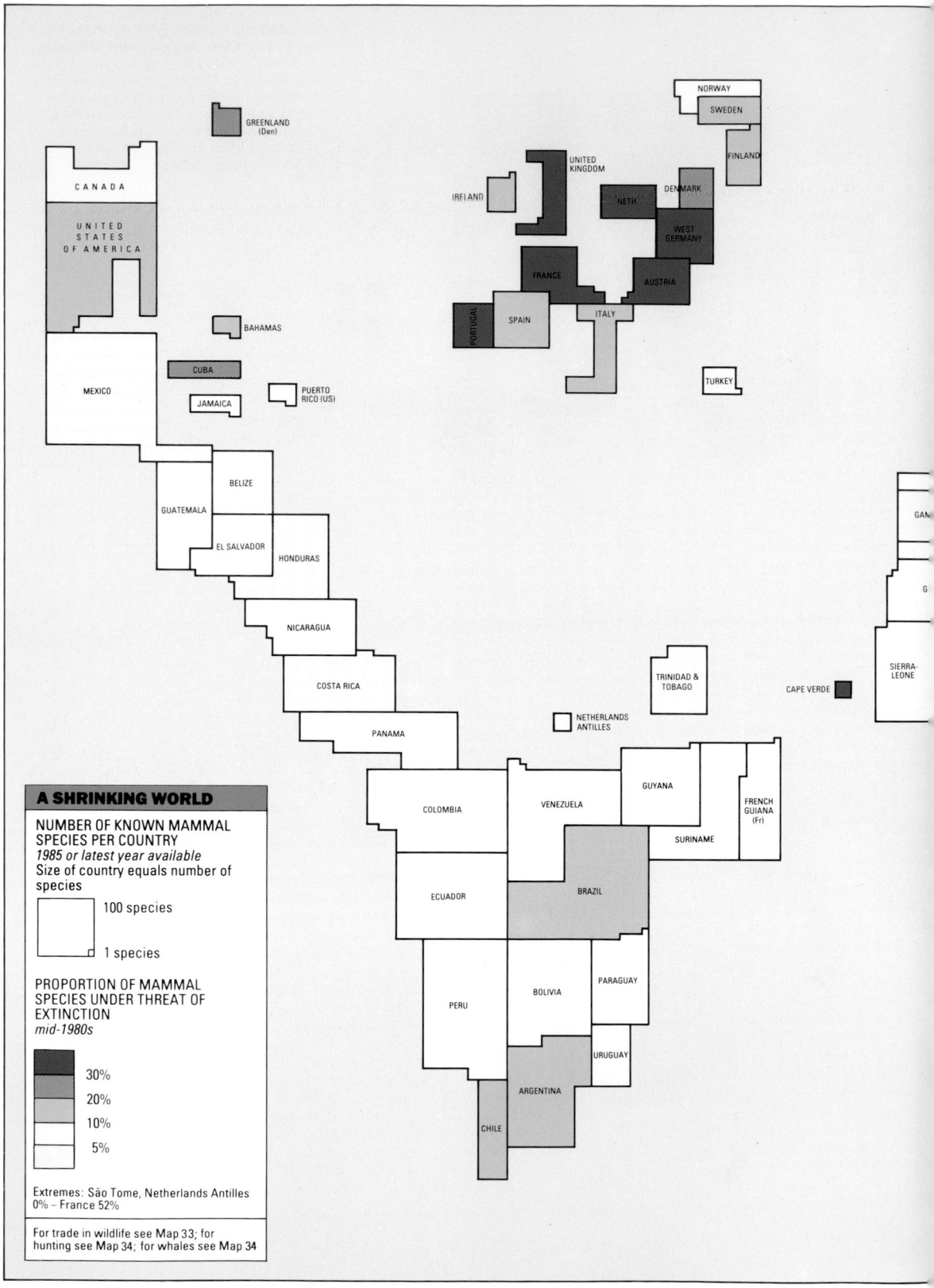

Data compiled by Andy Crump Main sources: IUCN Monitoring Centre (1988); OECD (1989); World Resources Institute (1987, 1988)

By the close of this century, 100 animal species a day may be facing extinction.

EMPTY NESTS

PROPORTION OF BIRD SPECIES UNDER THREAT OF EXTINCTION
OECD countries
mid-1980s

- 30%
- 20%
- 10%
- data not available/other

Extremes: Australia, Canada 3.3% – Austria 60.2%

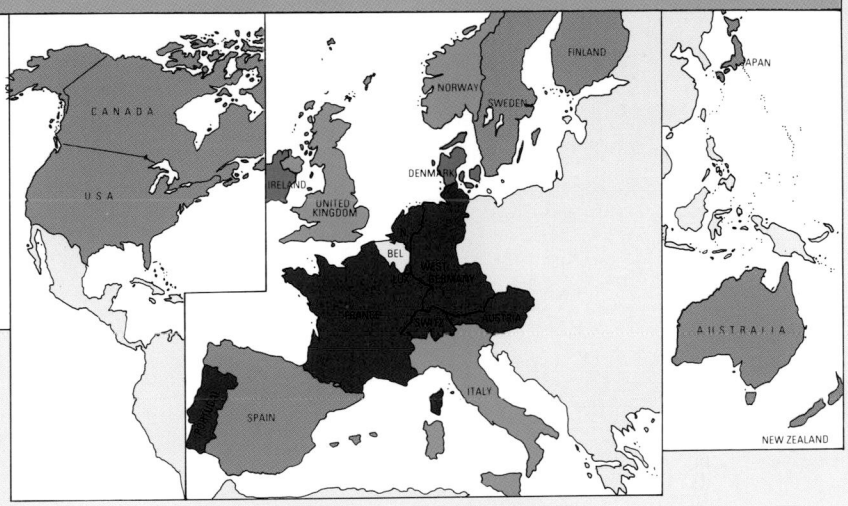

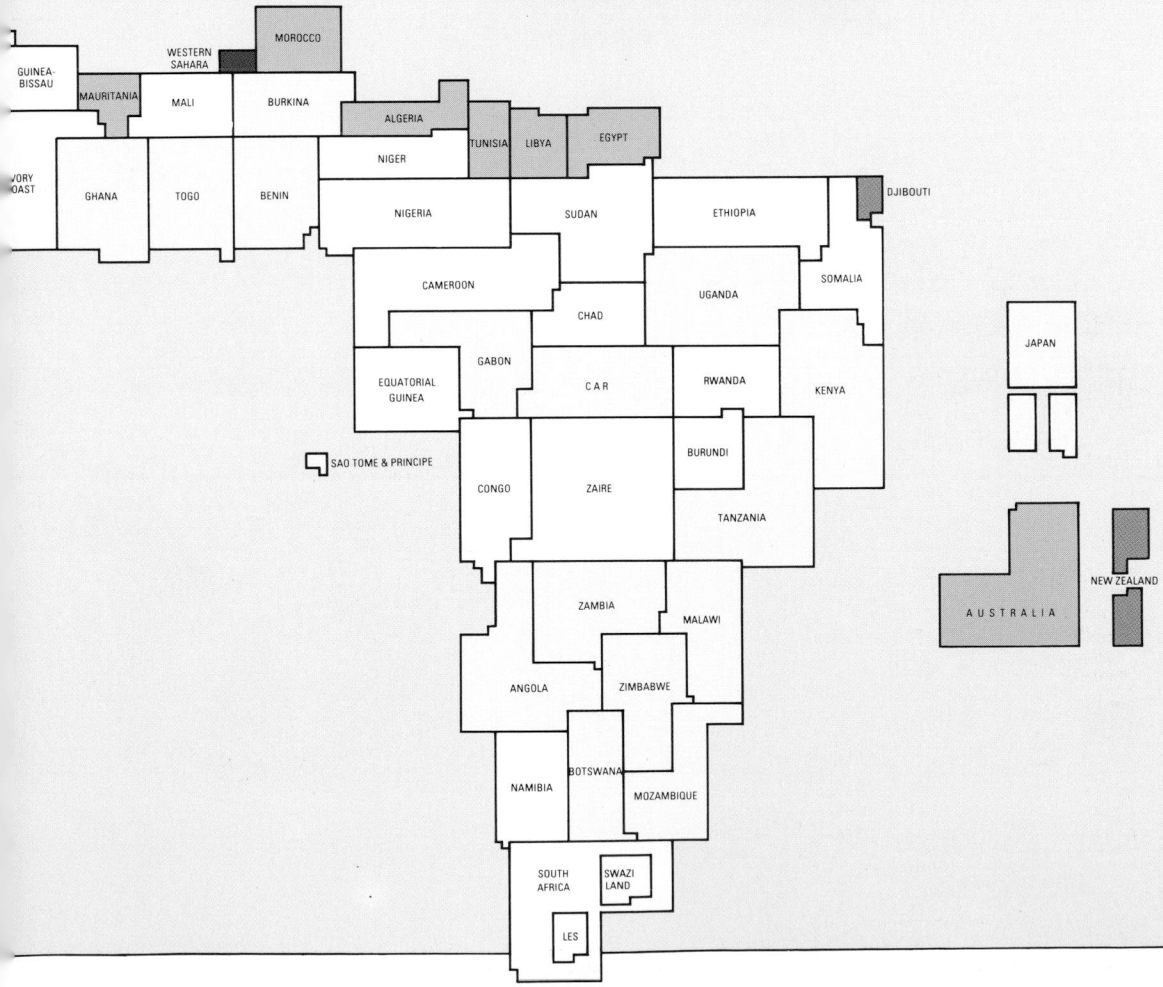

Copyright © Swanston Publishing Limited

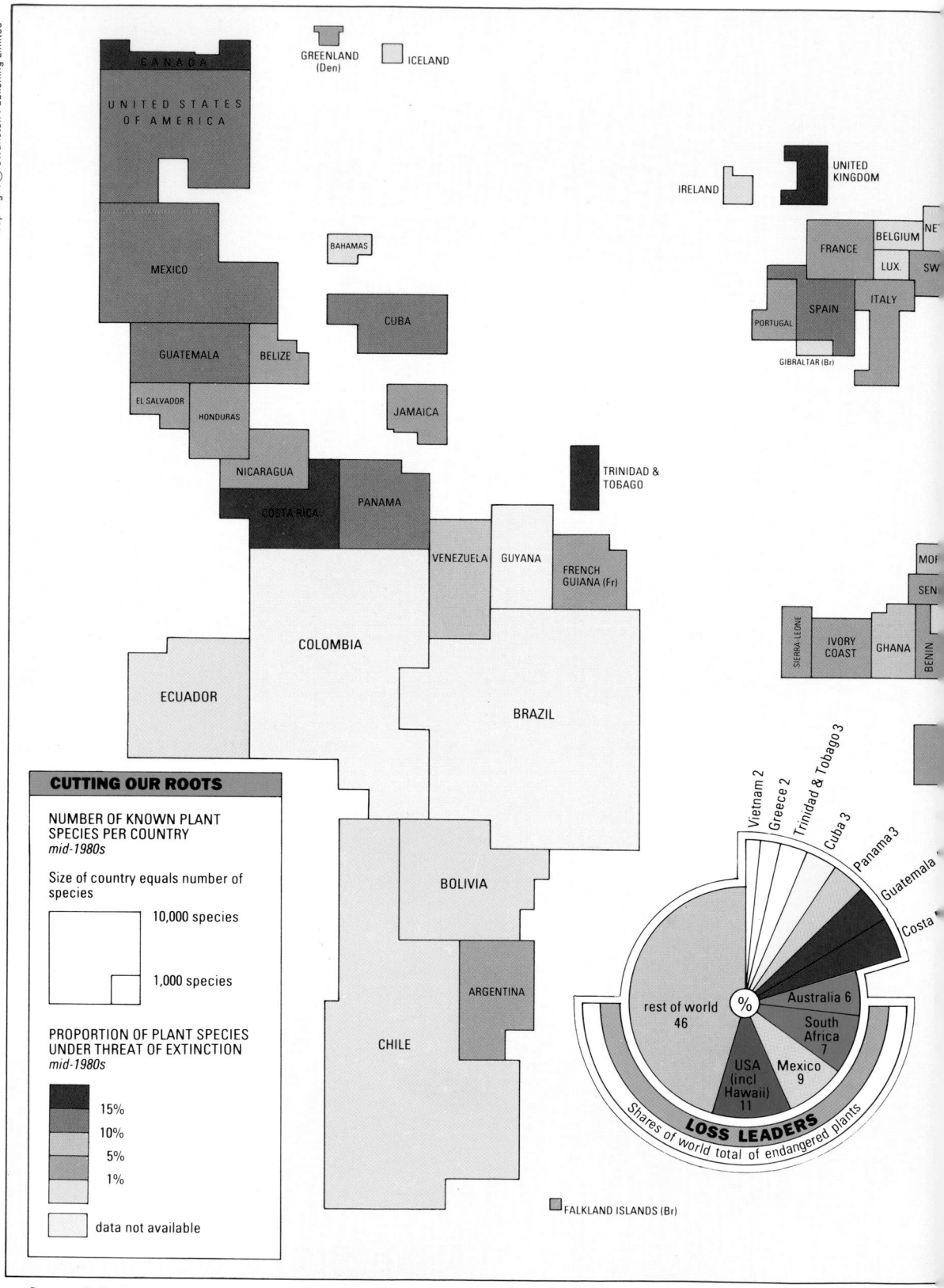

Data compiled by Simon Albrecht Main sources: Davis et al. (1979); World Resources Institute (1988).

CUTTING OUR ROOTS 4

Plants are the building blocks of all life on the planet.

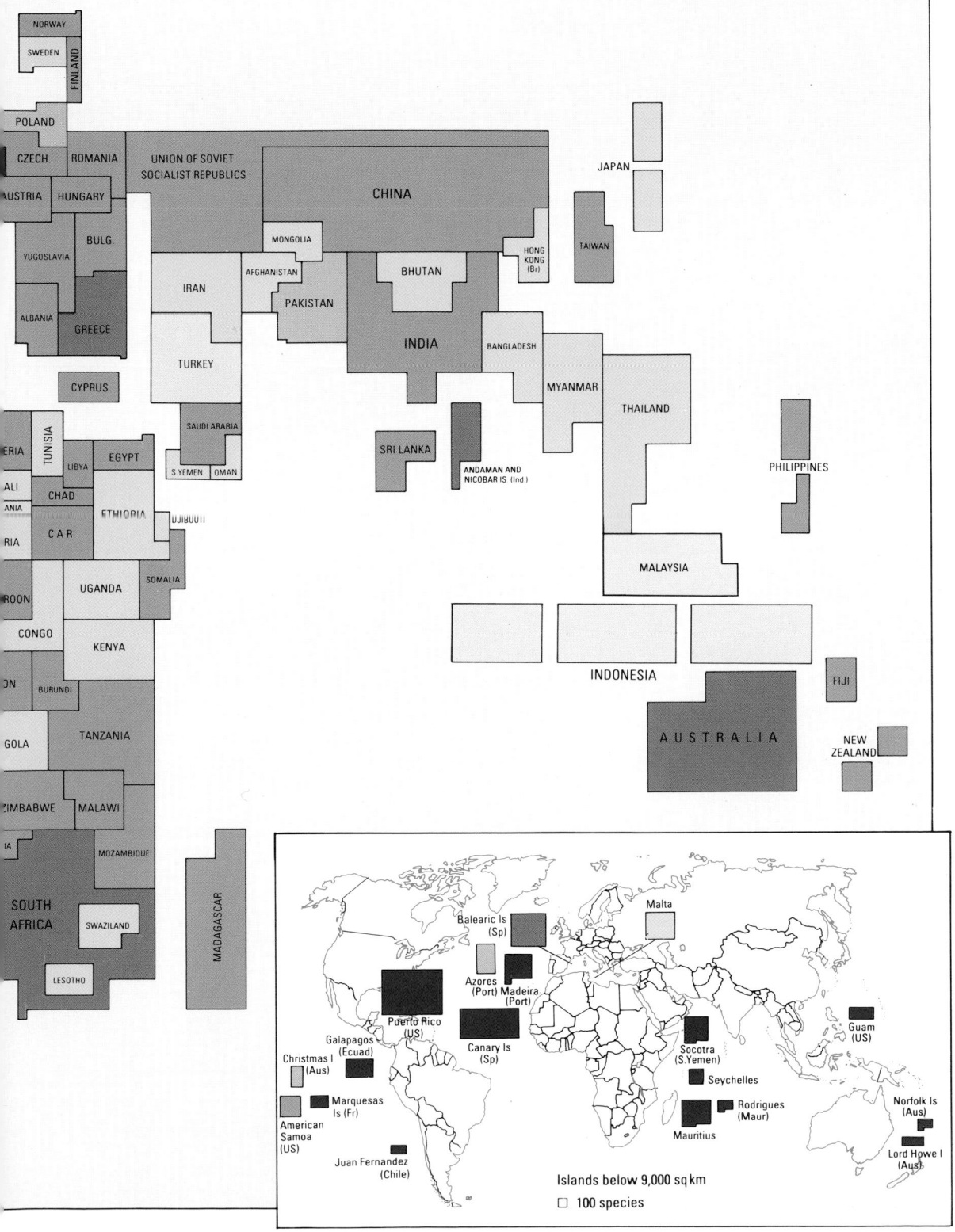

Copyright © Swanston Publishing Limited

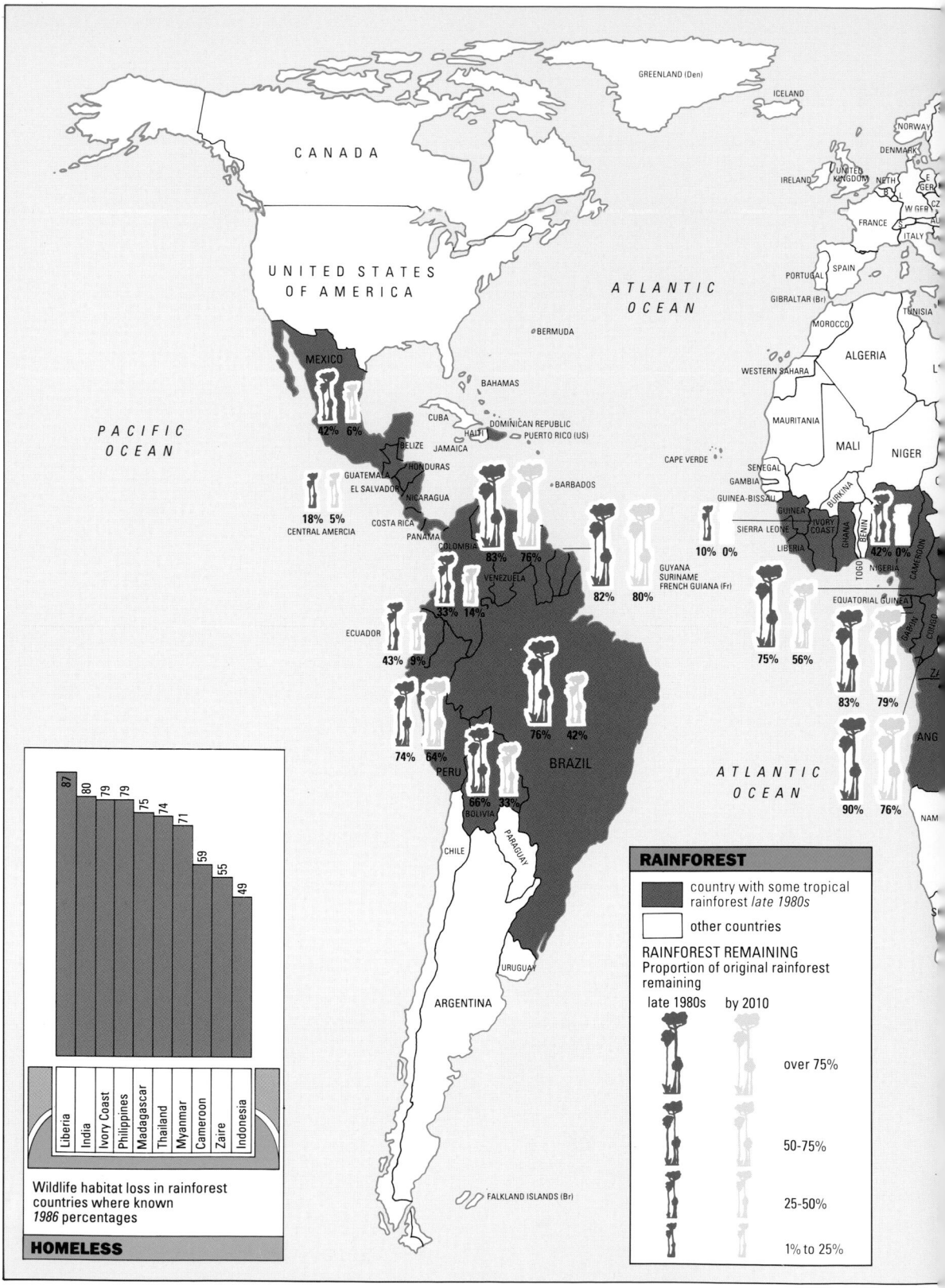

Data compiled by Friends of the Earth/Christine Lancaster Main sources: Campbell & Hammond (1989); Myers & Houghton (1989).

RAINFOREST 5

A hundred acres of tropical forest are destroyed every minute.

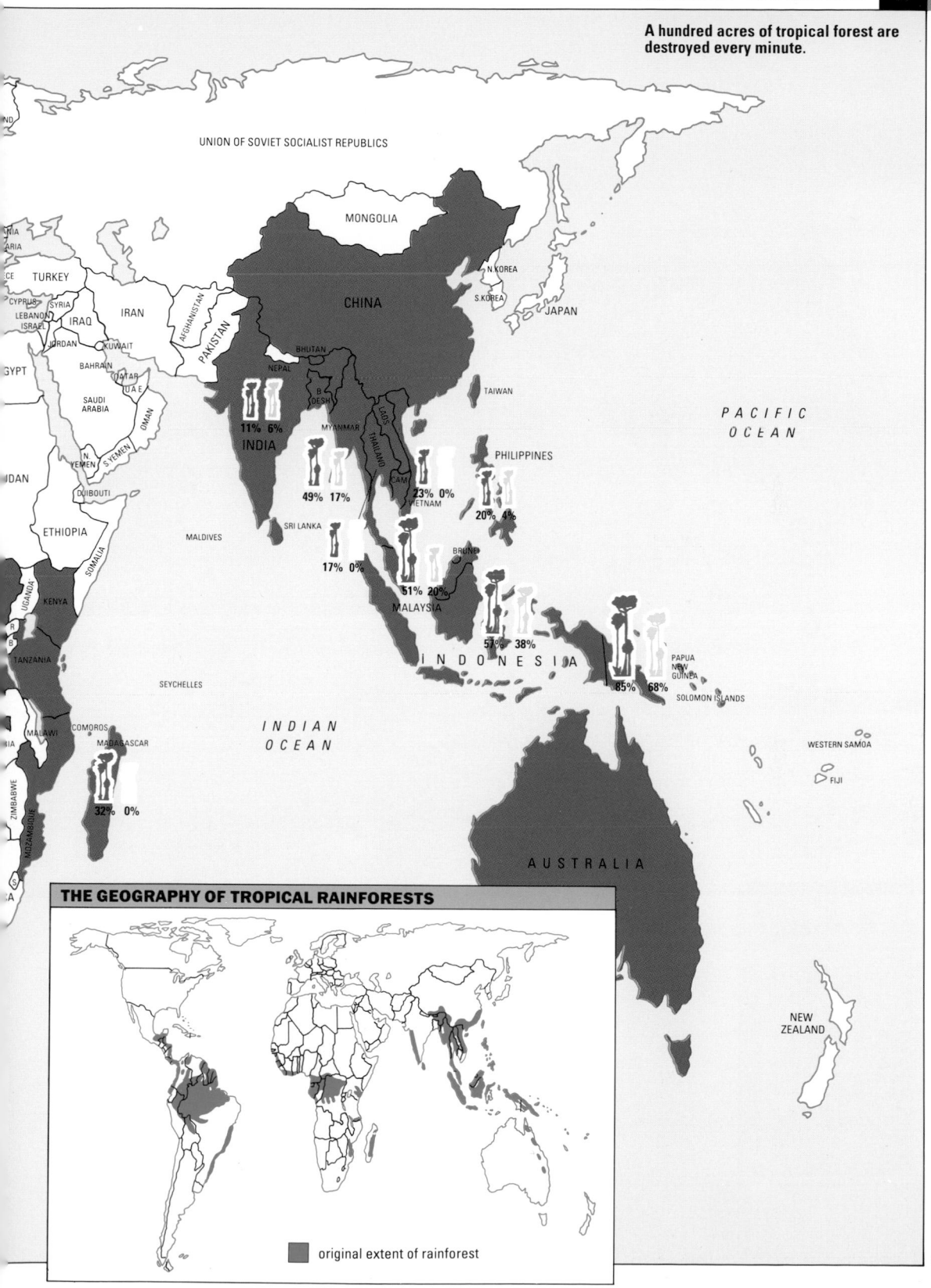

Copyright © Swanston Publishing Limited

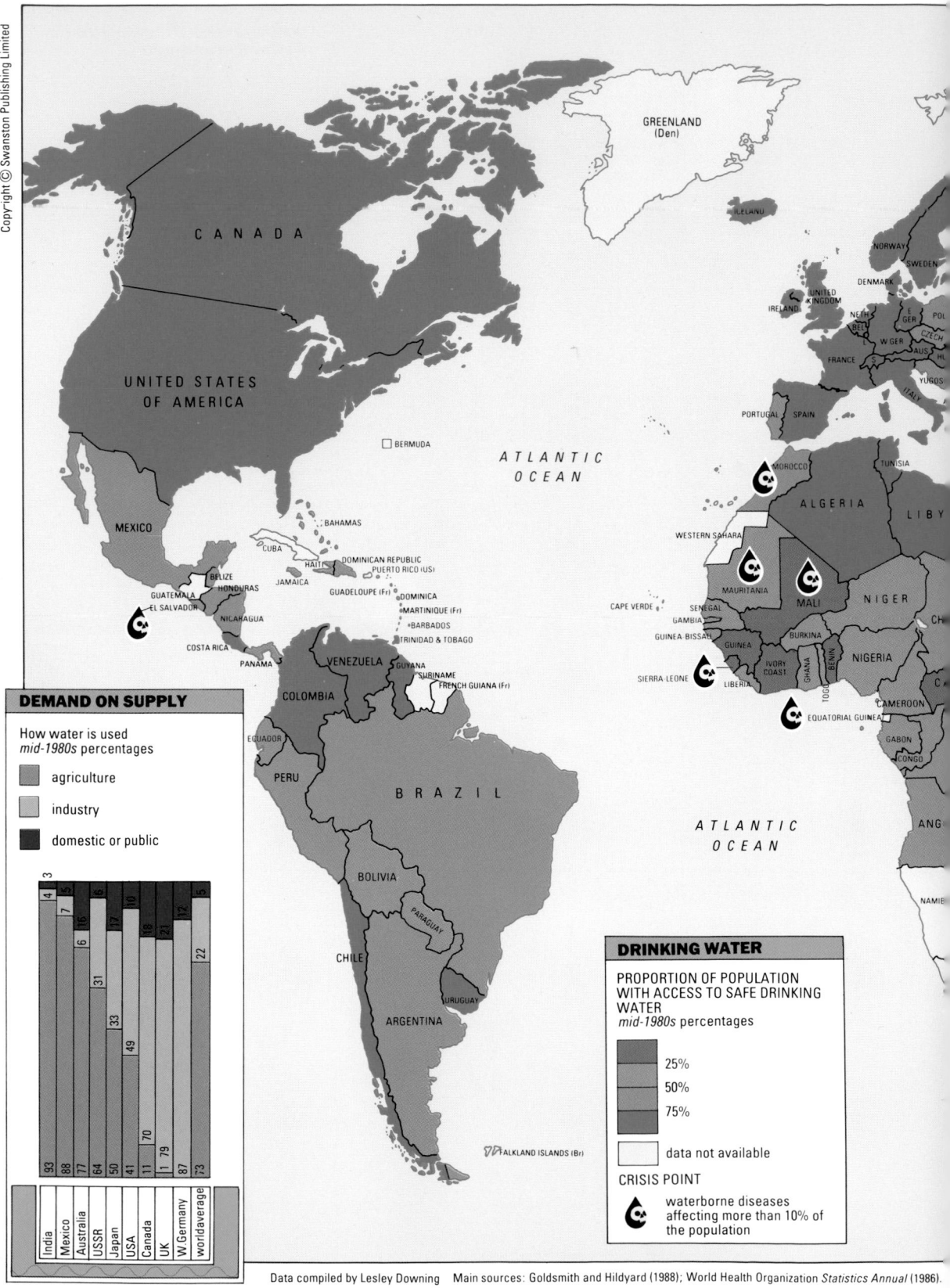

Data compiled by Lesley Downing Main sources: Goldsmith and Hildyard (1988); World Health Organization *Statistics Annual* (1986).

DRINKING WATER 6

The availability of safe drinking water cannot be taken for granted, even in the 'developed' world.

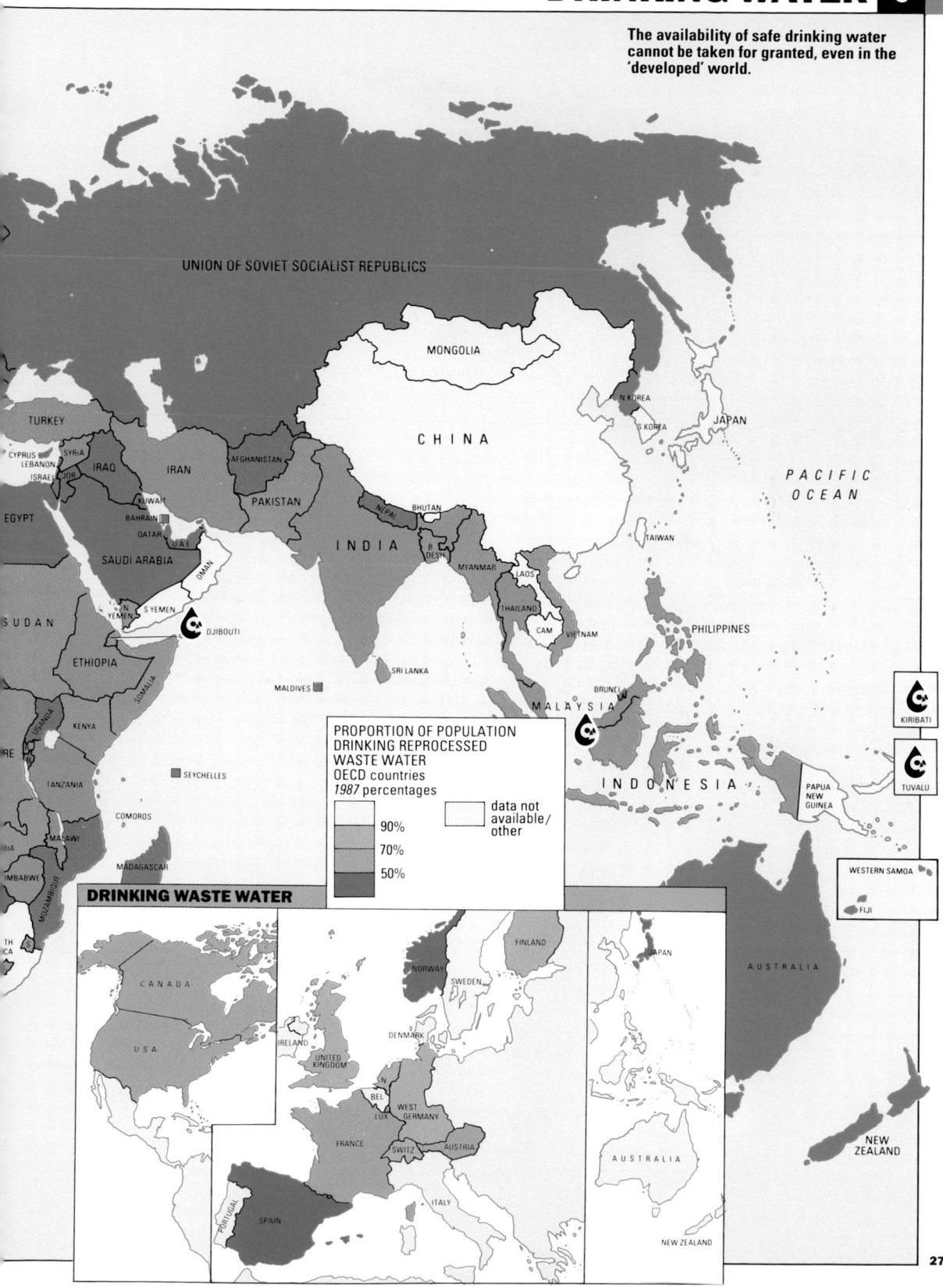

Copyright © Swanston Publishing Limited

Data compiled by Jeanne Kasperson and Joni Seager Main sources: FAO *Production Statistics* (1987); Kates (1989).

The persistence of hunger in a world of plenty represents the failure of social and economic systems.

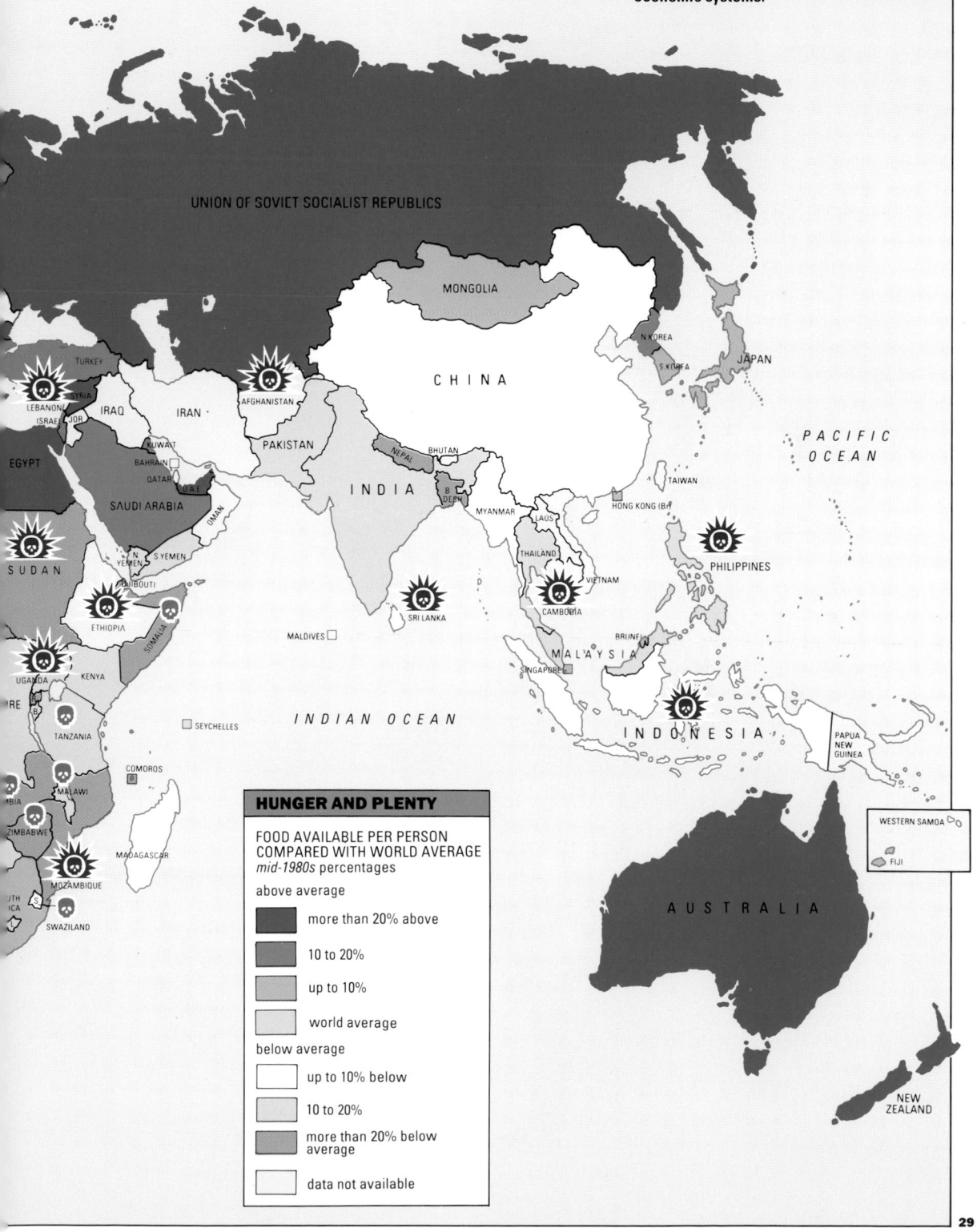

Copyright © Swanston Publishing Limited

Data compiled by Michael Shanabrook Main sources: FAO, *Production Statistics Yearbook* (1989); Gramfors (1989); Kurian (1984).

Agricultural land per person is shrinking the world over, although pressure on the land is not evenly distributed.

Copyright © Swanston Publishing Limited

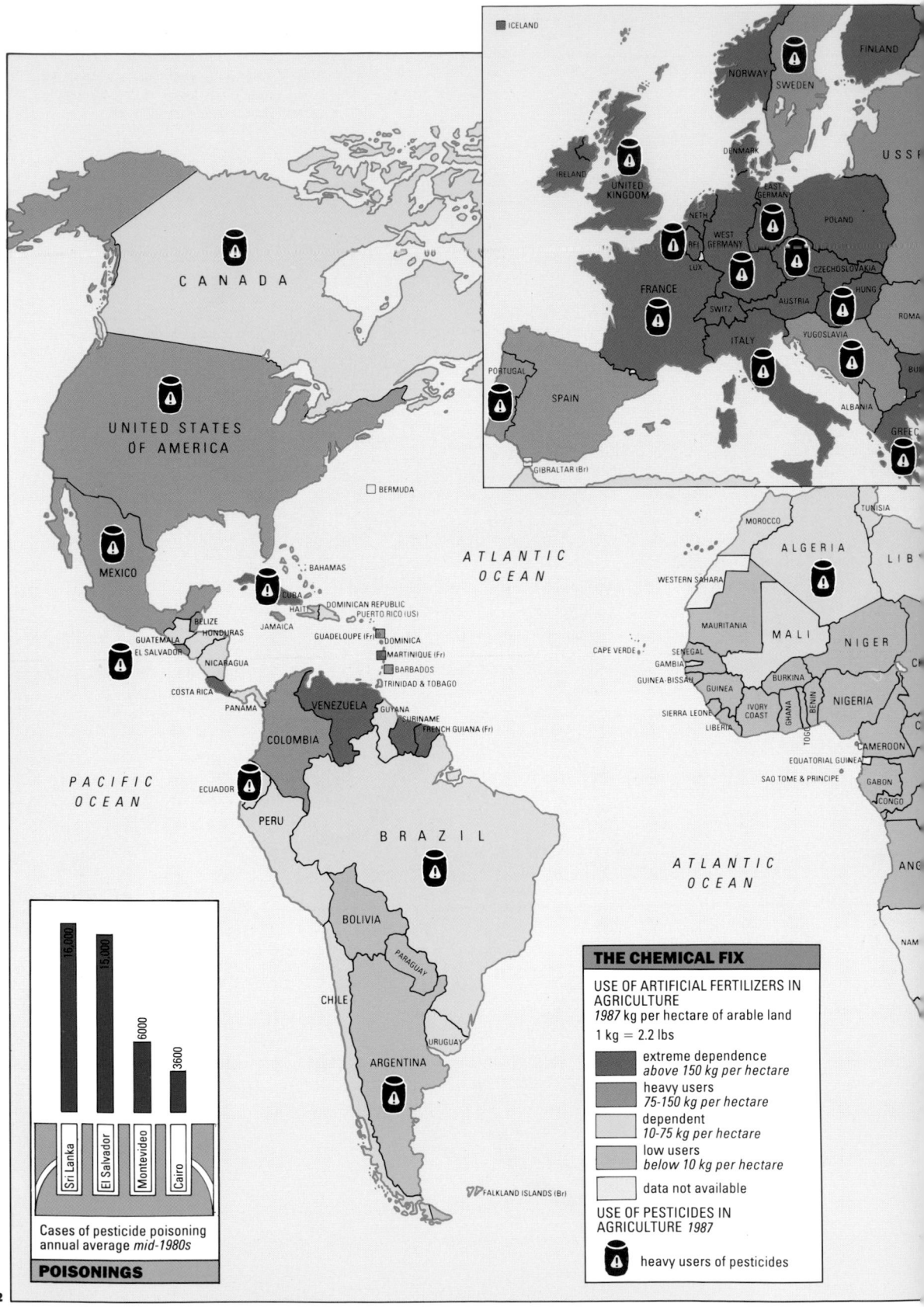

Data compiled by Joni Seager Main sources: FAO *Fertilizer Yearbook* (1988); FAO *Production Yearbook* (1987); FAO *Trade Statistics* (1988).

The more agricultural chemicals are used, the more they are needed.

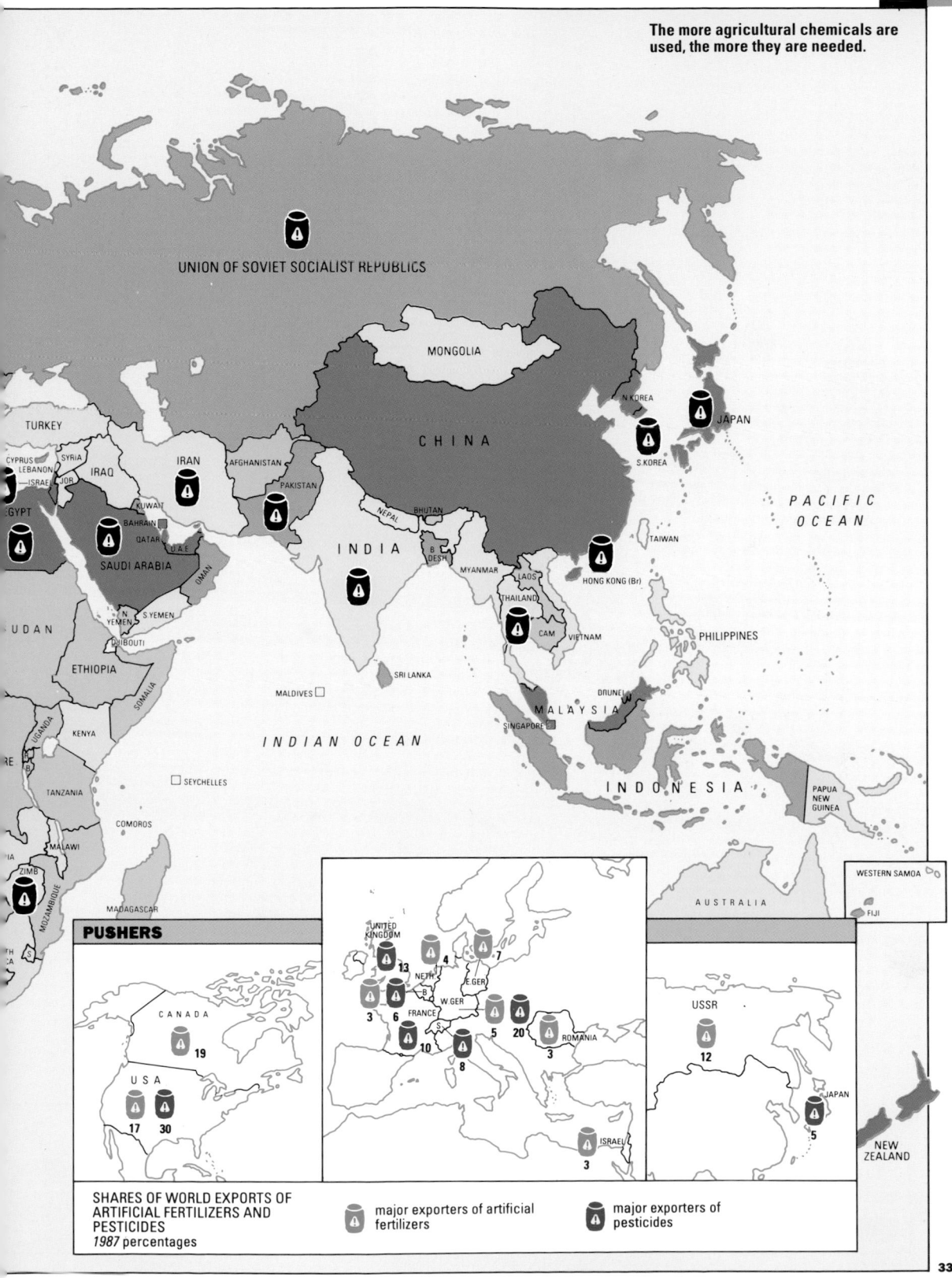

SHARES OF WORLD EXPORTS OF ARTIFICIAL FERTILIZERS AND PESTICIDES
1987 percentages

Copyright © Swanston Publishing Limited

Data compiled by Simon Albrecht Main sources: Prescott-Allen (1988); Myers (1984)

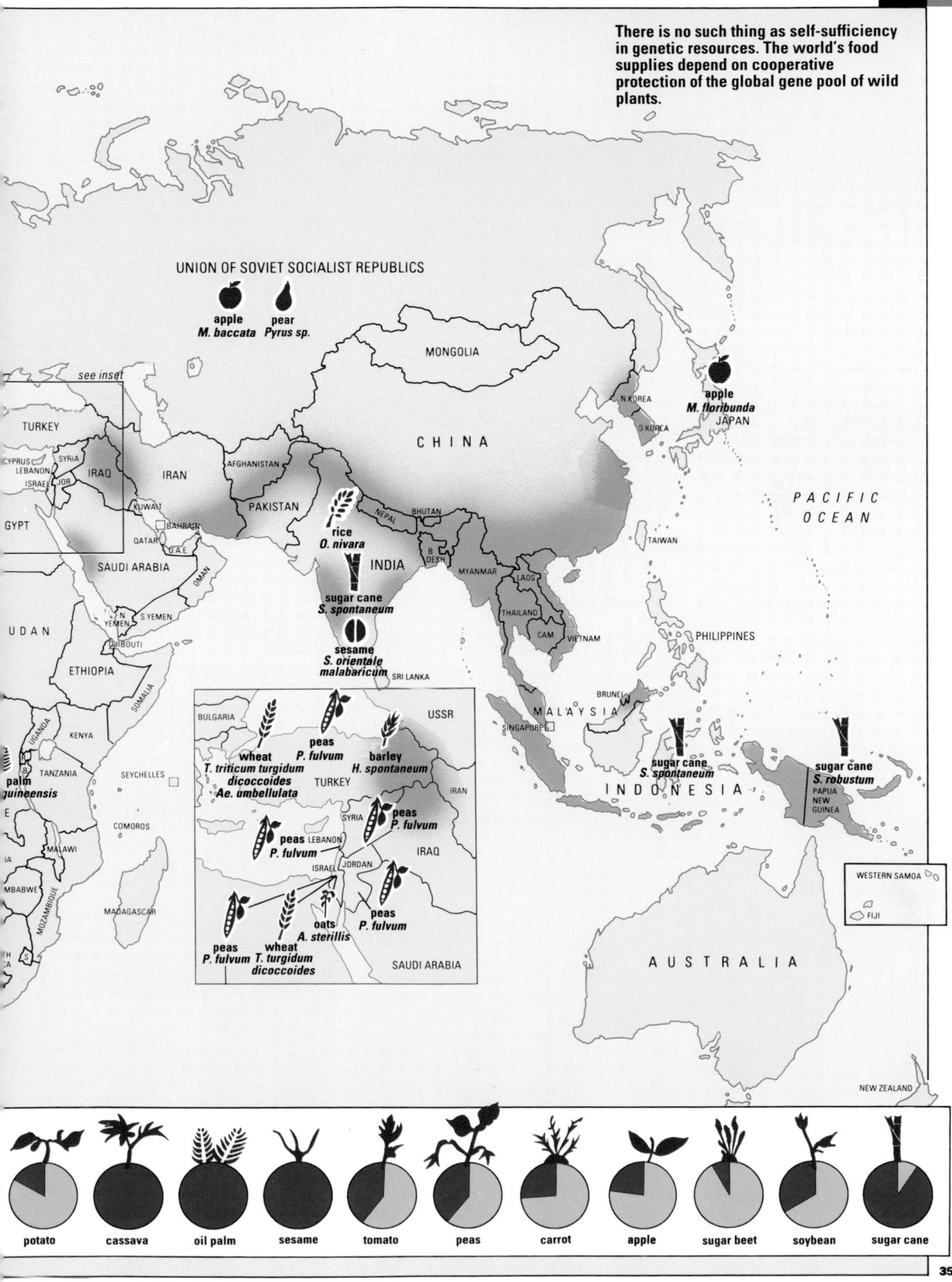
There is no such thing as self-sufficiency in genetic resources. The world's food supplies depend on cooperative protection of the global gene pool of wild plants.
UNION OF SOVIET SOCIALIST REPUBLICS
apple
M. baccata
pear
Pyrus sp.
MONGOLIA
see inset
TURKEY
CYPRUS
SYRIA
LEBANON
ISRAEL
JOR
IRAQ
IRAN
AFGHANISTAN
PAKISTAN
KUWAIT
BAHRAIN
QATAR
U.A.E.
SAUDI ARABIA
OMAN
N YEMEN
S YEMEN
DJIBOUTI
ETHIOPIA
SOMALIA
KENYA
UGANDA
TANZANIA
SEYCHELLES
COMOROS
MALAWI
MOZAMBIQUE
MADAGASCAR
palm
guineensis
CHINA
N KOREA
S KOREA
apple
M. floribunda
JAPAN
PACIFIC OCEAN
TAIWAN
NEPAL
BHUTAN
B DESH
MYANMAR
LAOS
THAILAND
CAM
VIETNAM
PHILIPPINES
rice
O. nivara
INDIA
sugar cane
S. spontaneum
sesame
S. orientale malabaricum
SRI LANKA
BRUNEI
MALAYSIA
SINGAPORE
INDONESIA
sugar cane
S. spontaneum
sugar cane
S. robustum
PAPUA NEW GUINEA
WESTERN SAMOA
FIJI
AUSTRALIA
NEW ZEALAND
BULGARIA
USSR
wheat
T. triticum turgidum dicoccoides
Ae. umbellulata
peas
P. fulvum
barley
H. spontaneum
TURKEY
IRAN
SYRIA
peas
P. fulvum
peas
P. fulvum
LEBANON
IRAQ
ISRAEL
JORDAN
peas
P. fulvum
oats
A. sterillis
peas
P. fulvum
wheat
T. turgidum dicoccoides
SAUDI ARABIA
potato
cassava
oil palm
sesame
tomato
peas
carrot
apple
sugar beet
soybean
sugar cane

Copyright © Swanston Publishing Limited

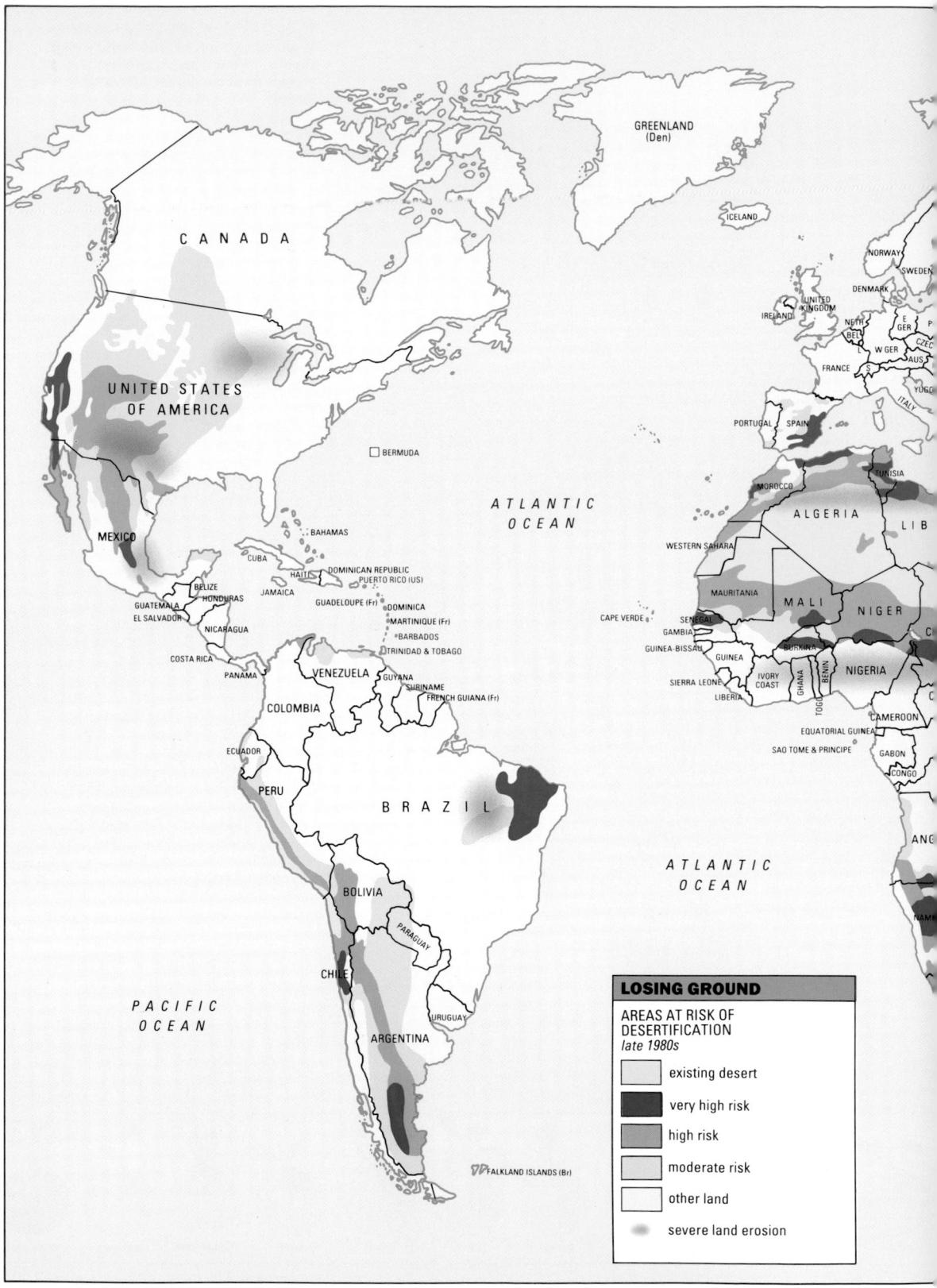

Data compiled by Andy Crump Main sources: UNEP *World Conservation Strategy* (1980); World Resources Institute (1988); Myers (1984).

By the year 2000 one-third of the world's agricultural land will have turned to dust.

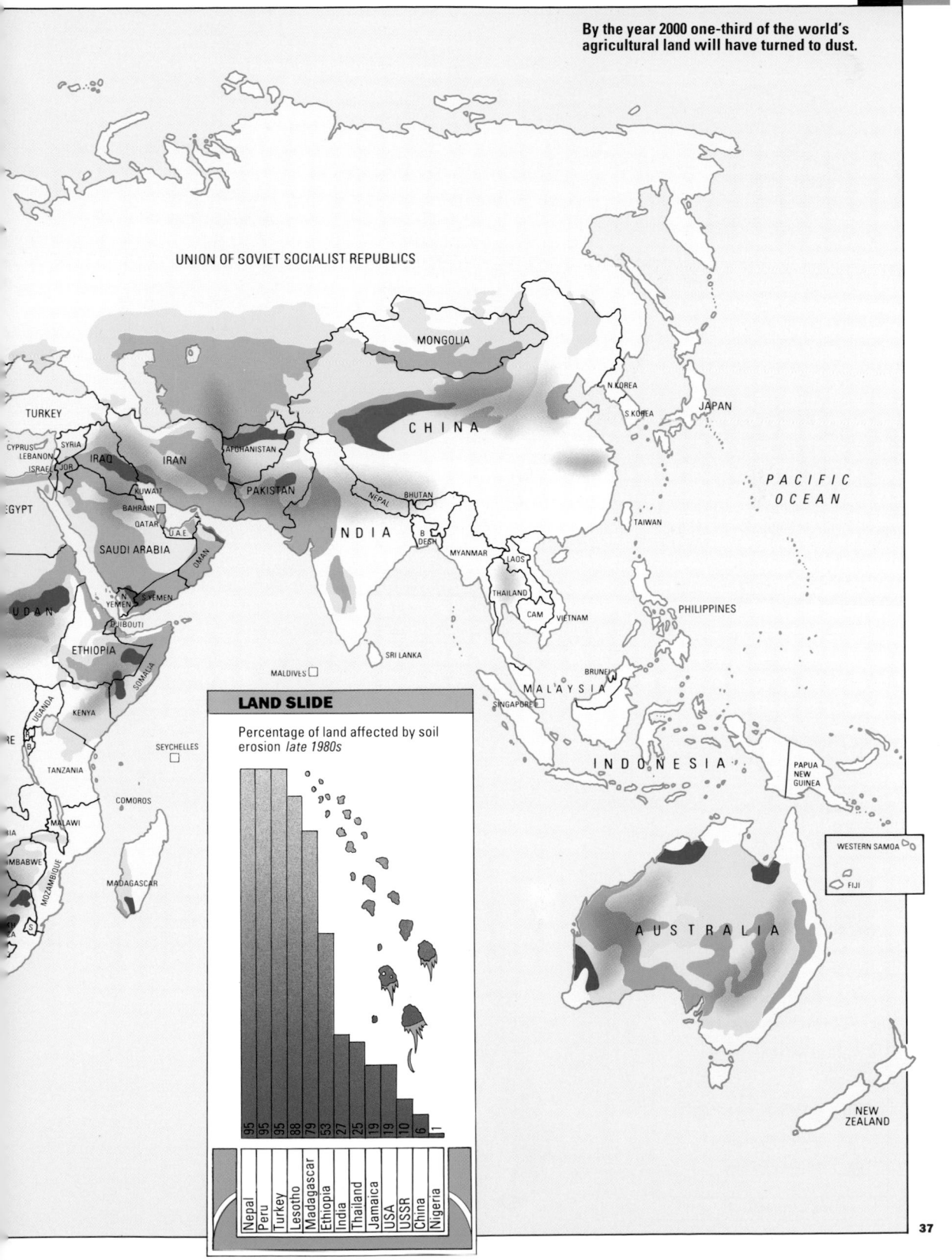

Copyright © Swanston Publishing Limited

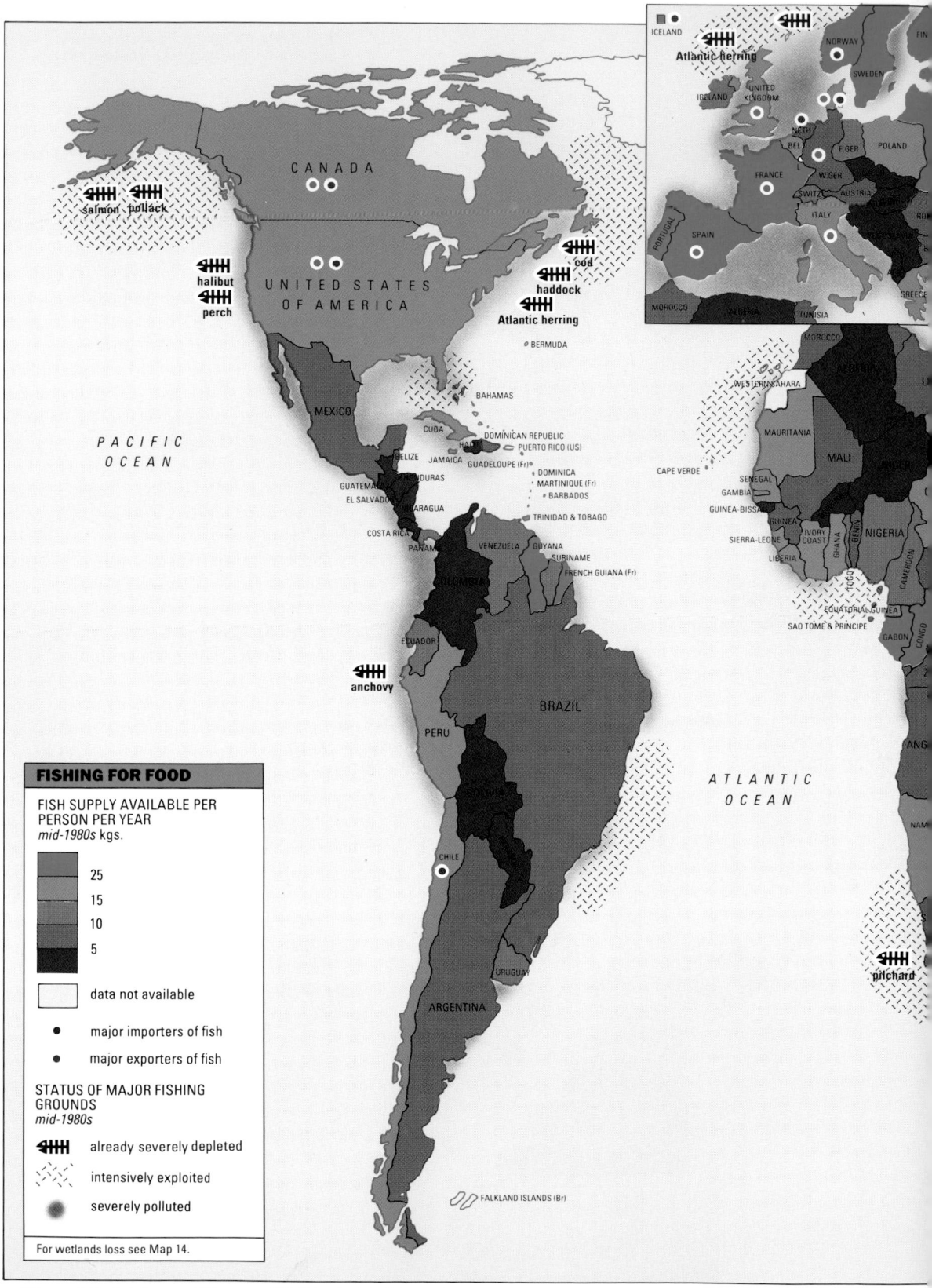

Data compiled by Andy Crump Main sources: FAO *Fishery Statistics* (1986, 1987); Myers (1984).

FISHING FOR FOOD 12

Fisheries provide almost a quarter of the world's supply of animal protein, but face threats from many sources.

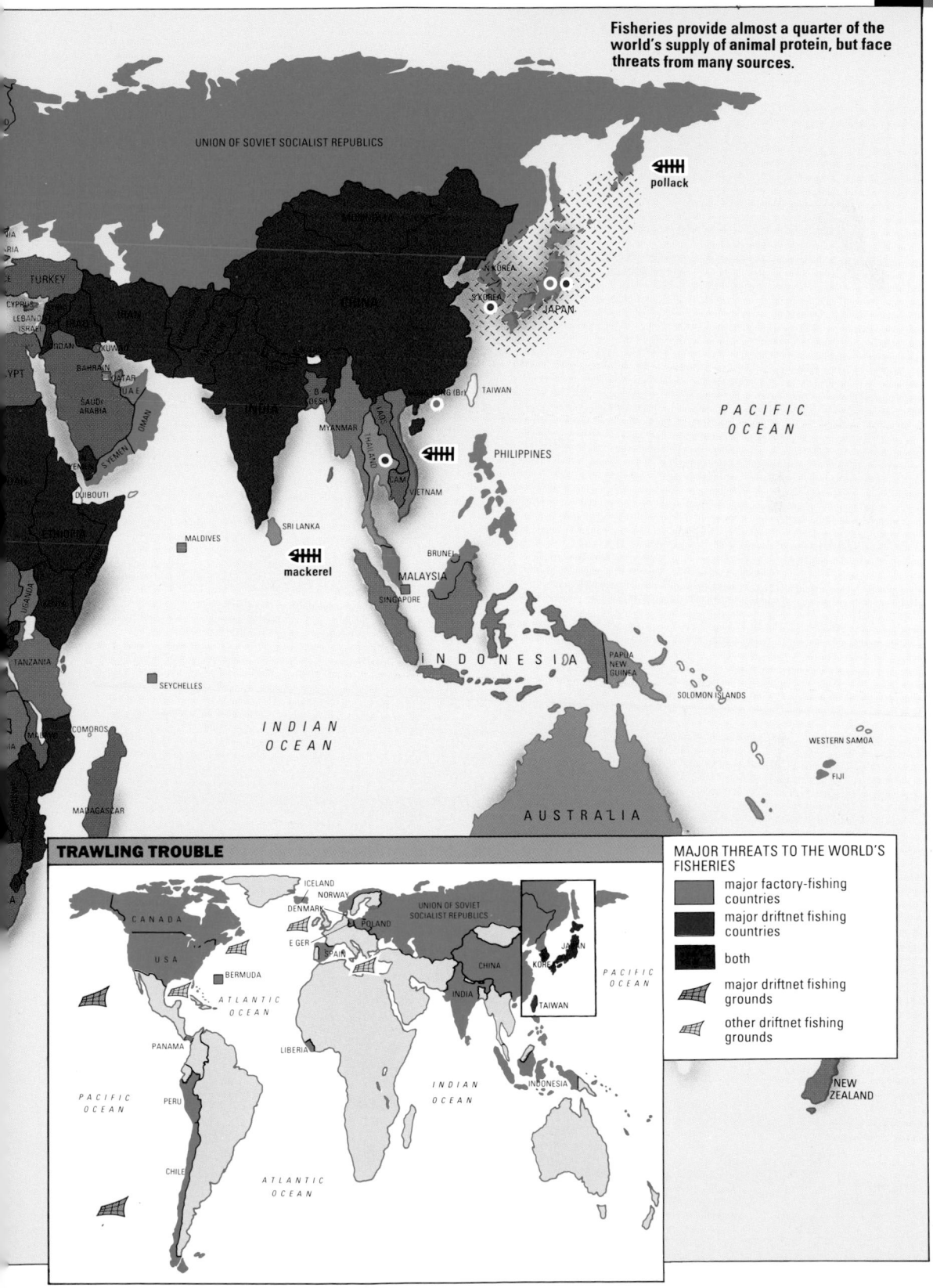

Copyright © Swanston Publishing Limited

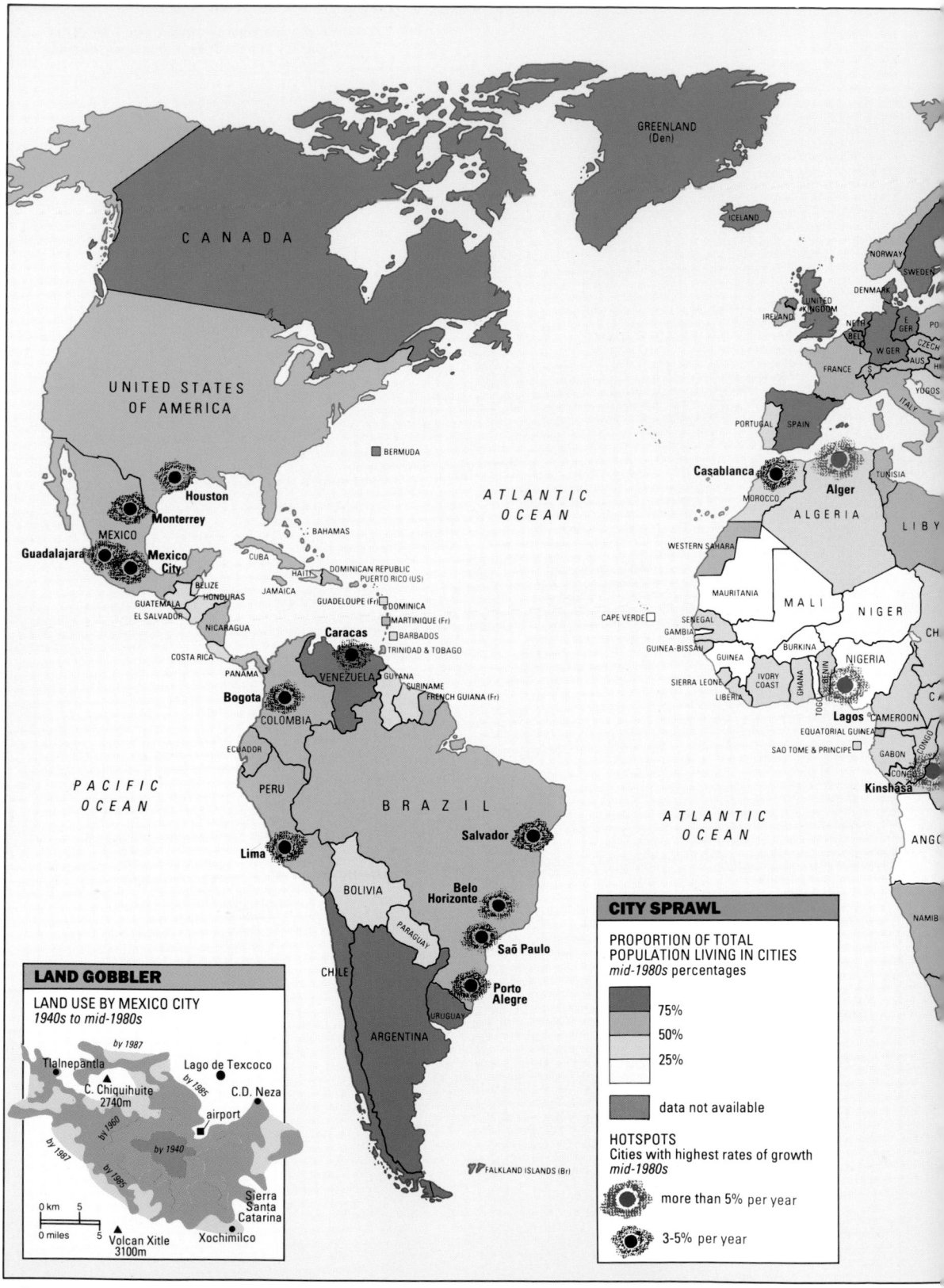

Data compiled by Michael Steinitz Main sources: UN *Prospects of World Urbanization* (1988); *National Geographic* (1984).

CITY SPRAWL 13

By the year 2000, half the world's population will live in cities.

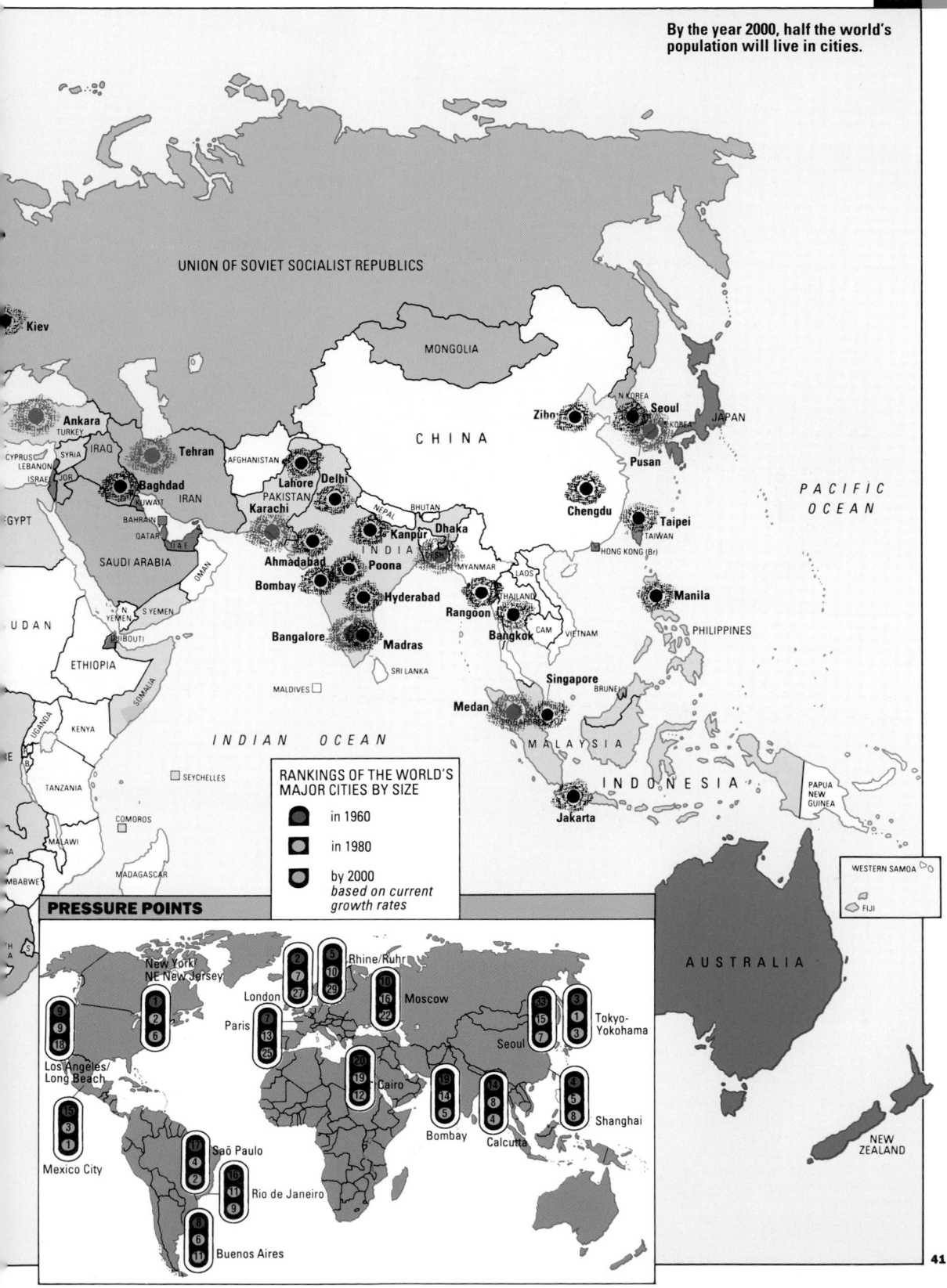

Copyright © Swanston Publishing Limited

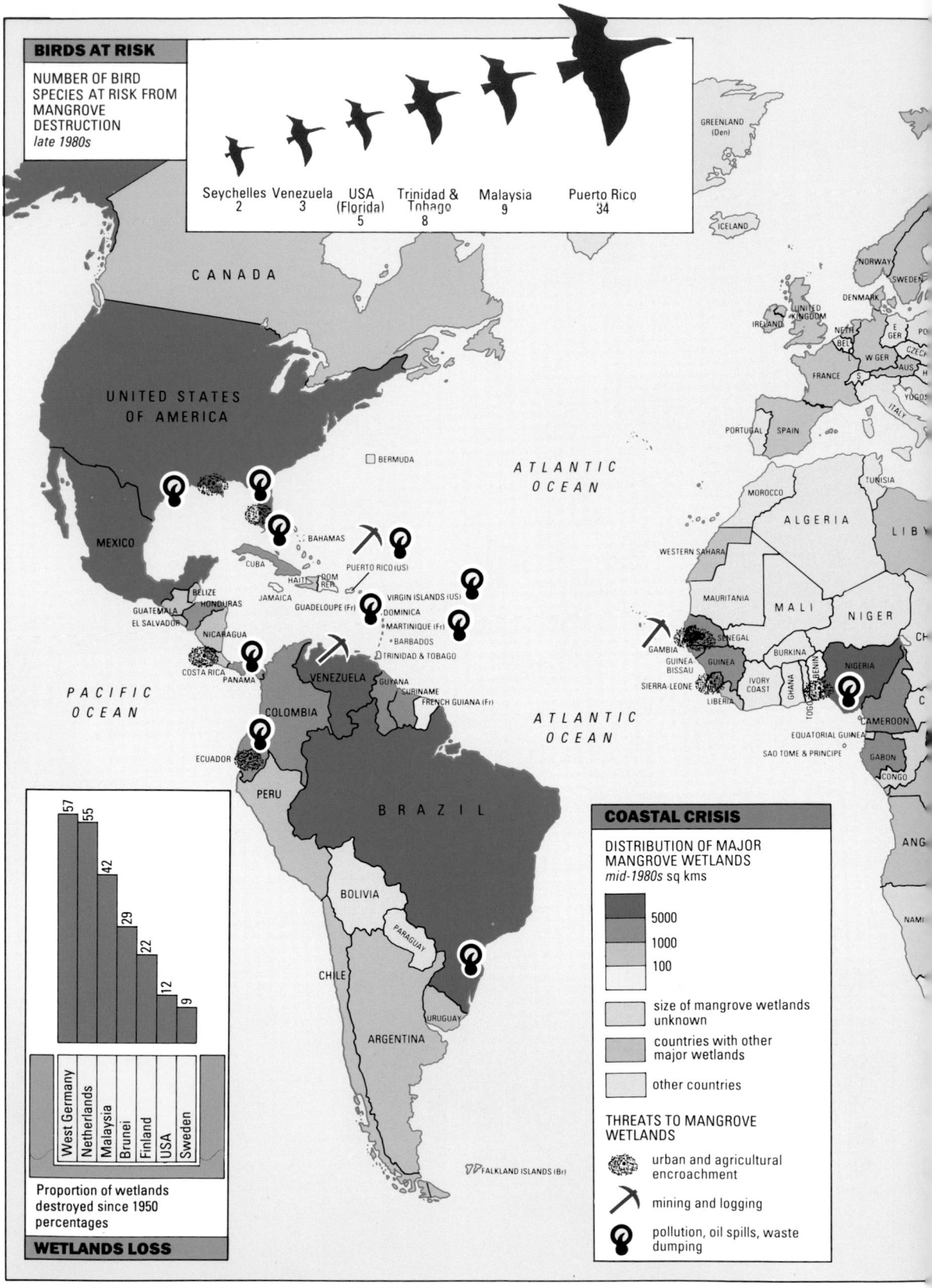

Data compiled by Michael Steinitz Main sources: Saenger (1983); AMBIO (1988).

COASTAL CRISIS 14

The world's wetlands are being drained and paved over for development. More than half have already been destroyed.

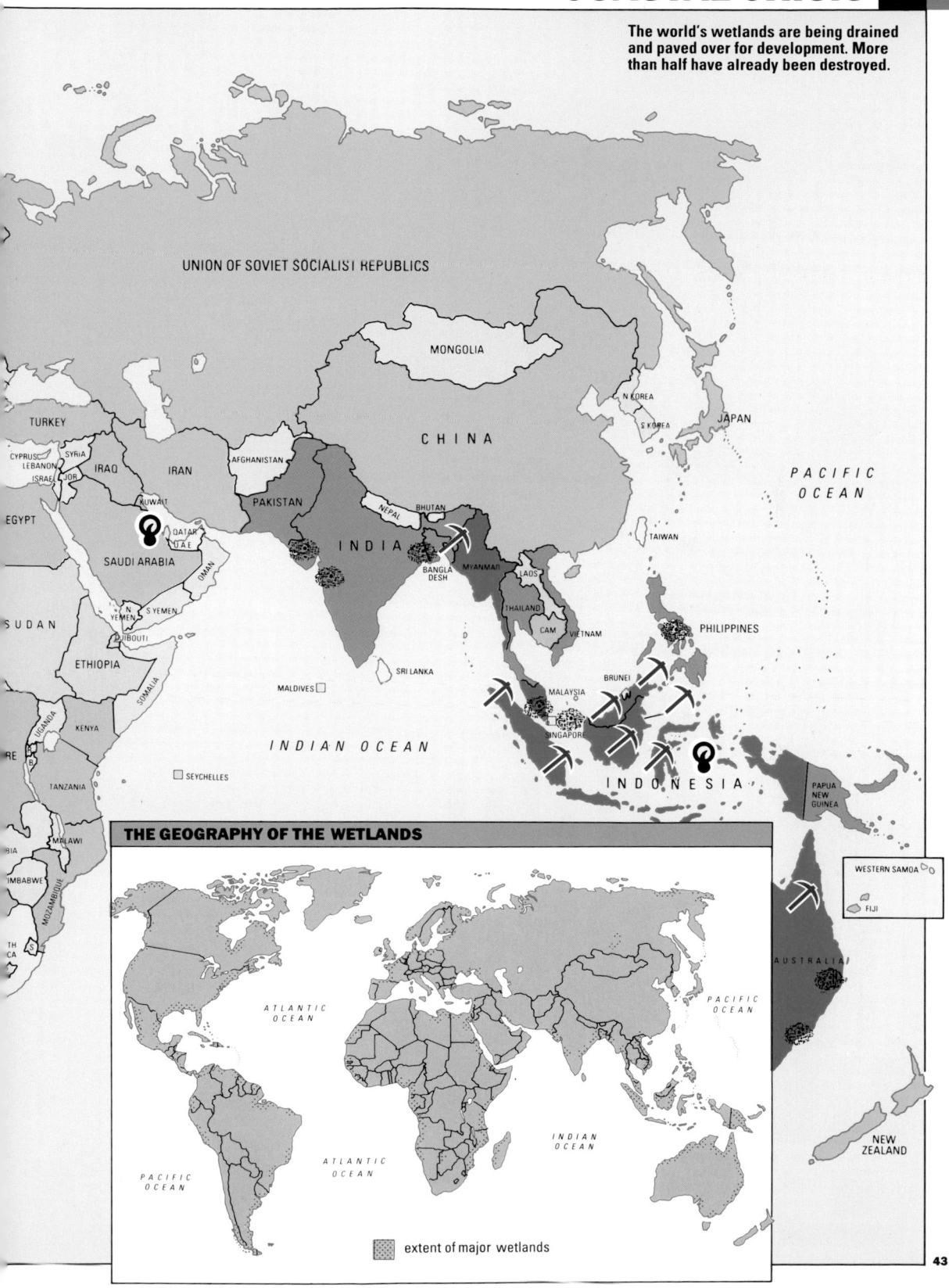

Copyright © Swanston Publishing Limited

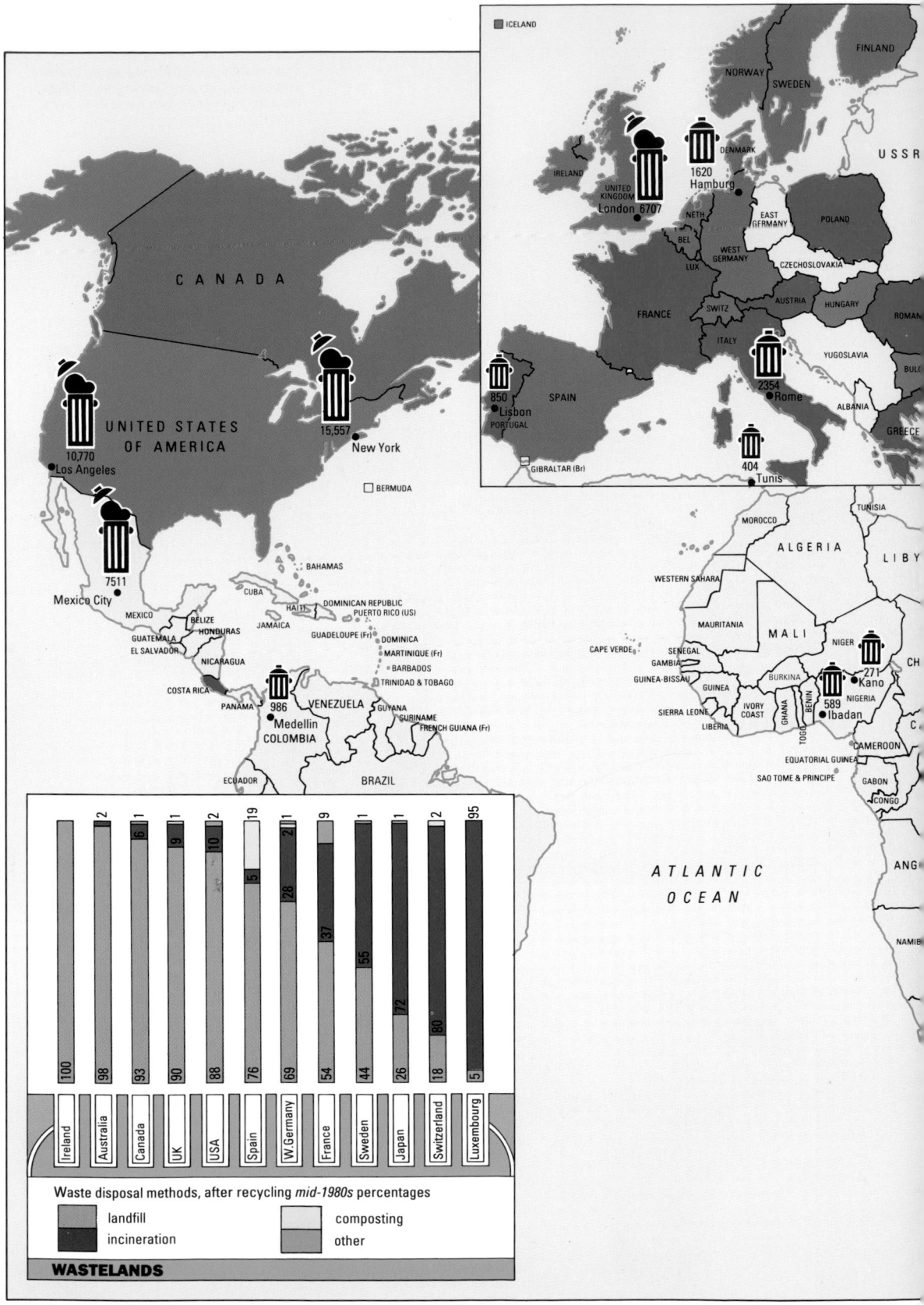

Data compiled by Joni Seager Main sources: Cointreau (1987); Levenson, US Congress Office of Technology Assessment; OECD *Environmental Data Compendium* (1989).

WASTE 15

The richer the country the more garbage it produces. But getting rid of it safely is a global problem.

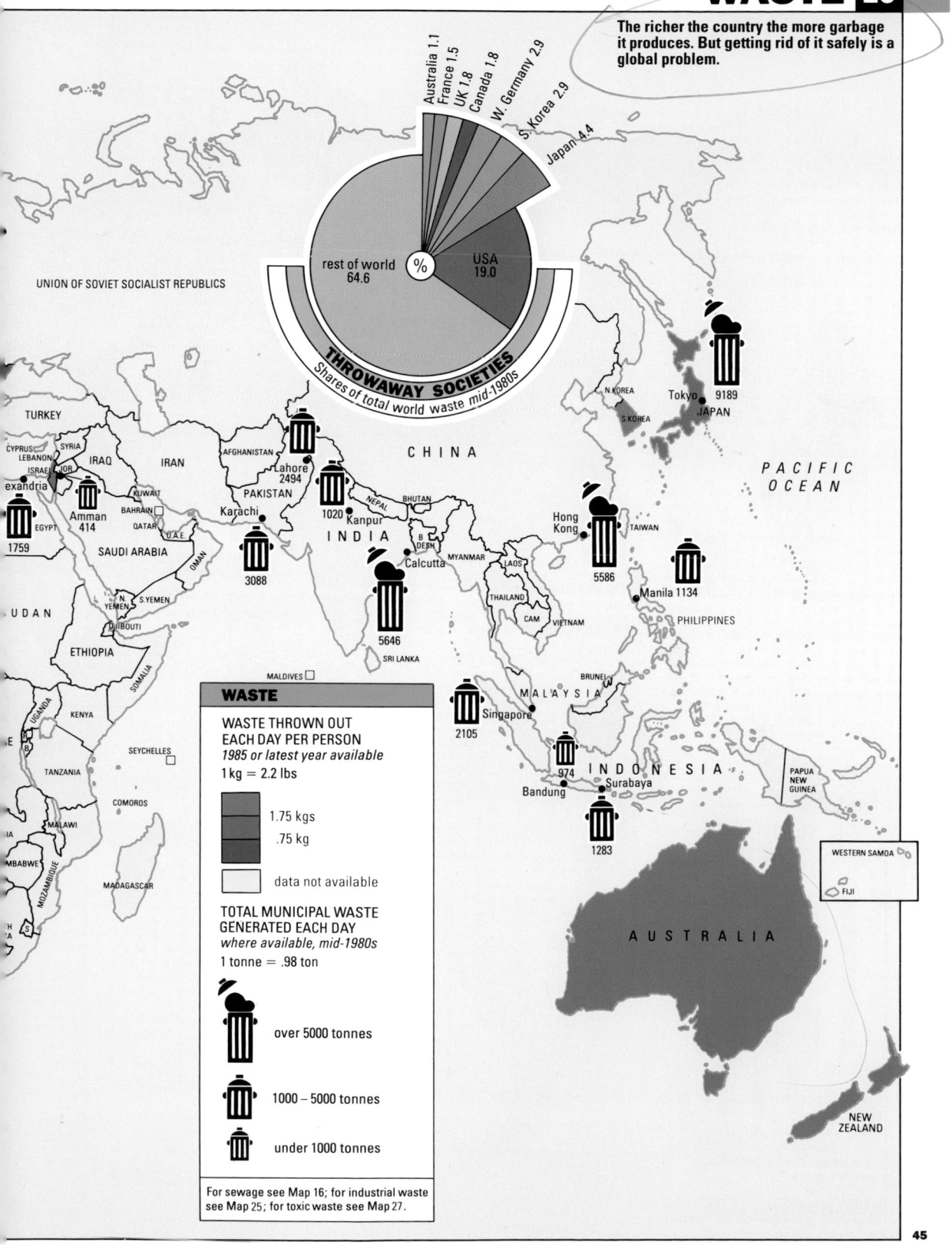

Copyright © Swanston Publishing Limited

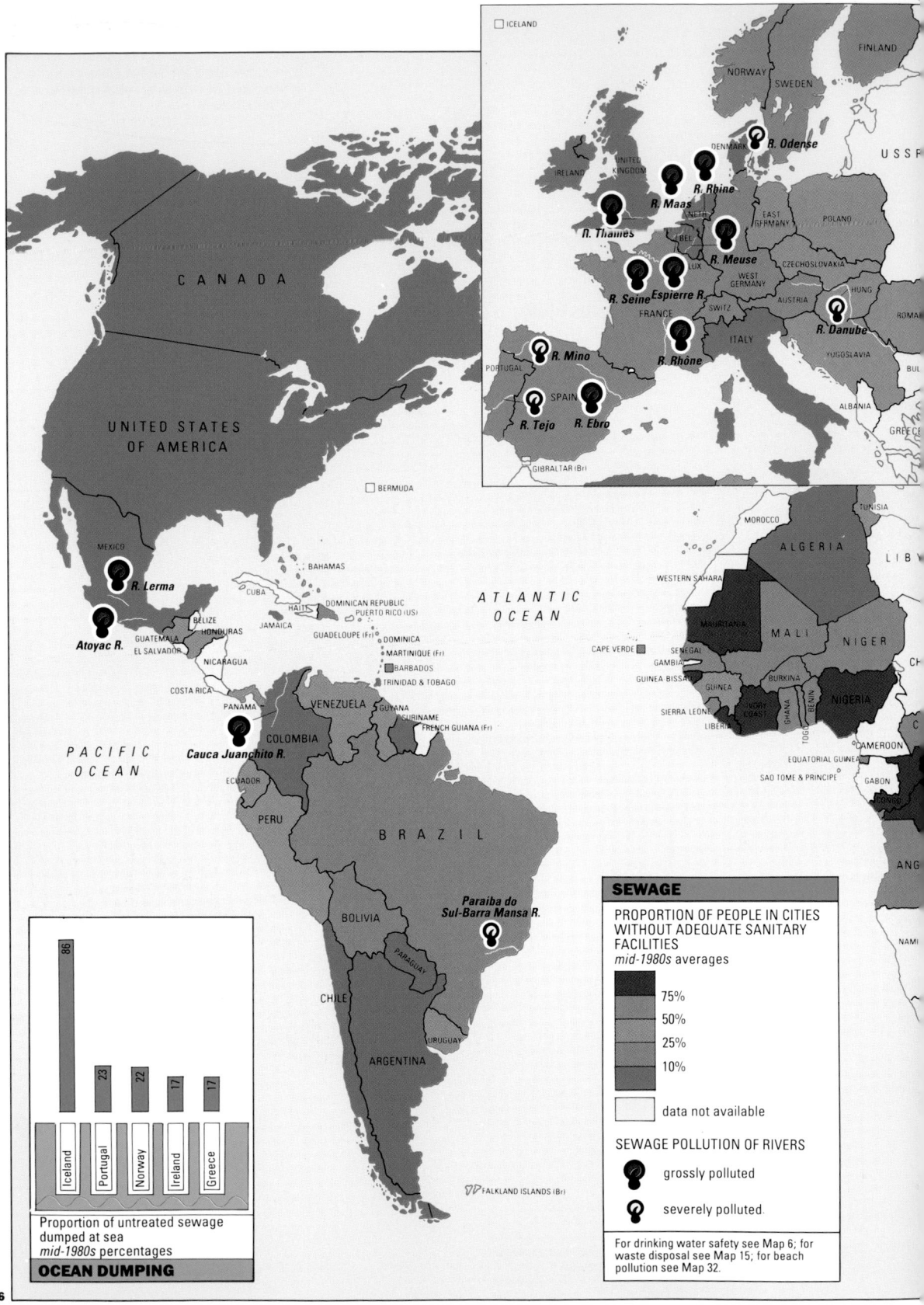

Data compiled by Lesley Downing Main sources: Monitoring and Assessment Research Centre (1987); UNEP(1989); WHO *World Health Statistics Annual (1986).*

The growth of city populations is overwhelming existing systems for safe disposal of sewage. Many urban rivers have become virtual open sewers.

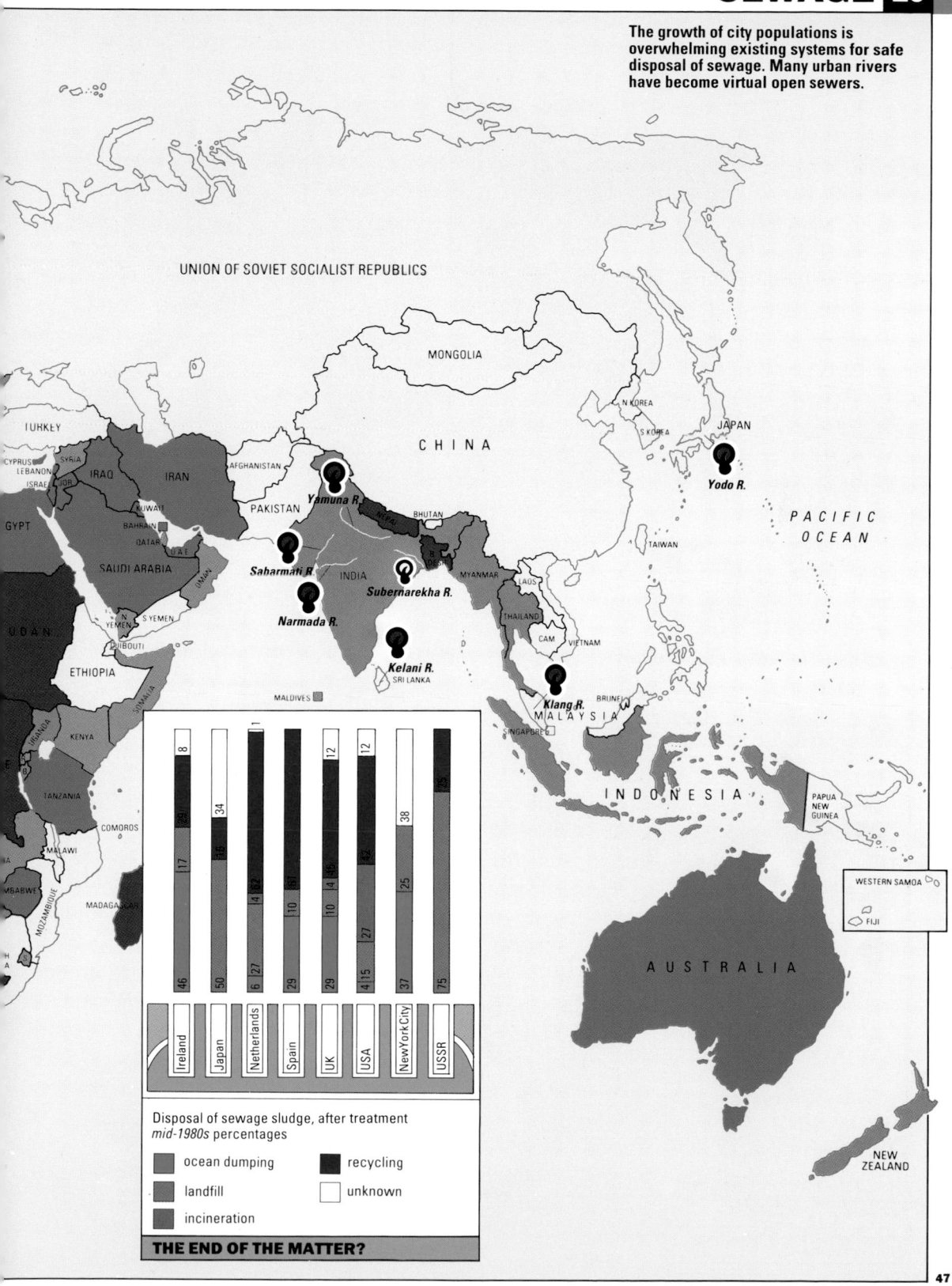

THE END OF THE MATTER?

Copyright © Swanston Publishing Limited

AIR QUALITY

CITIES WITH AIR QUALITY PROBLEMS
Annual averages *mid-1980s*
Known pollution is greatest from high levels of

- sulphur dioxide
- nitrogen oxides
- both

High level exceeds international safe health guidelines

medium levels of:

- sulphur dioxide
- nitrogen oxides
- both

Most sulphur dioxide comes from burning fossil fuels; most nitrogen oxides come from cars.

For acid rain see Map 24; for fossil fuel pollution see Map 23.

Data compiled by Claire Holman Main sources: GEMS (1988); World Resources Institute (1988); OECD (1989).

In many cities, just breathing is a health hazard.

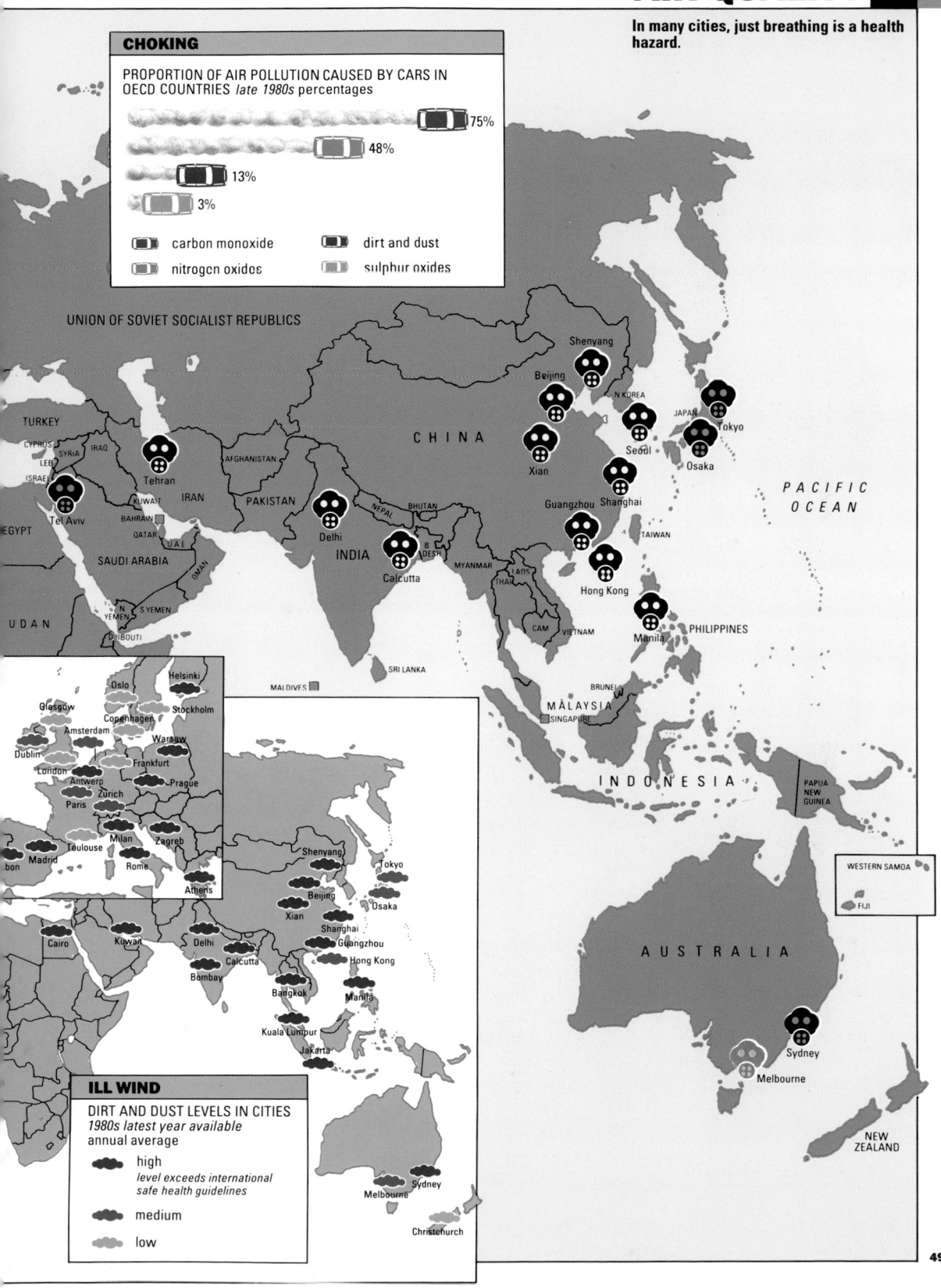

Copyright © Swanston Publishing Limited

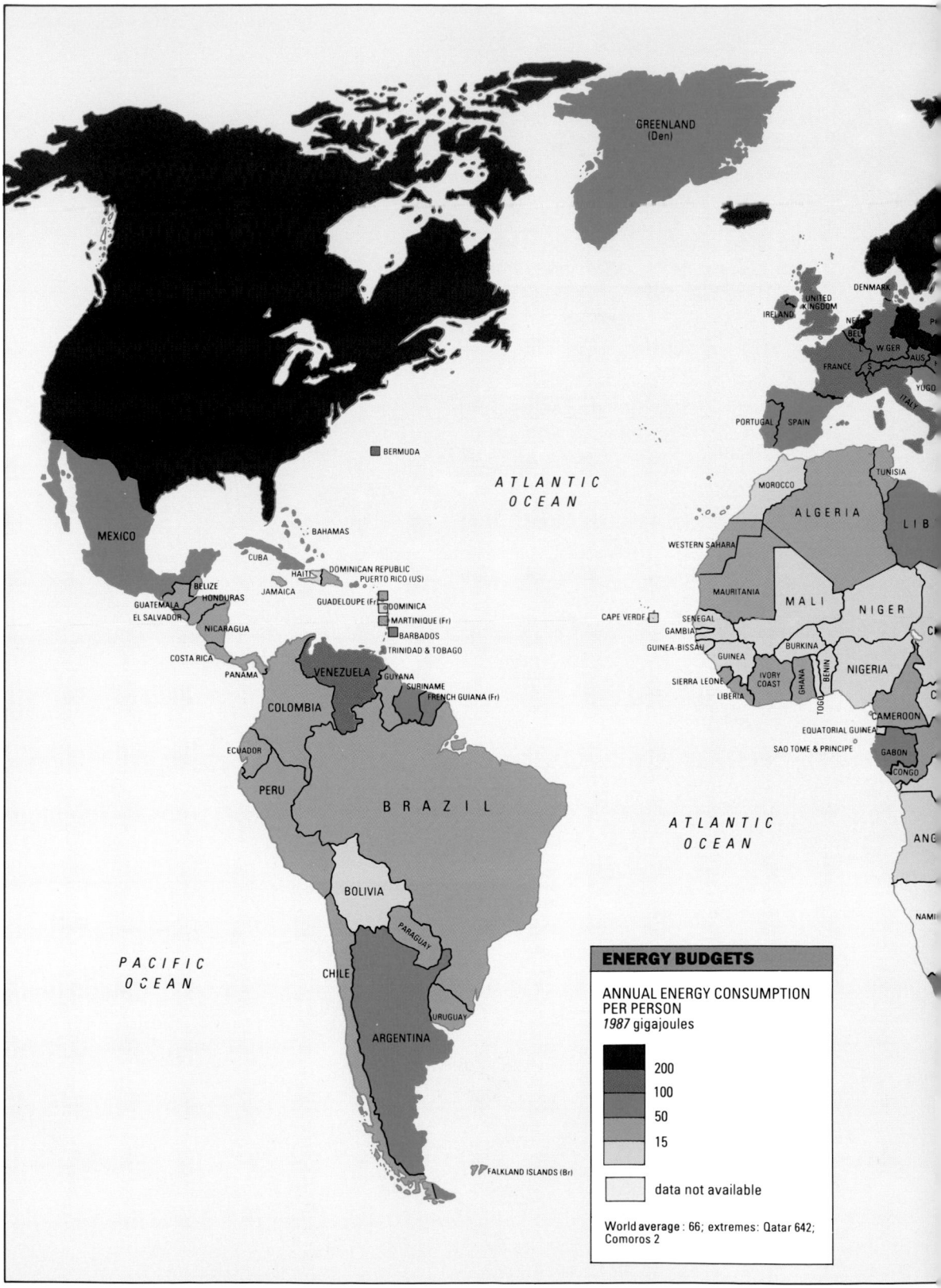

Data compiled by Lisa Greber Main sources: IEA (1989); UN *Energy Statistics Yearbook* (1989).

There is neither social nor environmental balance in today's global energy budget.

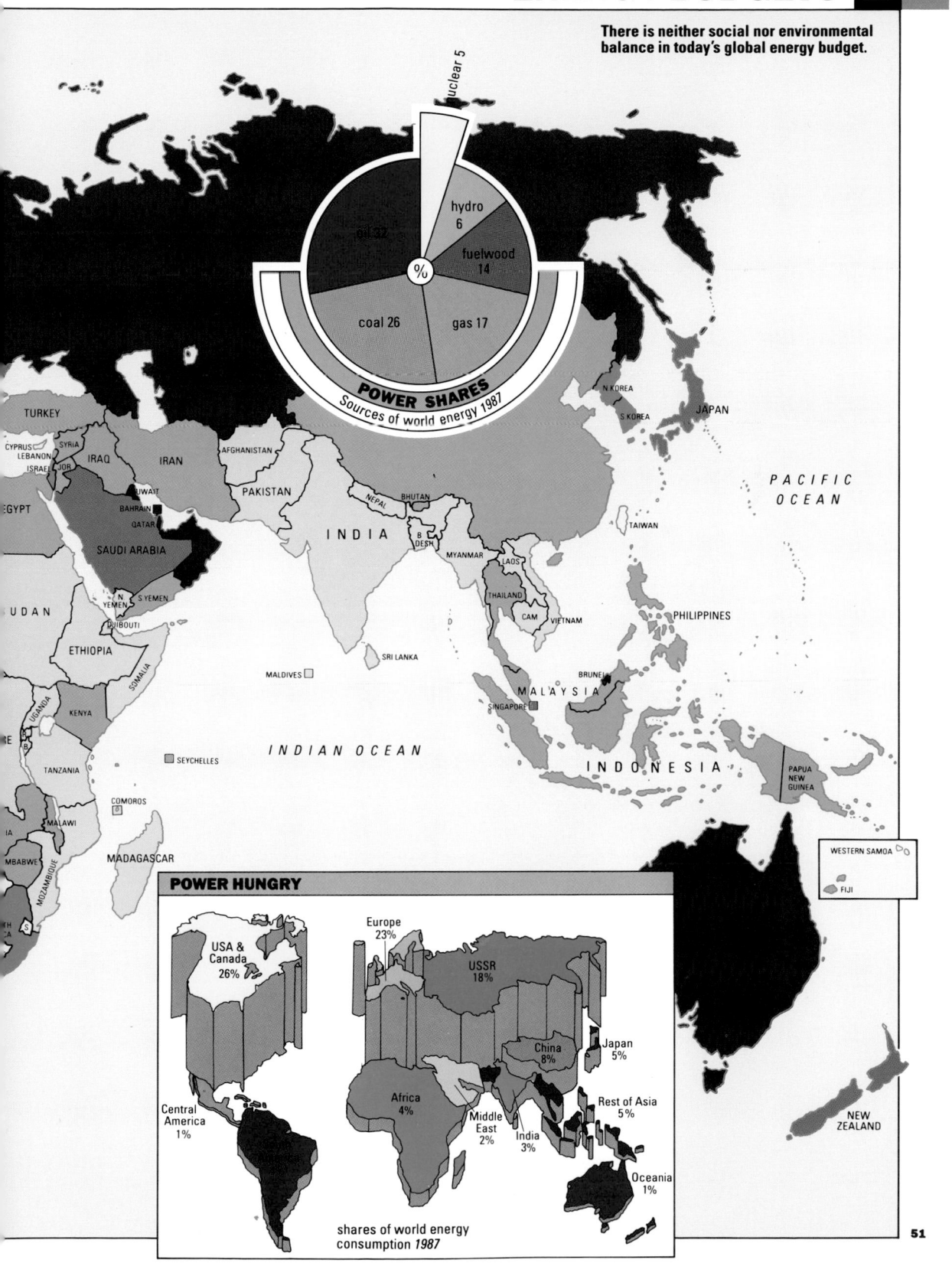

Copyright © Swanston Publishing Limited

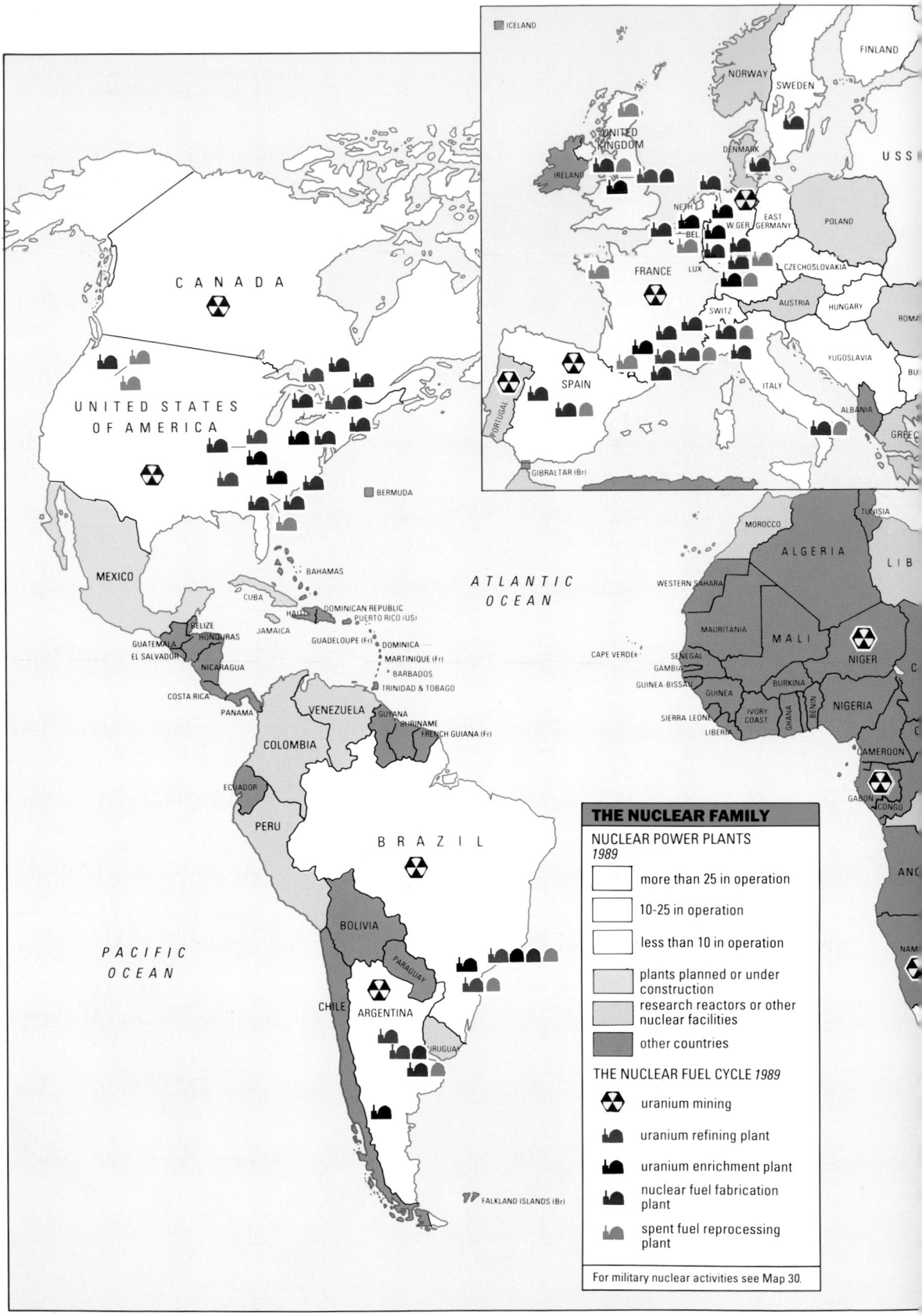

Data compiled by Lisa Greber Main sources: International Atomic Energy Agency (1989); *Nuclear News* (August 1989).

THE NUCLEAR FAMILY 19

There are more than 400 nuclear power plants operating in 26 countries. But an even greater number of states participate in the supply and support of the nuclear industry.

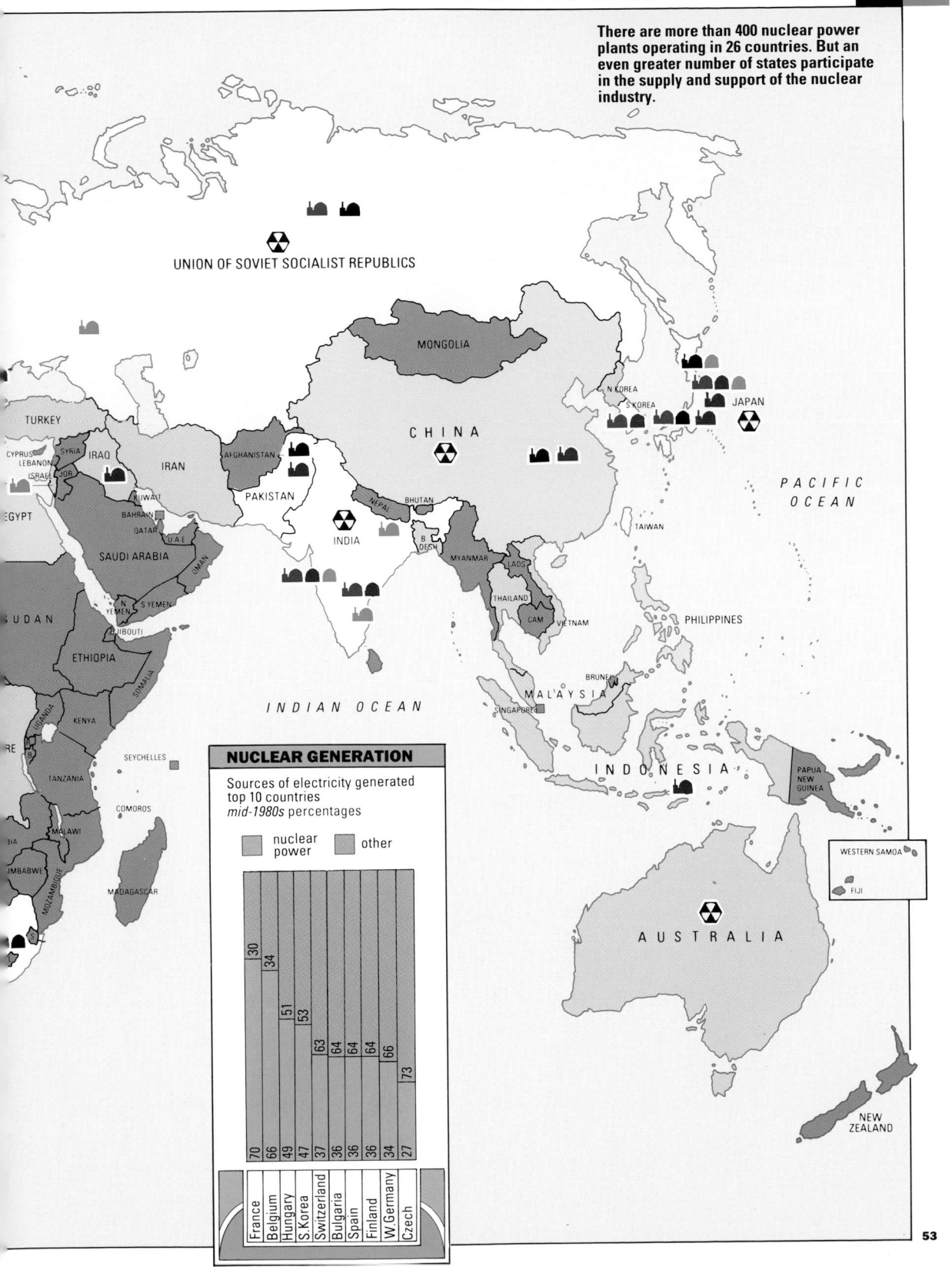

Copyright © Swanston Publishing Limited

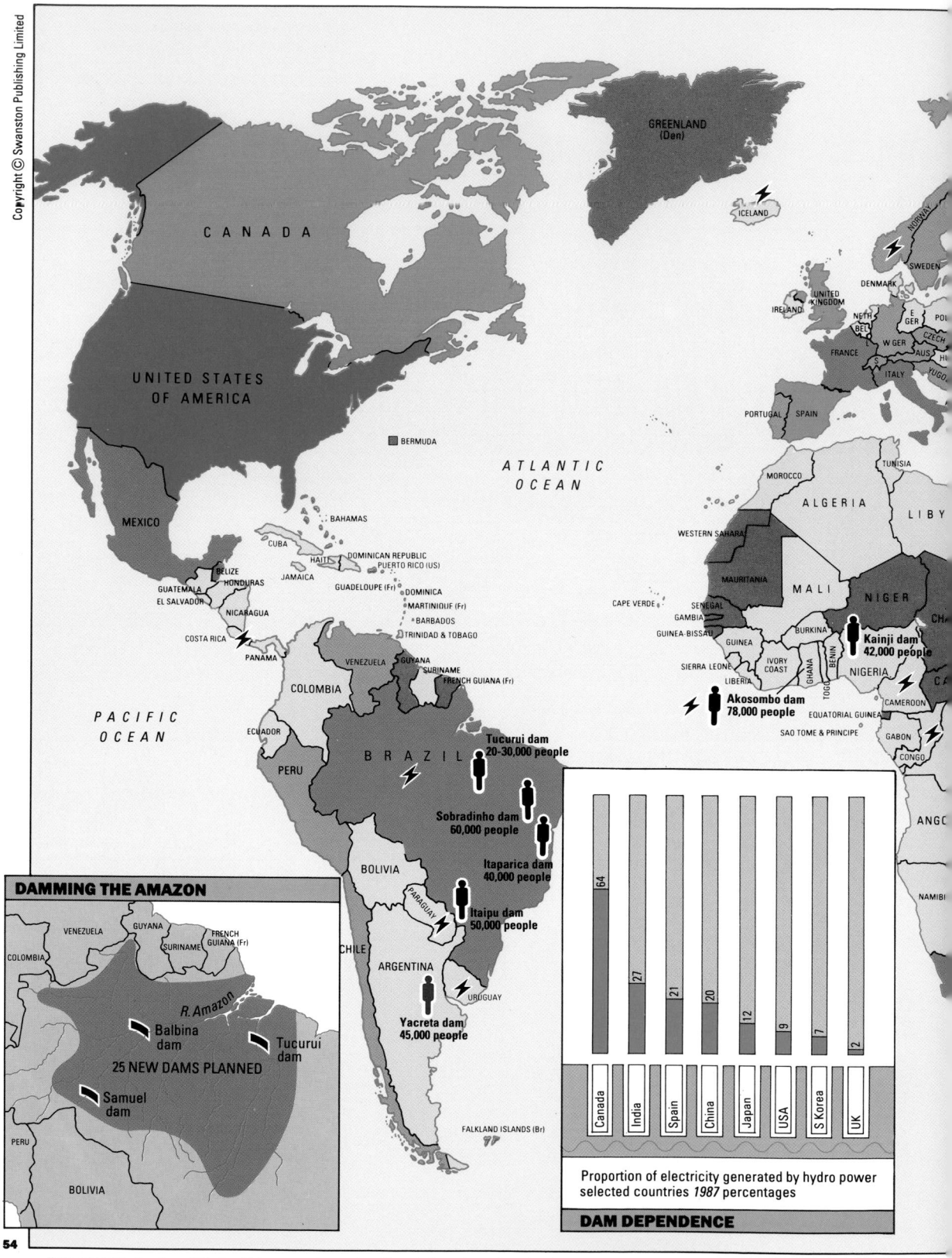

Data compiled by Constance E Hunt Main sources: International Commission on Large Dams (1984); Mermel (1989); Simons (1989);

Hydro power is a cheap and renewable energy source, but dams often carry a high social and environmental price tag.

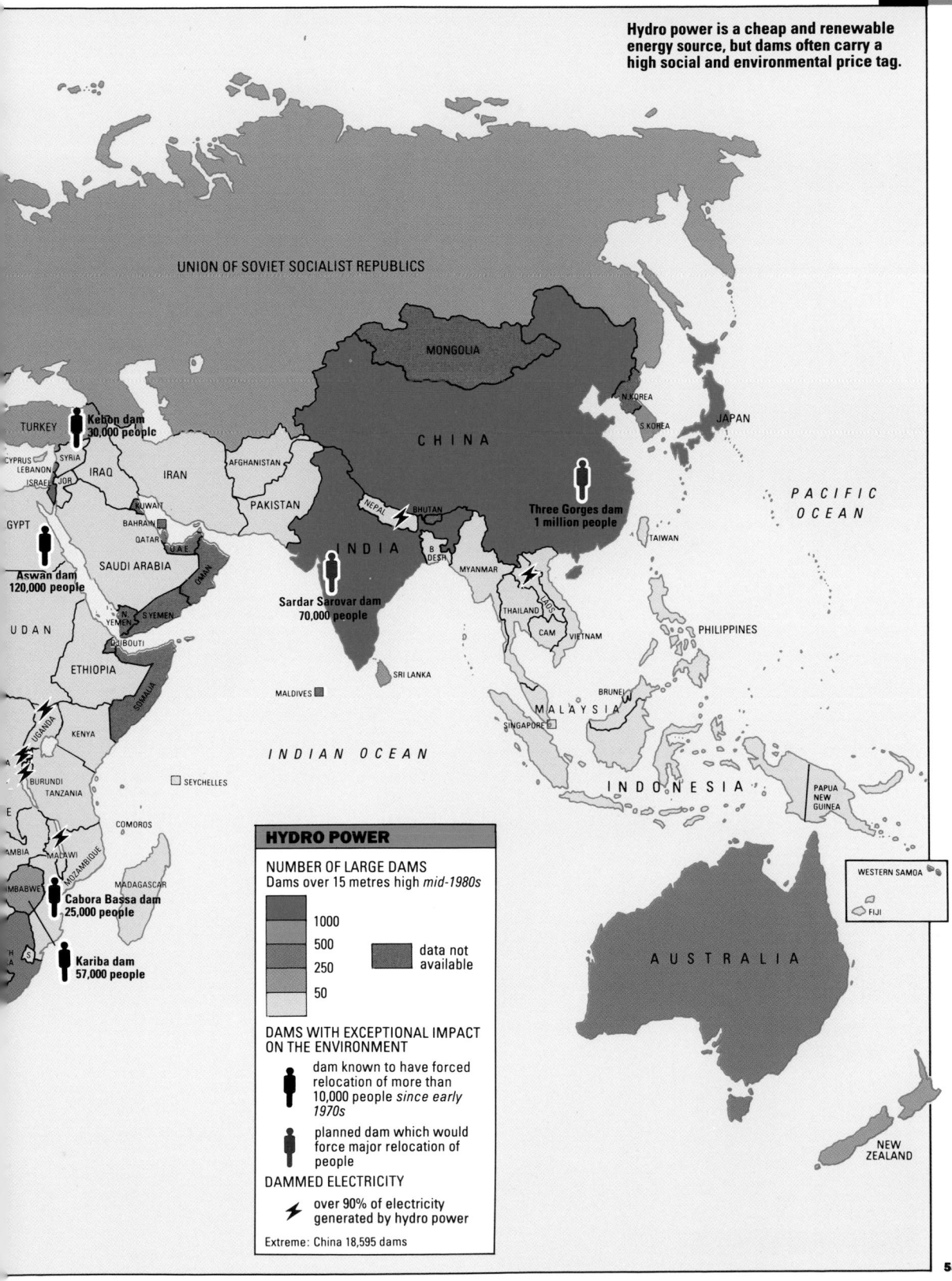

Copyright © Swanston Publishing Limited

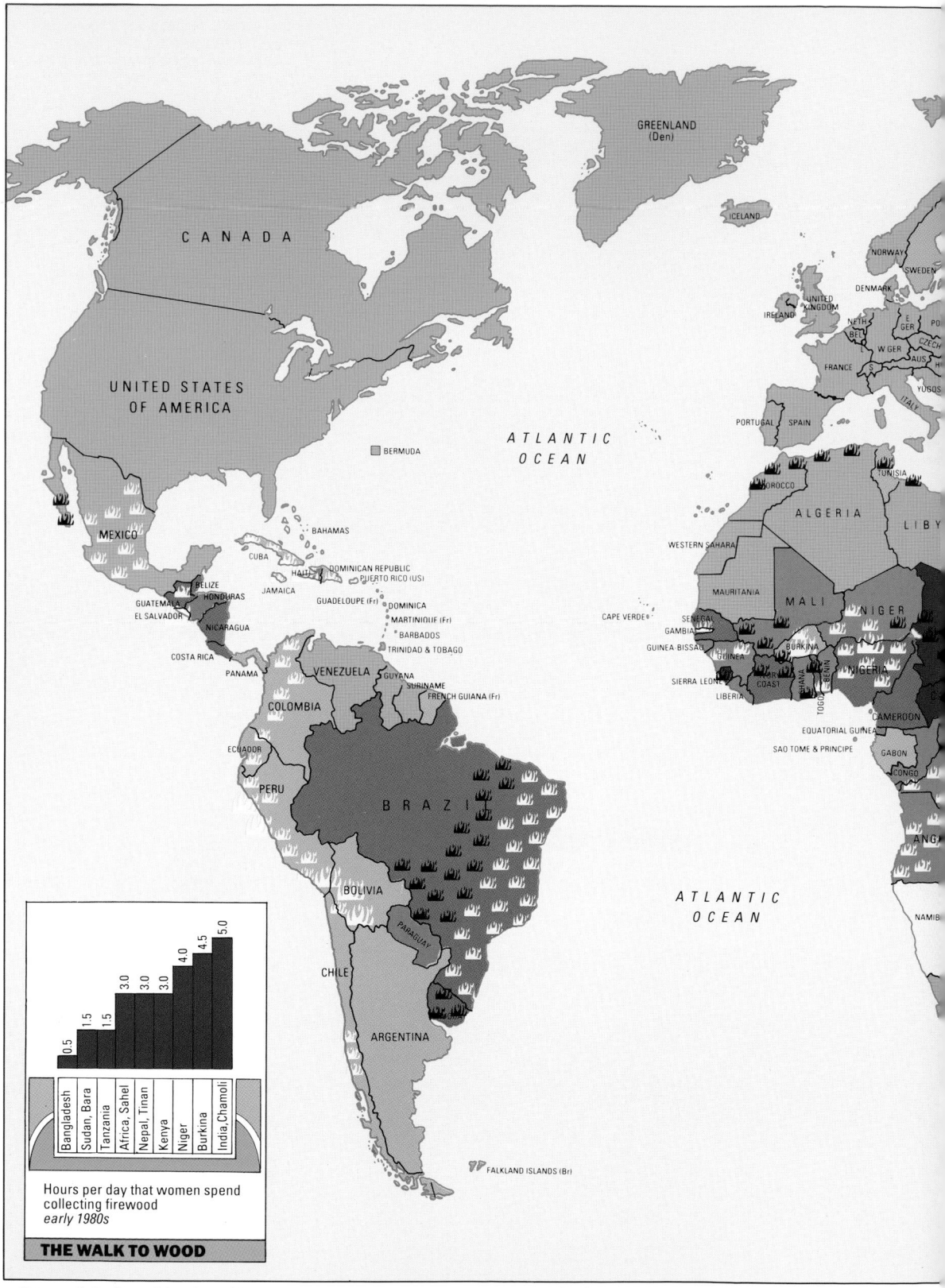

THE WALK TO WOOD

Data compiled by Thomas E Downing Main sources: Agarwal (1986); FAO (1981); UN Statistical Office (1987).

Firewood, the primary source of energy for many people in the world, is increasingly short in supply.

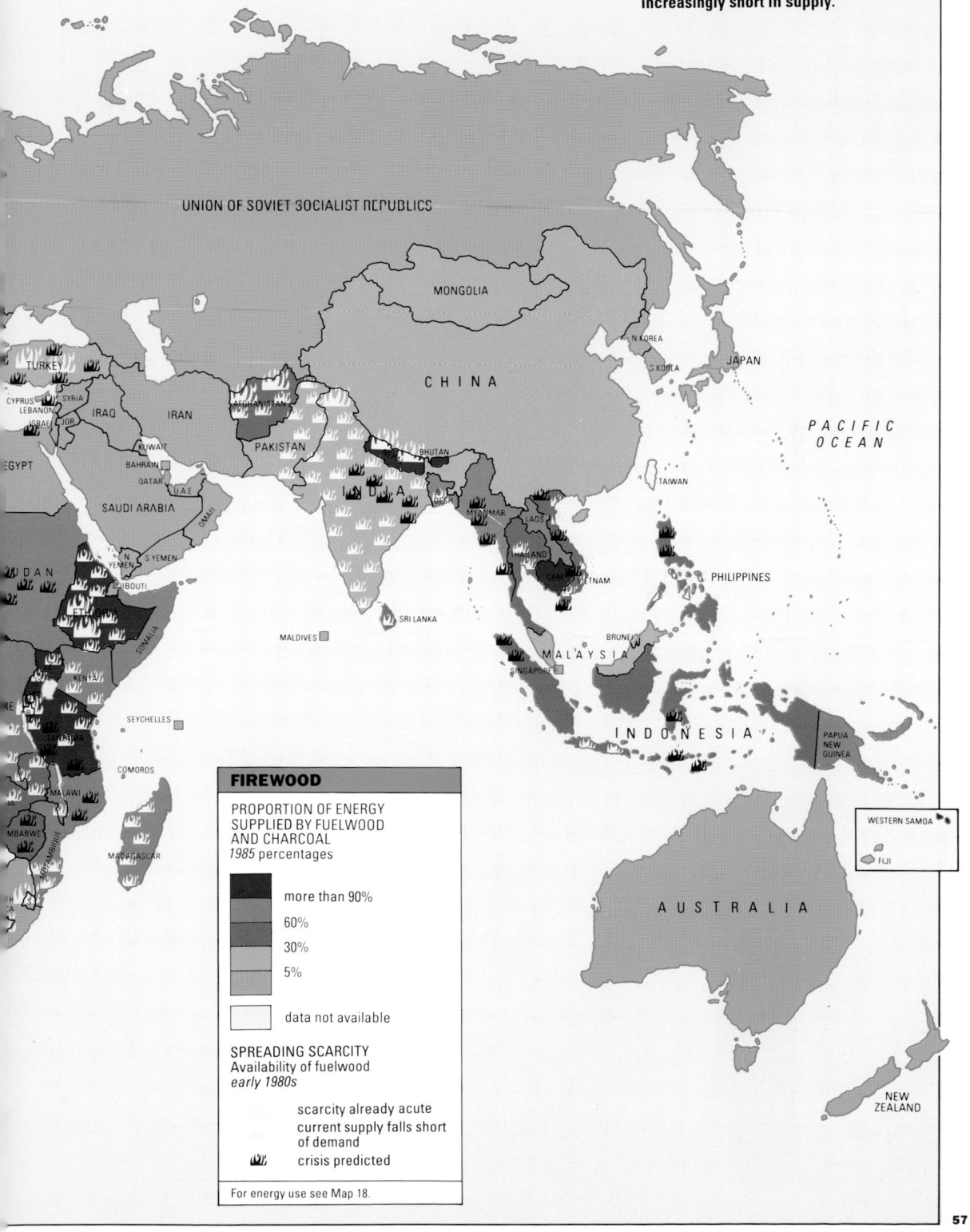

Copyright © Swanston Publishing Limited

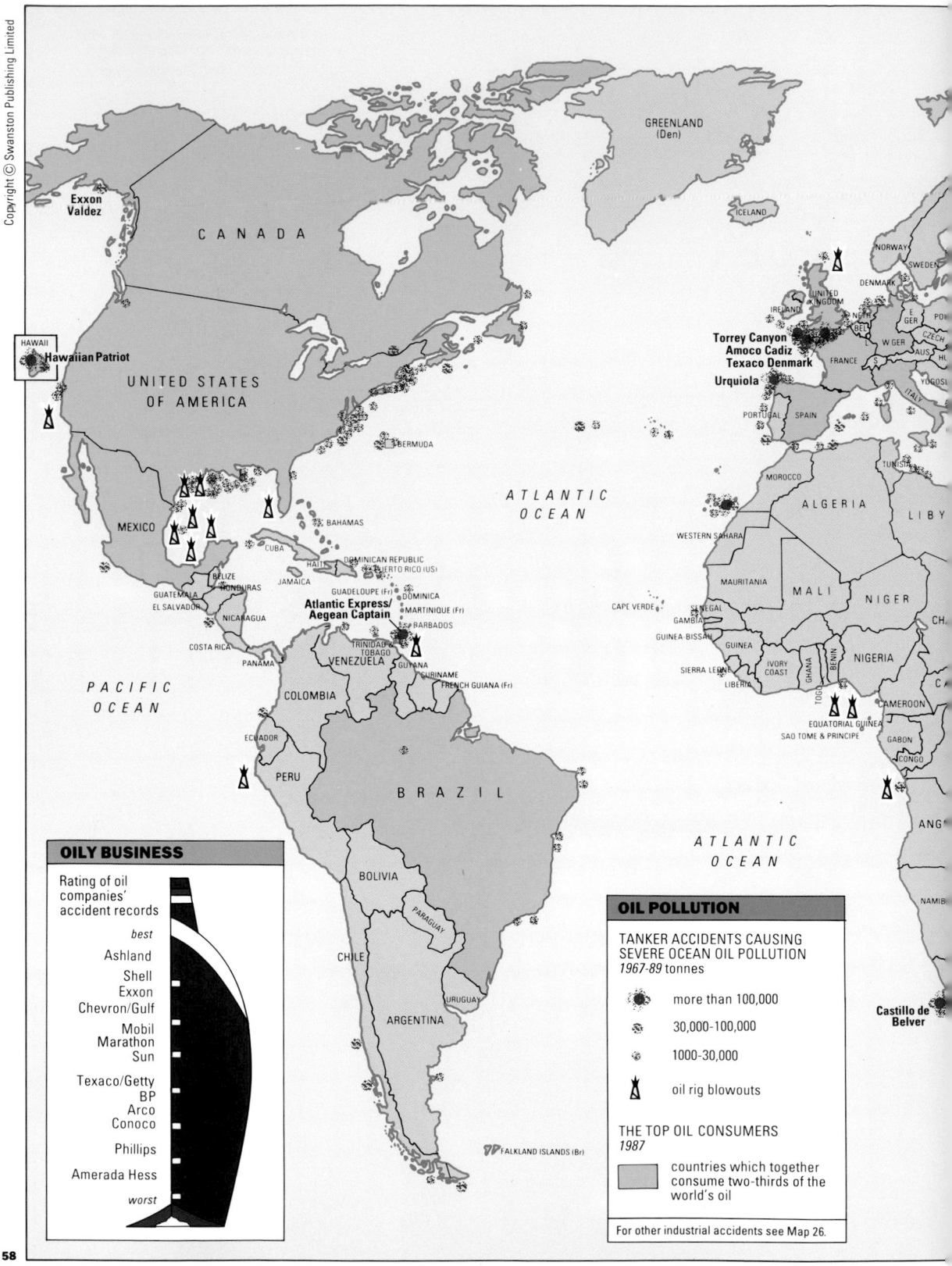

Data compiled by Dominic Golding

Main sources: Couper (1983); ITOPF (1983); Levy (1984); McKenzie (1989); NAS (1985); OECD *Environmental Data Compendium* (1989); Tanker Advisory Center (1989); UNEP *Environmental Data Report* (1989).

Dependence on oil is a defining feature of modern industrial economies, as is the pollution it leaves in its wake.

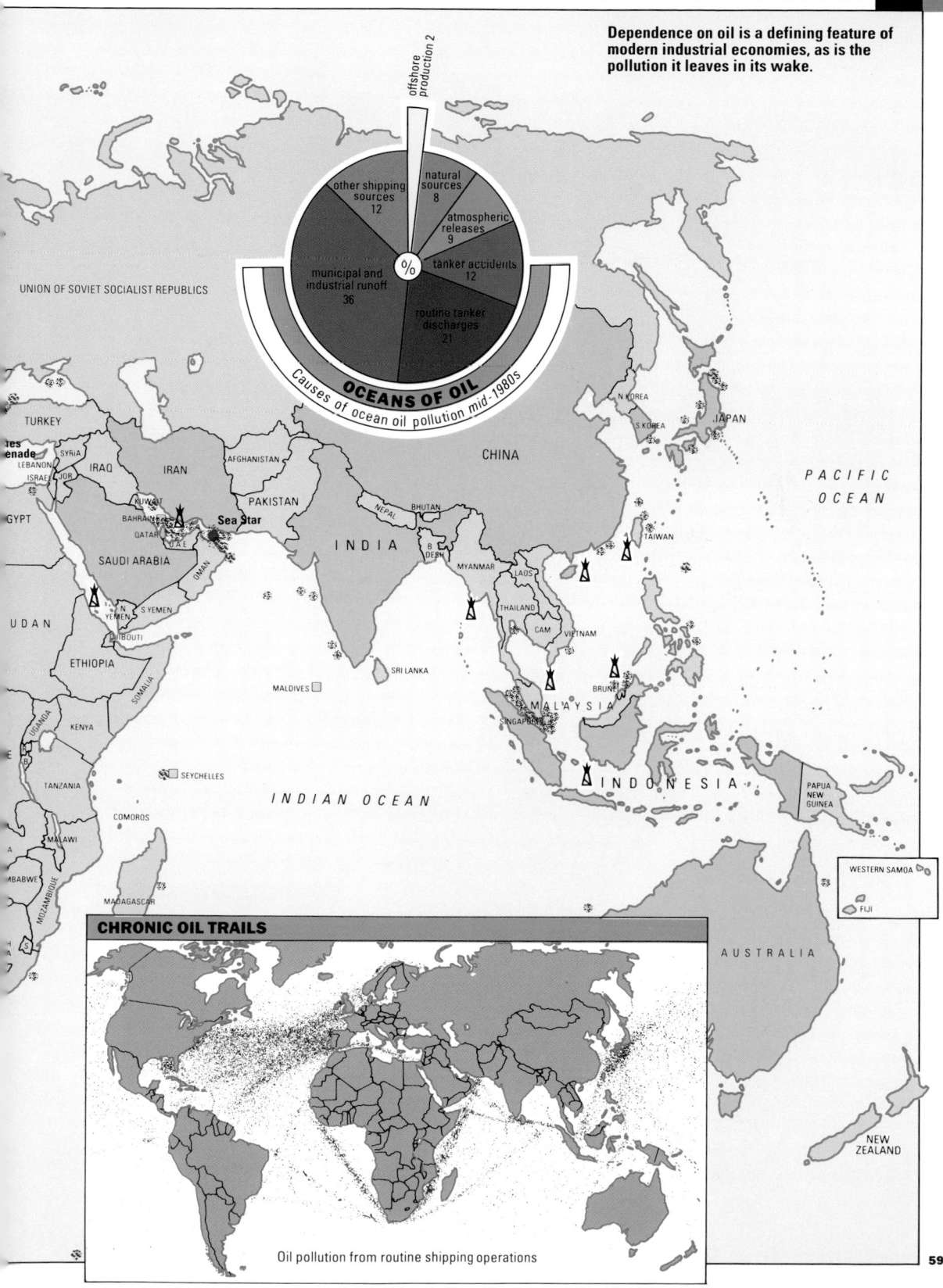

Copyright © Swanston Publishing Limited

Data compiled by Claire Holman Main sources: Eliasson et.al. (1988); GEMS (1988); Oak Ridge National Laboratory (1988).

FOSSIL FUEL POLLUTION 23

There is now 25 per cent more carbon dioxide in the atmosphere than there was at the beginning of the Industrial Revolution. It is the major cause of global warming.

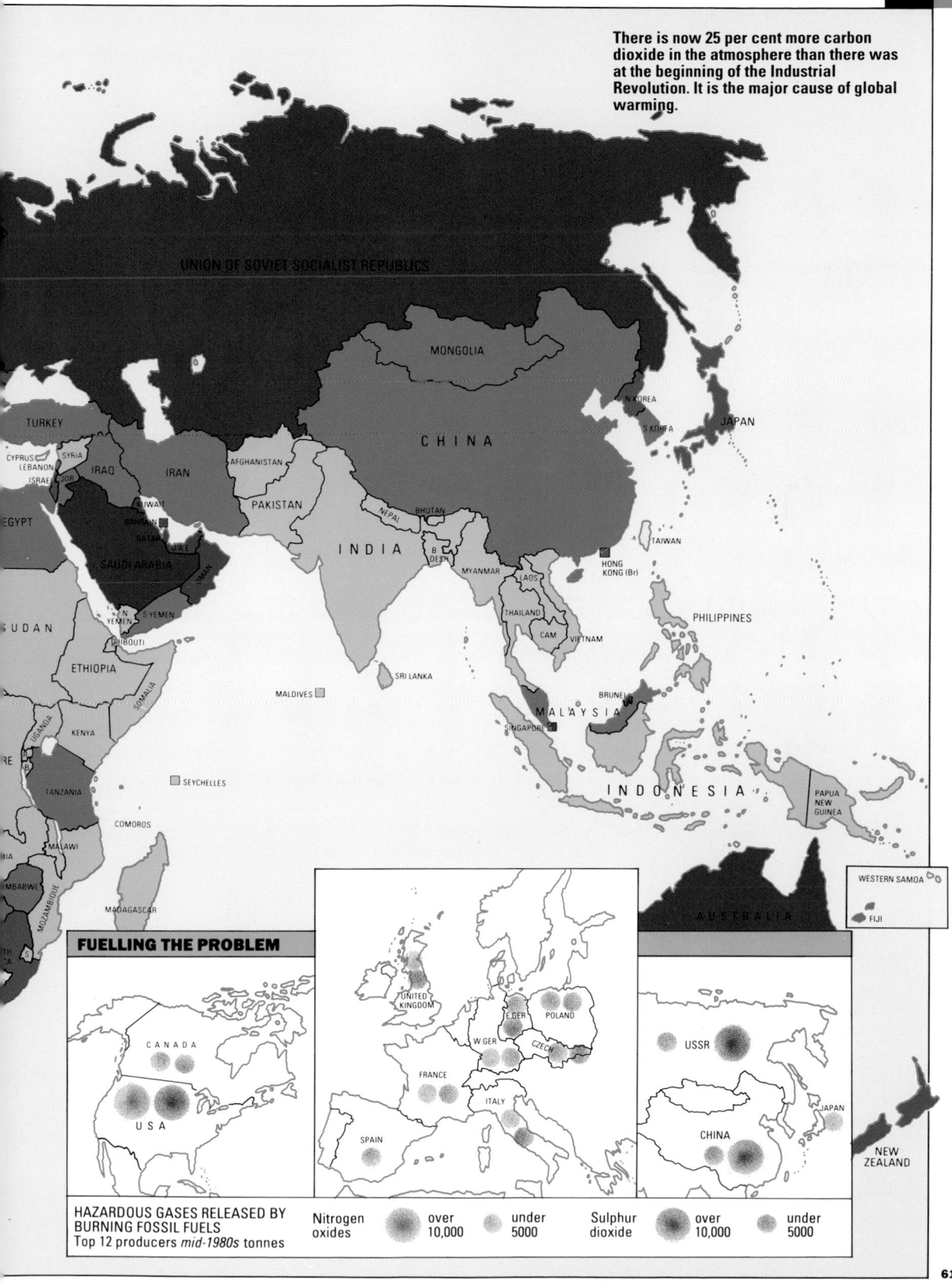

Copyright © Swanston Publishing Limited

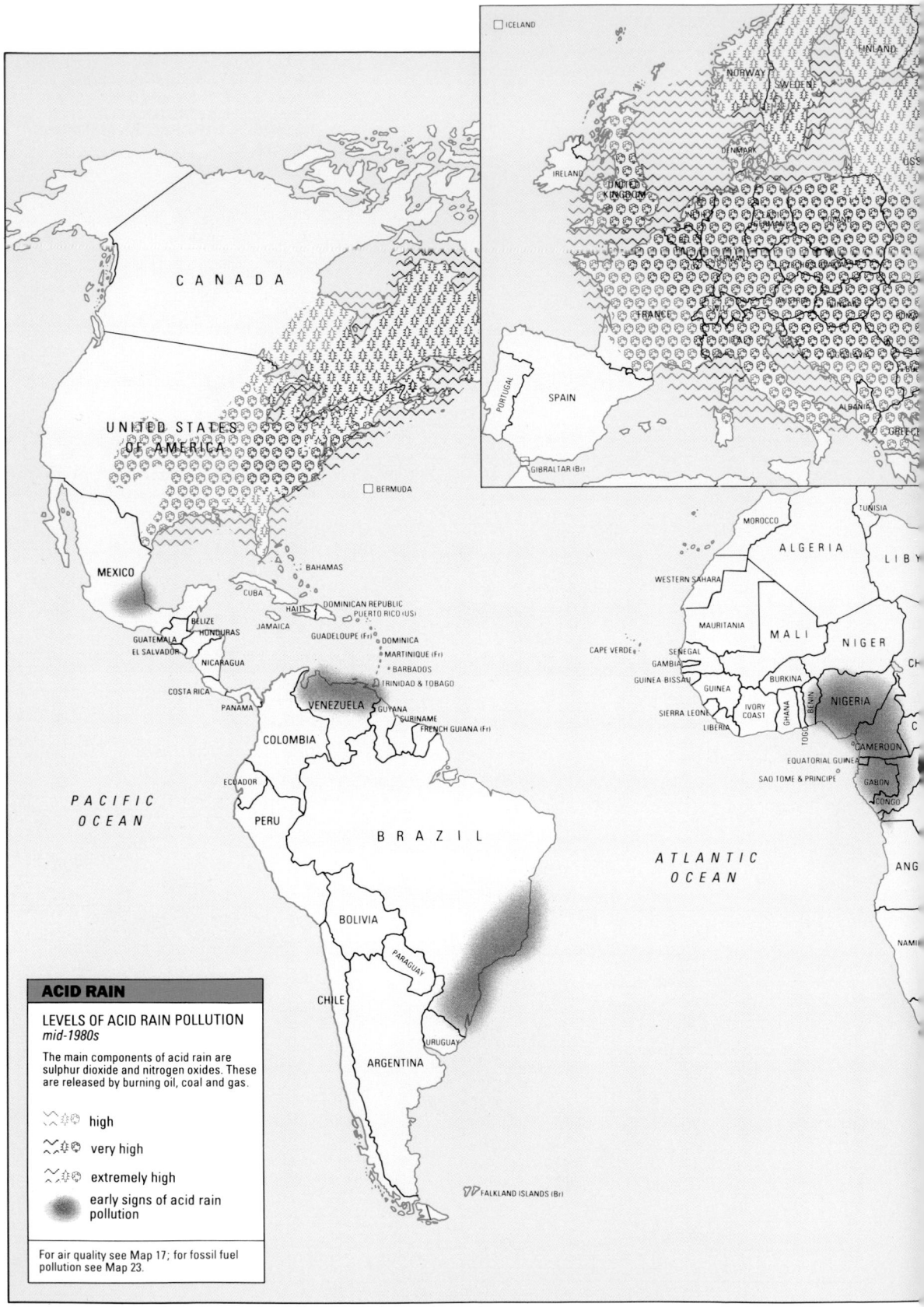

Data compiled by Friends of the Earth/Mike Birkin

Main sources: Goldsmith & Hildyard eds. (1988); UNEP, *Forest Damage & Air Pollution* (1989); McCormick (1989); World Resources Institute (1988).

ACID RAIN 24

Acid rain is the fallout of industrial and fossil-fuel dependent economies. After falling on Europe for more than 100 years it is now becoming a global phenomenon.

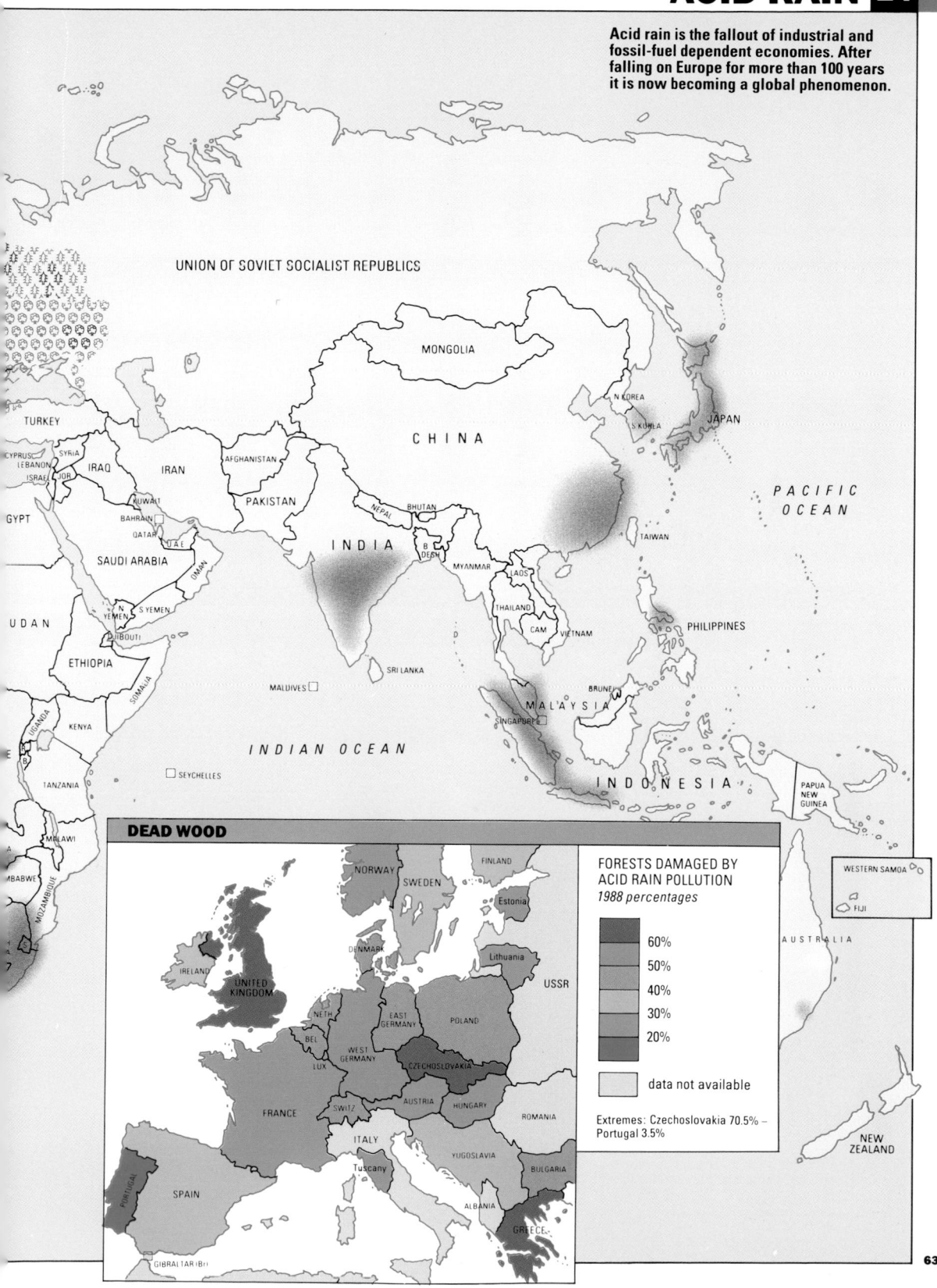

Copyright © Swanston Publishing Limited

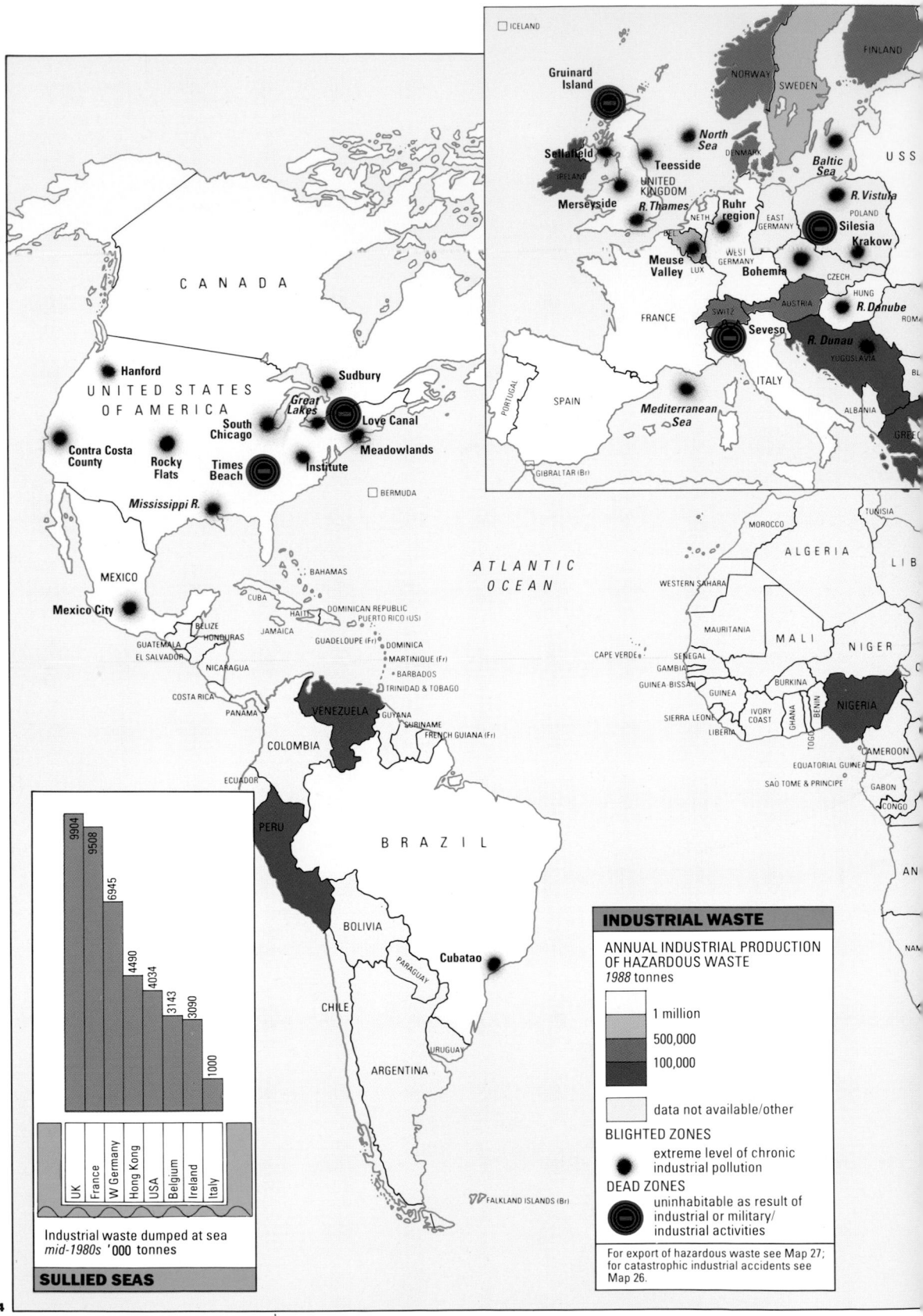

Data compiled by Joni Seager Main sources: National Wildlife Federation *The Toxic 500 1987* (1989); UNEP *Environmental Data Report* (1989).

Chronic pollution and a worldwide trail of hazardous waste are hallmarks of the industrial age.

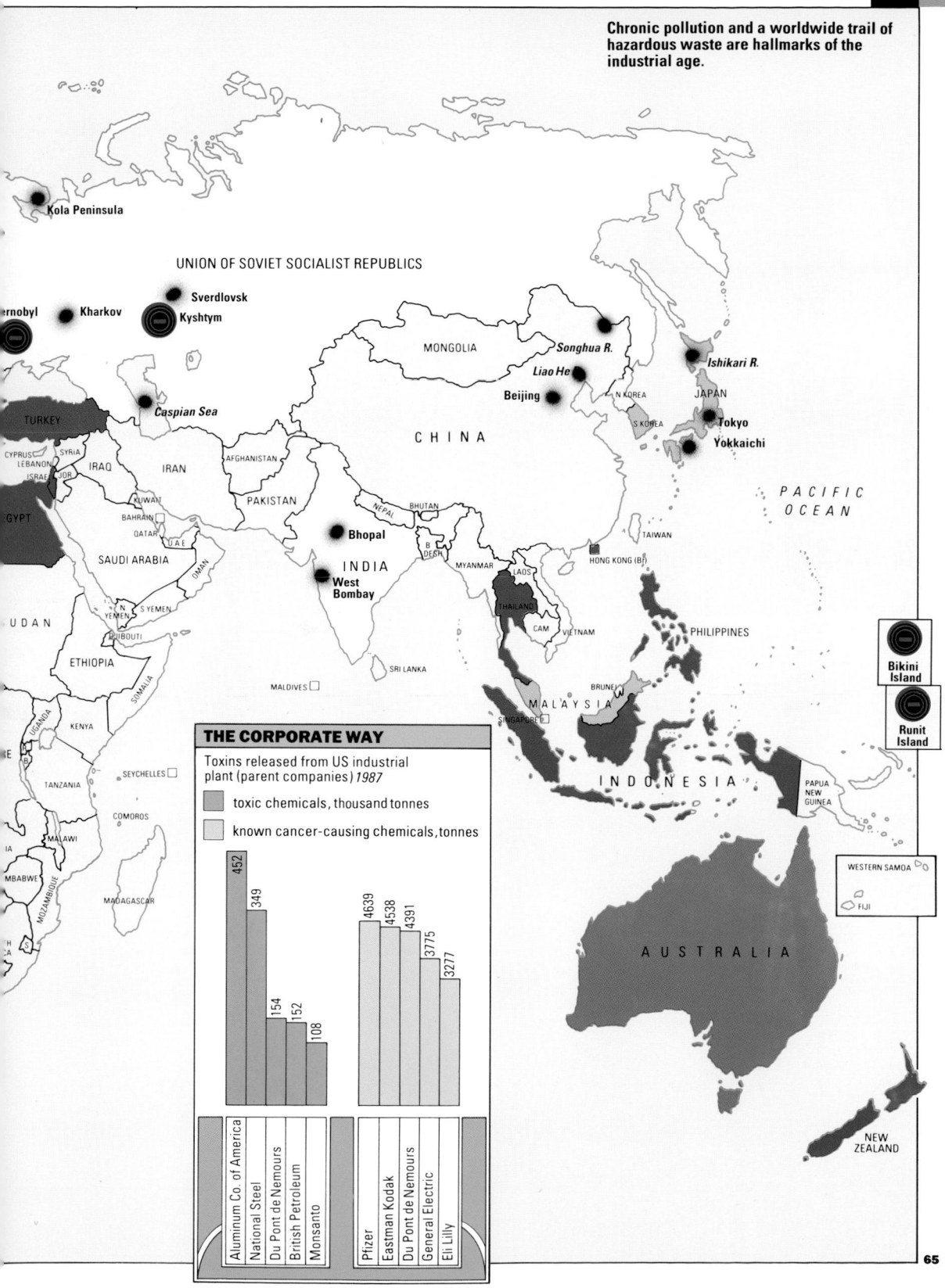

Copyright © Swanston Publishing Limited

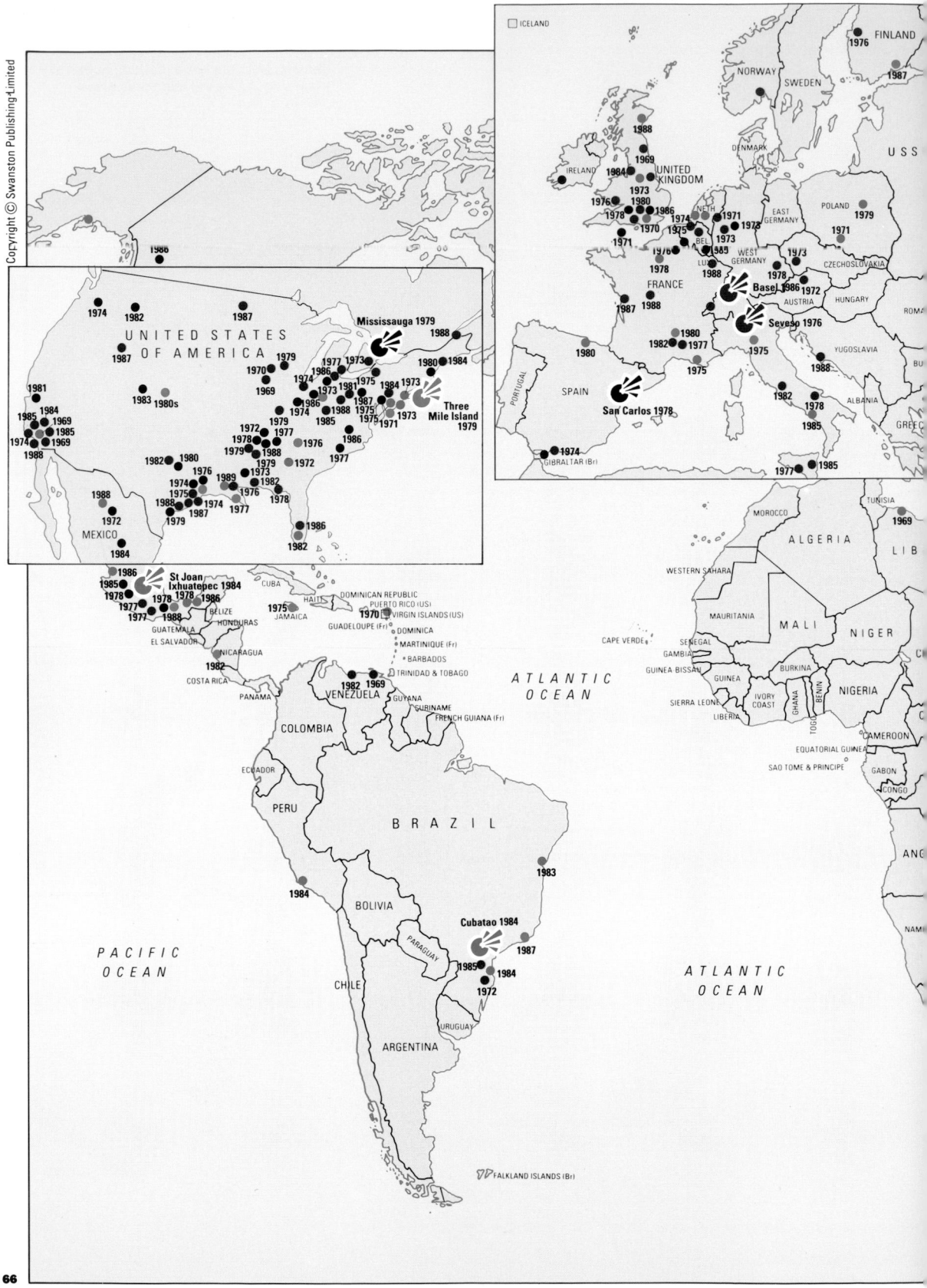

Data compiled by Dominic Golding Main sources: OECD *Environmental Data Compendium* (1989); UNEP *Environmental Data Report* (1988/90); Lagadec (1982); Gittus (1988).

Accidents are usually characterized as unprecedented events. But as industrialization spreads and the products of industry become more toxic, 'accidents' are becoming a normal part of industrial culture.

DEADLY INDUSTRY

MAJOR INDUSTRIAL ACCIDENTS
resulting in damage to human health, life and the environment *1969-89*
date given where known

major industrial accident	catastrophic industrial accident	
●		manufacturing plant or storage facility accident
●		transportation accident
●		accident in natural gas/oil refining facility, pipeline or storage tank
●		other accident in manufacture and transportation of hazardous materials

For oil spills and oil-rig blowouts, see Map 22

Copyright © Swanston Publishing Limited

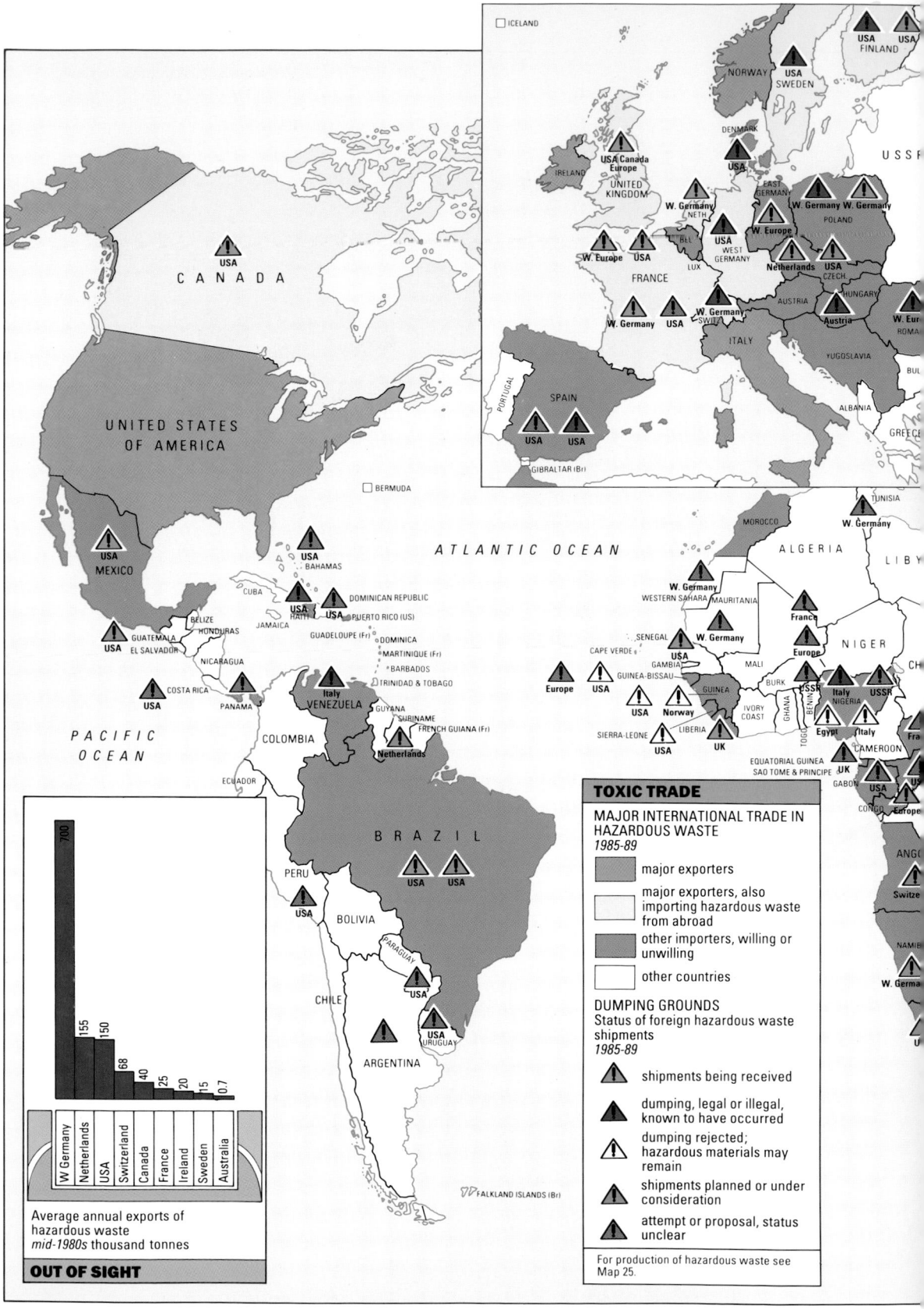

Data compiled by Marina Alberti Main sources: Greenpeace (1989); OECD *Environmental Data Compendium* (1989).

Poor countries have become dumping grounds as industrialized countries try to ship their toxic wastes out of sight out of mind.

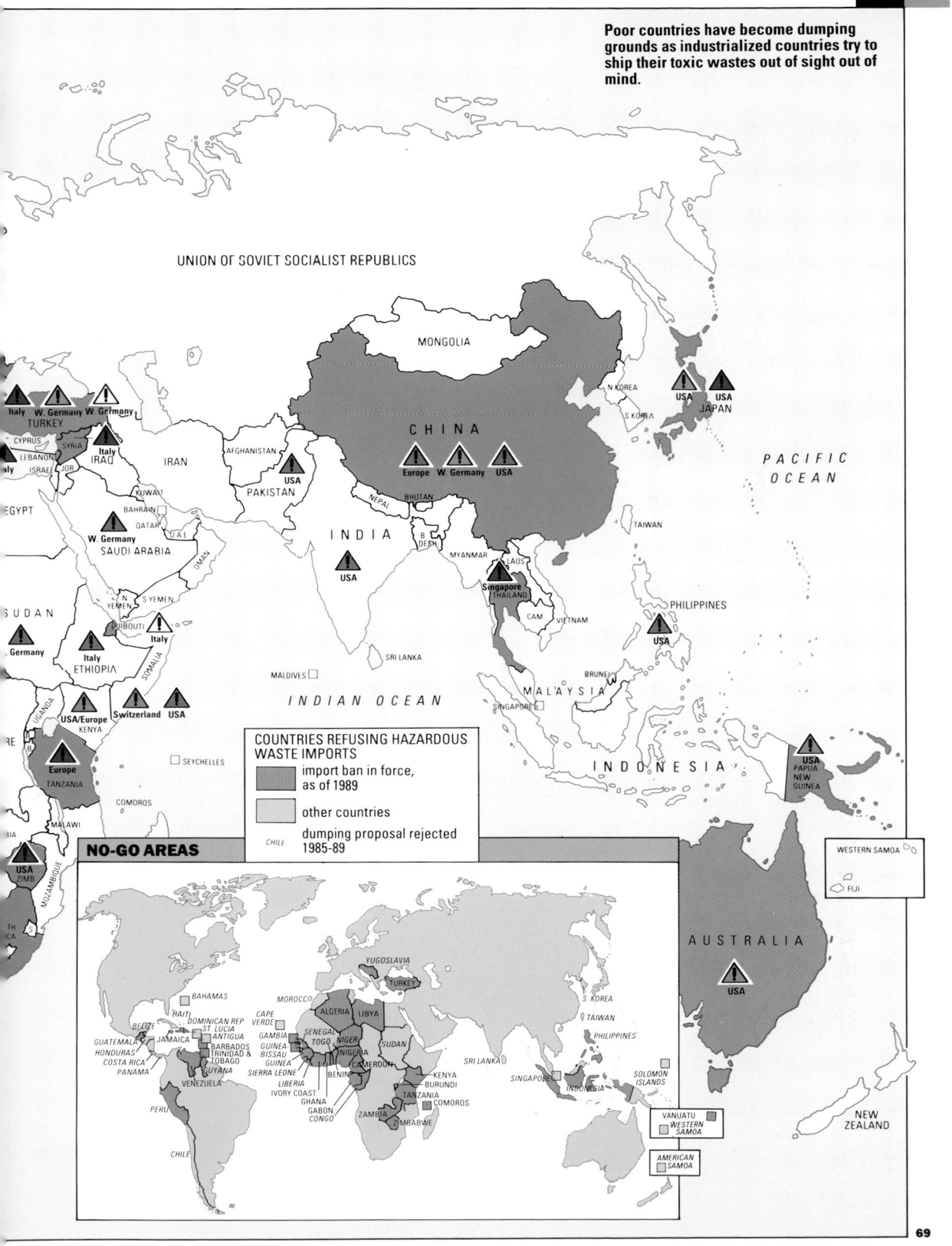

Copyright © Swanston Publishing Limited

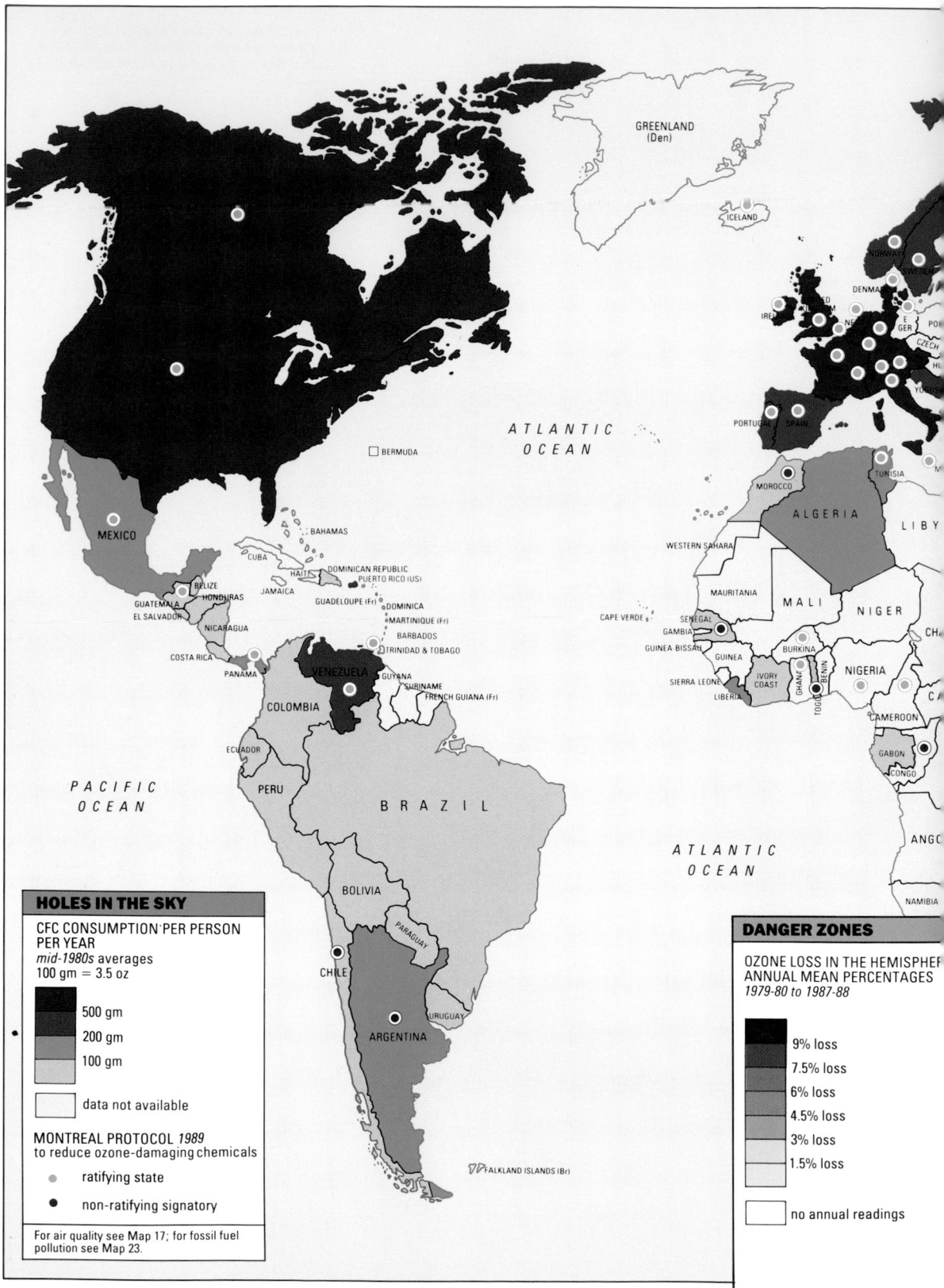

Data compiled by Nigel Dudley Main sources: US Environmental Protection Agency (1986); NASA Ozone Trends Panel; John Gille, US National Center for Atmospheric Research.

HOLES IN THE SKY 28

The chemicals that are now destroying the ozone layer do not occur naturally – they are entirely the creation of modern industry.

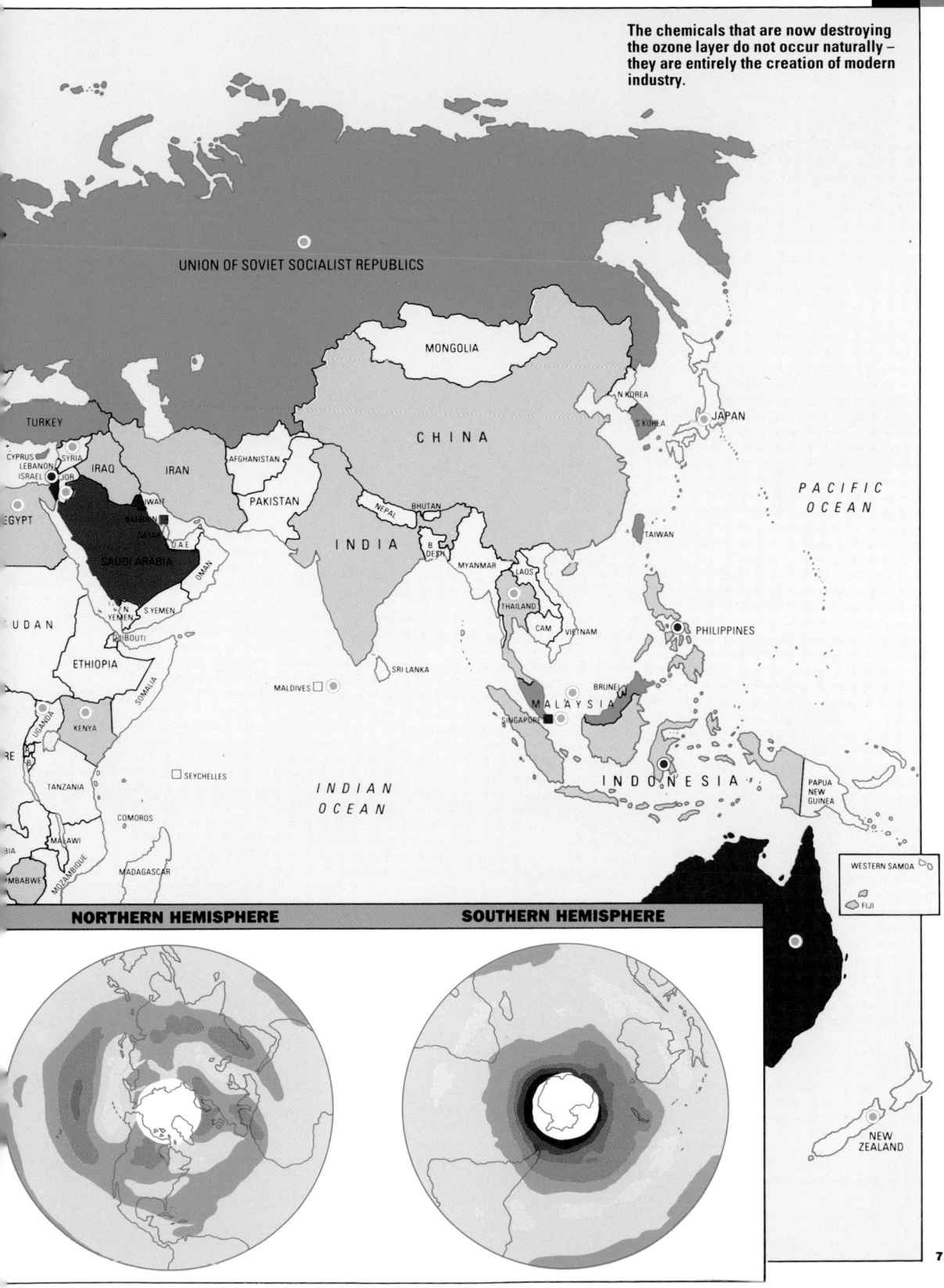

Copyright © Swanston Publishing Limited

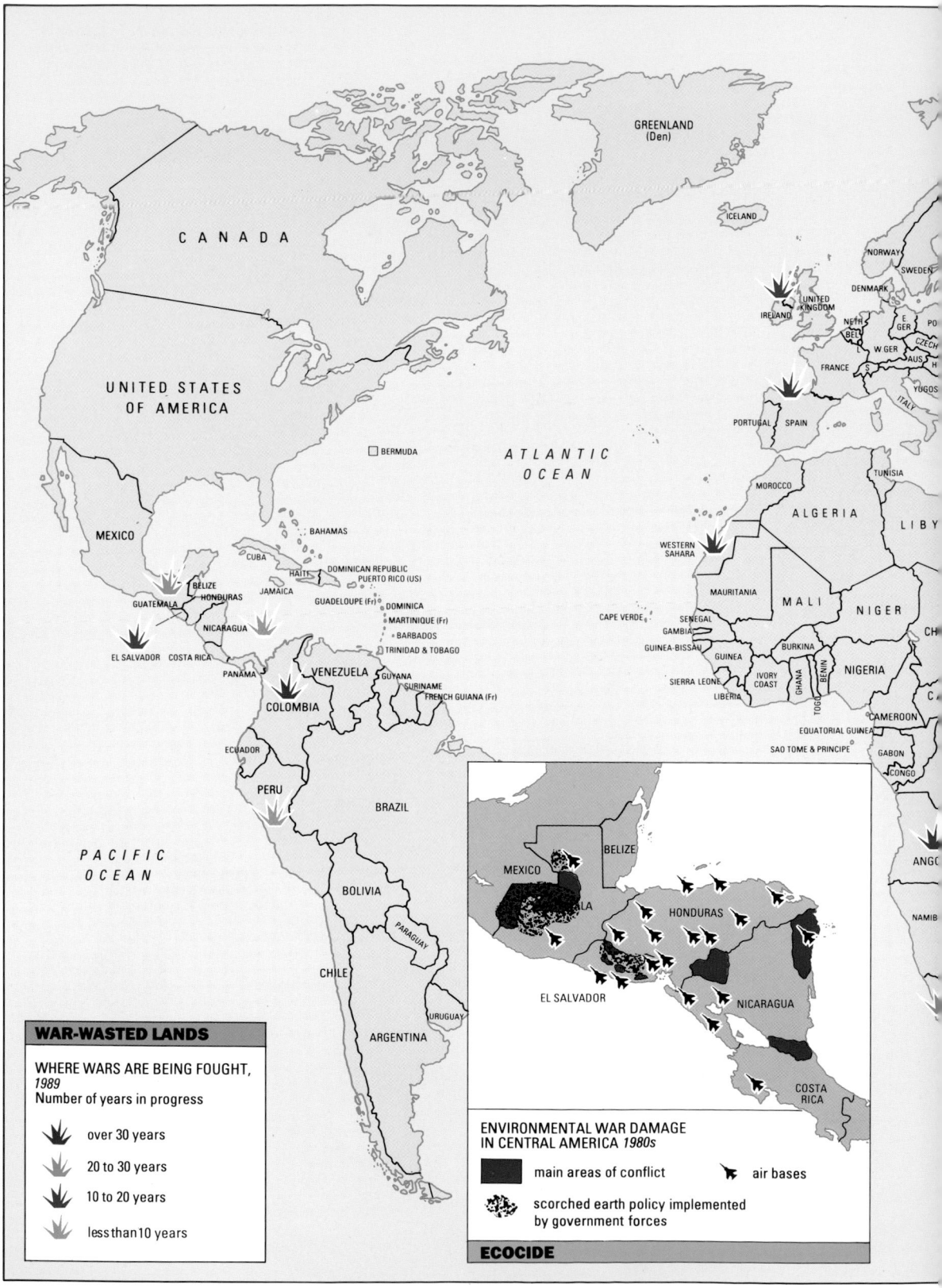

Data compiled by Dan Smith Main sources: EPOCA (1989); SIPRI *Yearbook* (1987, 1988, 1989); Sivard (1989); Wallensteen (1988)

As the weapons of war become more powerful, so the environmental damage they cause escalates. Often the environment itself is a military target.

Copyright © Swanston Publishing Limited

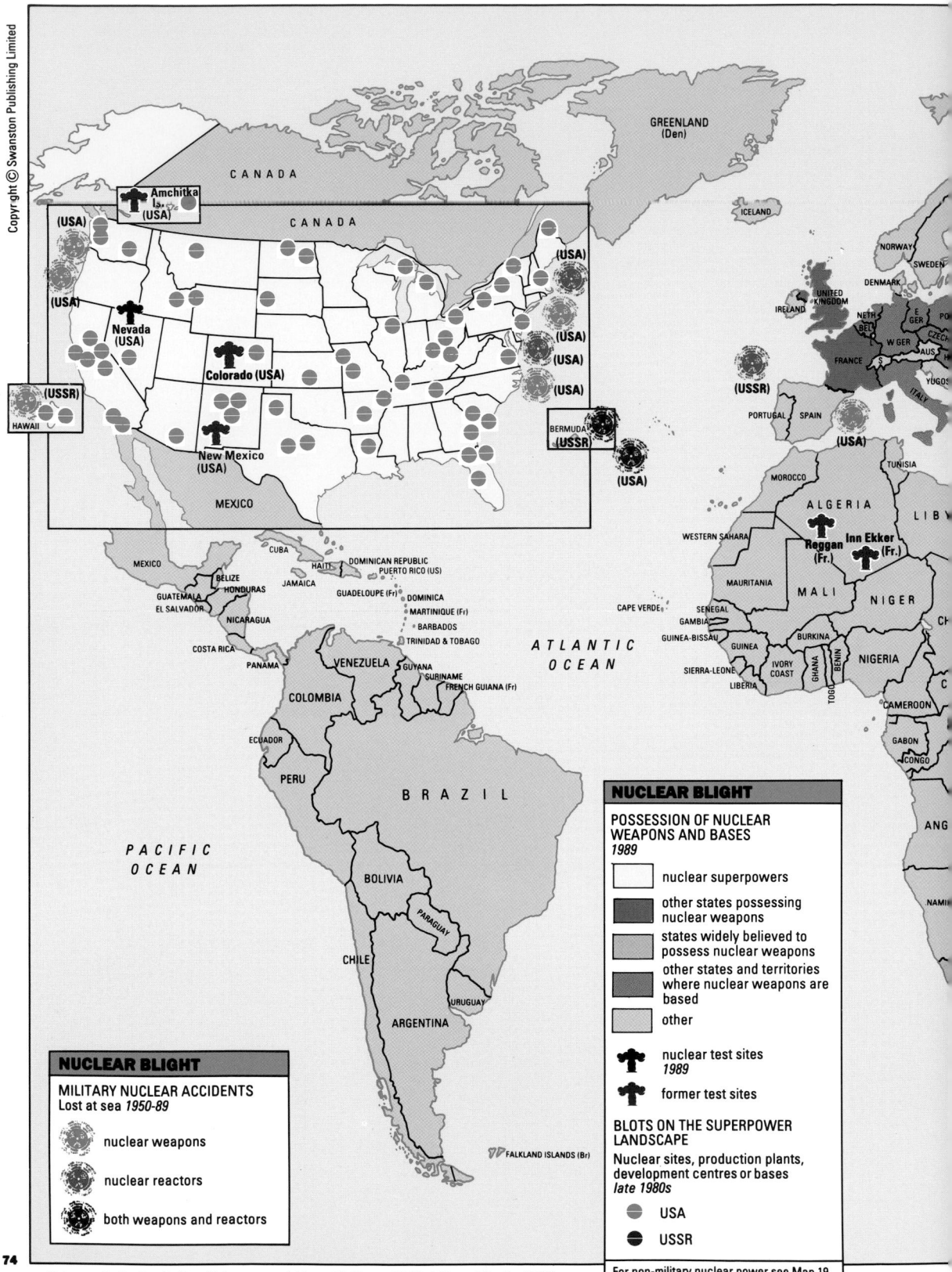

Data compiled by Dan Smith Main sources: Arkin and Fieldhouse (1985); Arkin and Handler (1989); *SIPRI Yearbooks*

NUCLEAR BLIGHT 30

The nuclear activities of a few military states pose a real and present danger to the global environment.

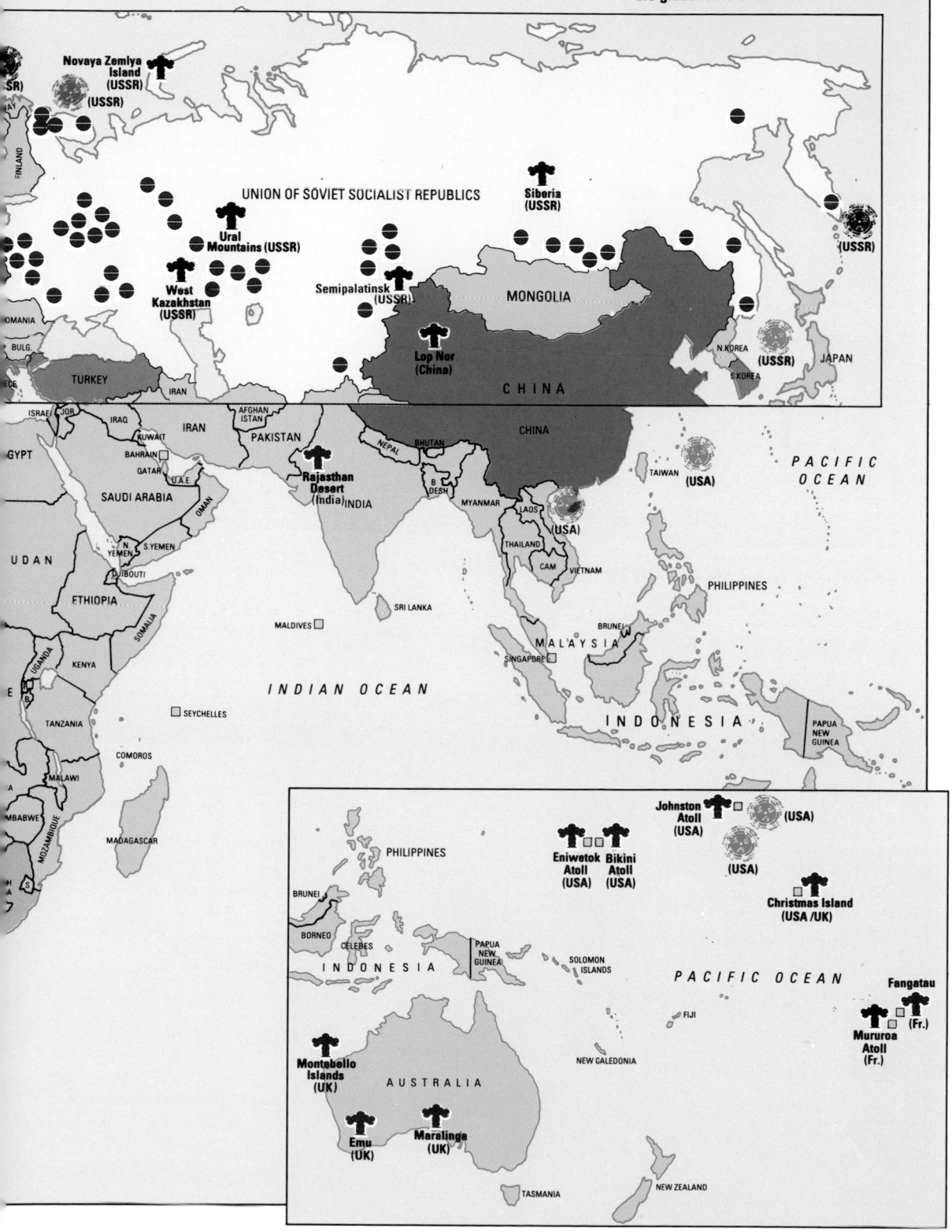

Copyright © Swanston Publishing Limited

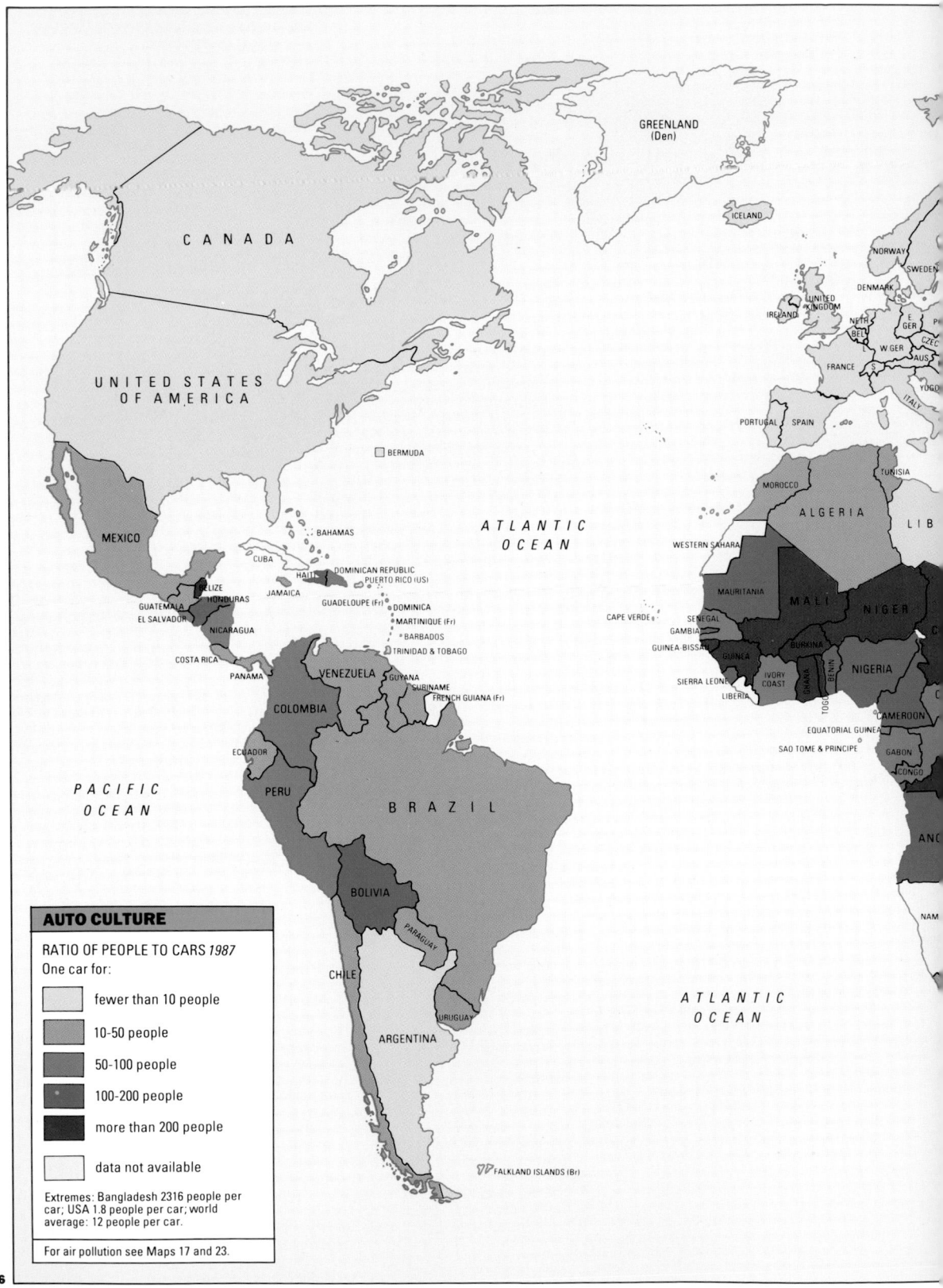

Data compiled by Joni Seager Main sources: *World Motor Vehicle Data* (1989).

The number of cars in the world has doubled in the past 20 years.

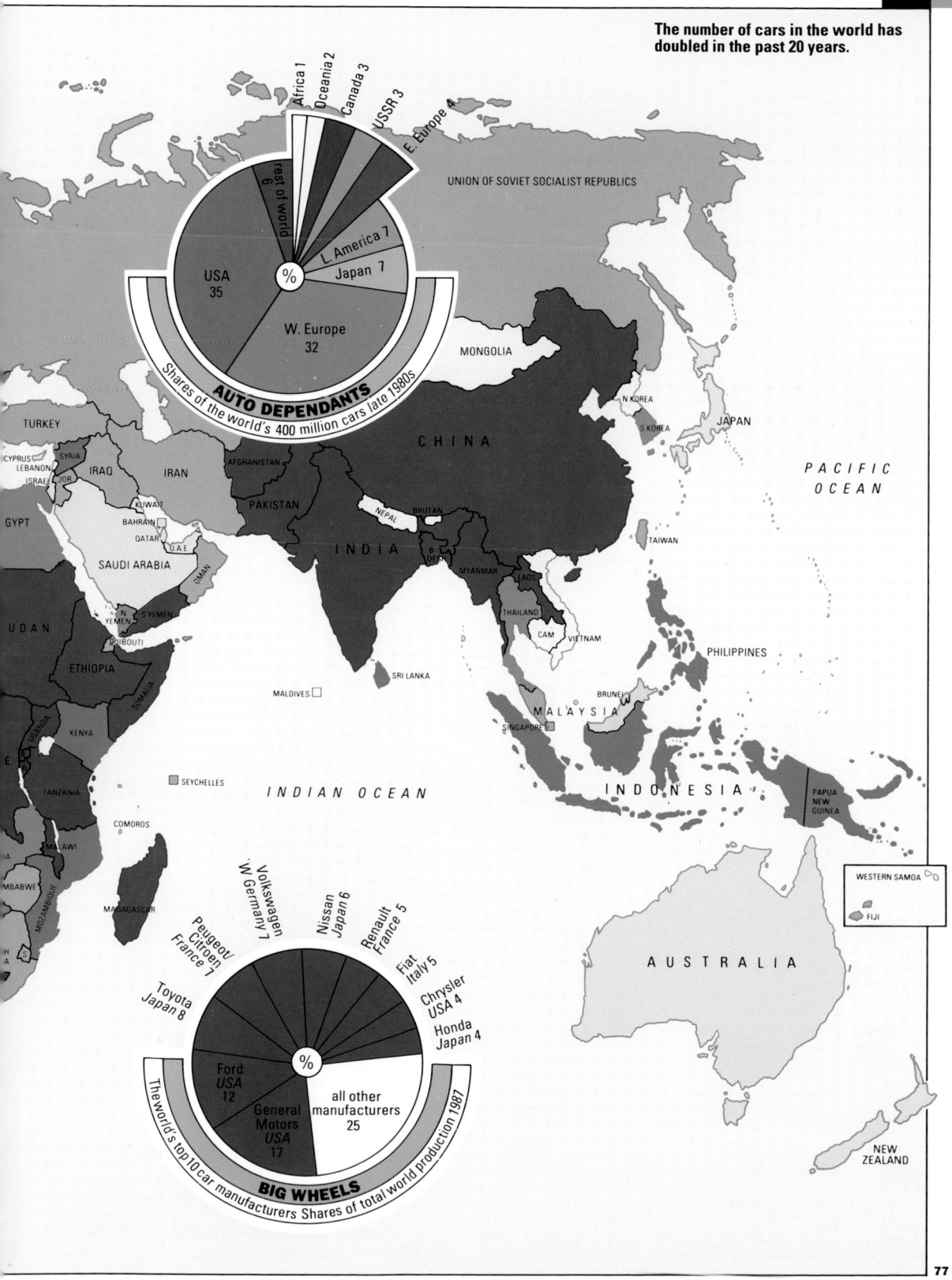

Copyright © Swanston Publishing Limited

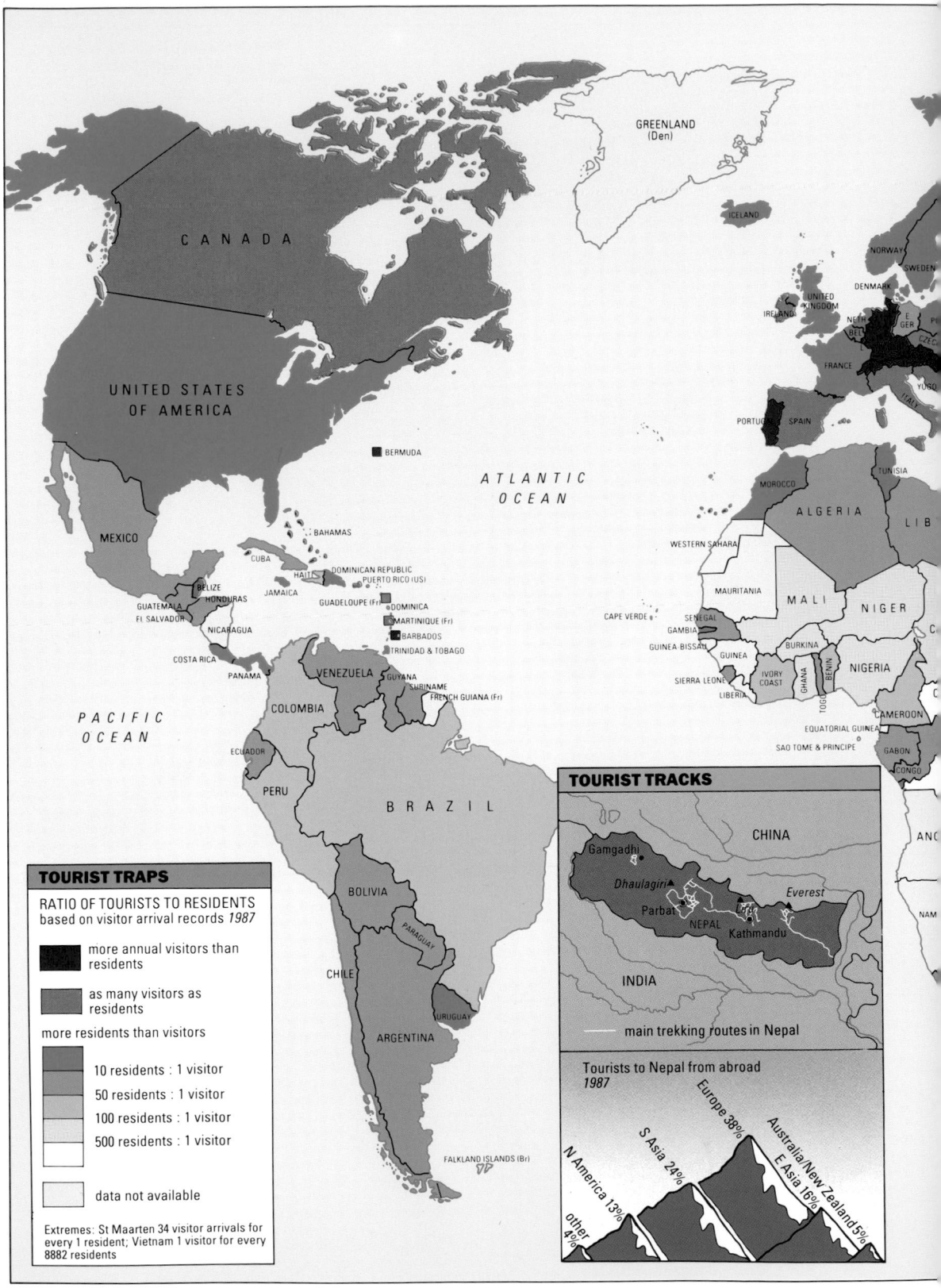

Data compiled by Nigel Dudley and Mark Davis Main sources: Commission of the European Communities *Quality of Bathing Water* (1987); World Tourism Organisation (1988).

TOURIST TRAPS 32

The needs of tourists, especially rich tourists in poor countries, can deplete local resources and leave a global trail of litter and waste.

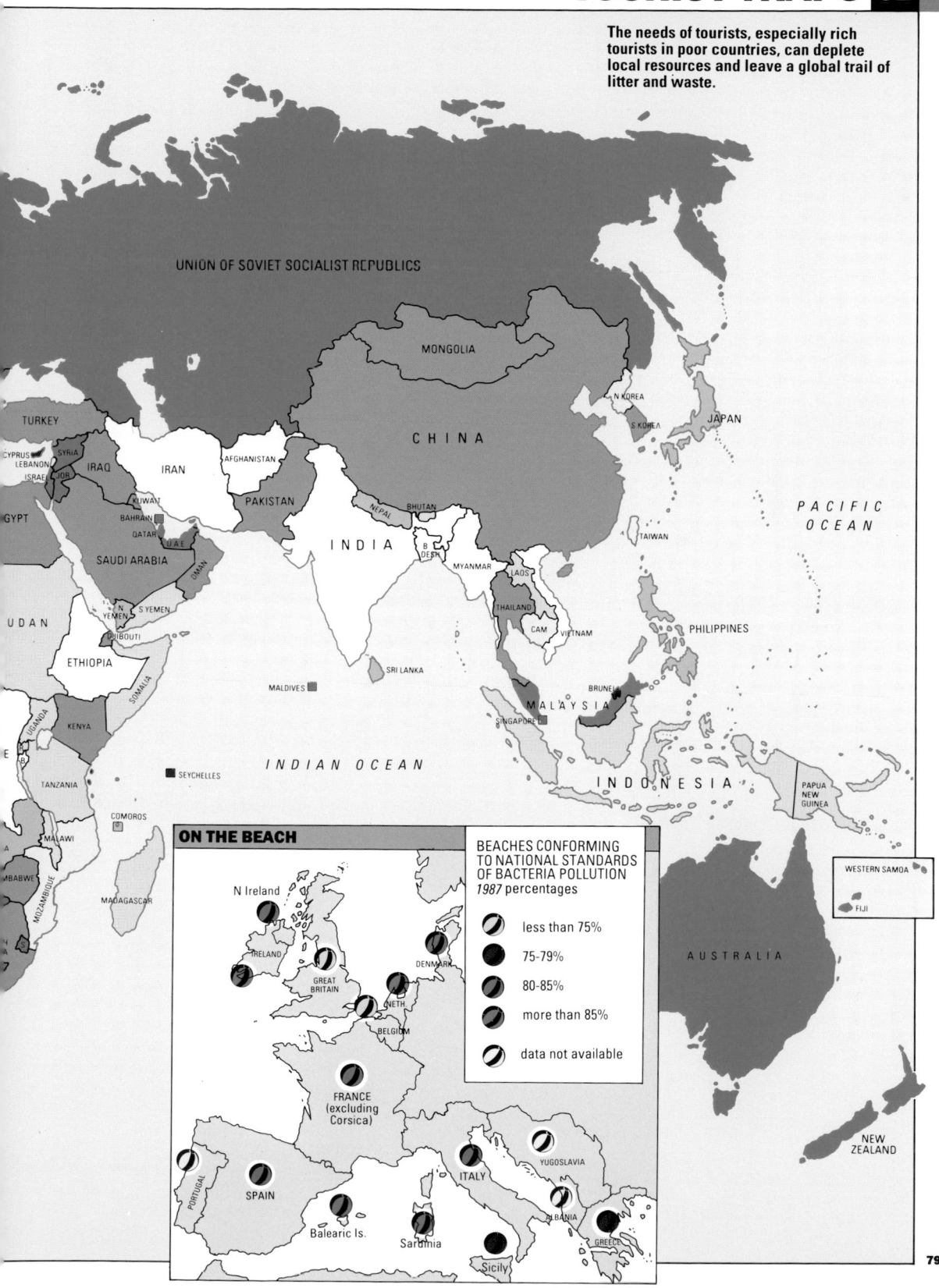

Copyright © Swanston Publishing Limited

Data compiled by Andy Crump Main sources: World Resources Institute (1988); IUCN Monitoring Centre

The trade in wildlife and wildlife products is a $5 billion industry that threatens whole species and ecosystems.

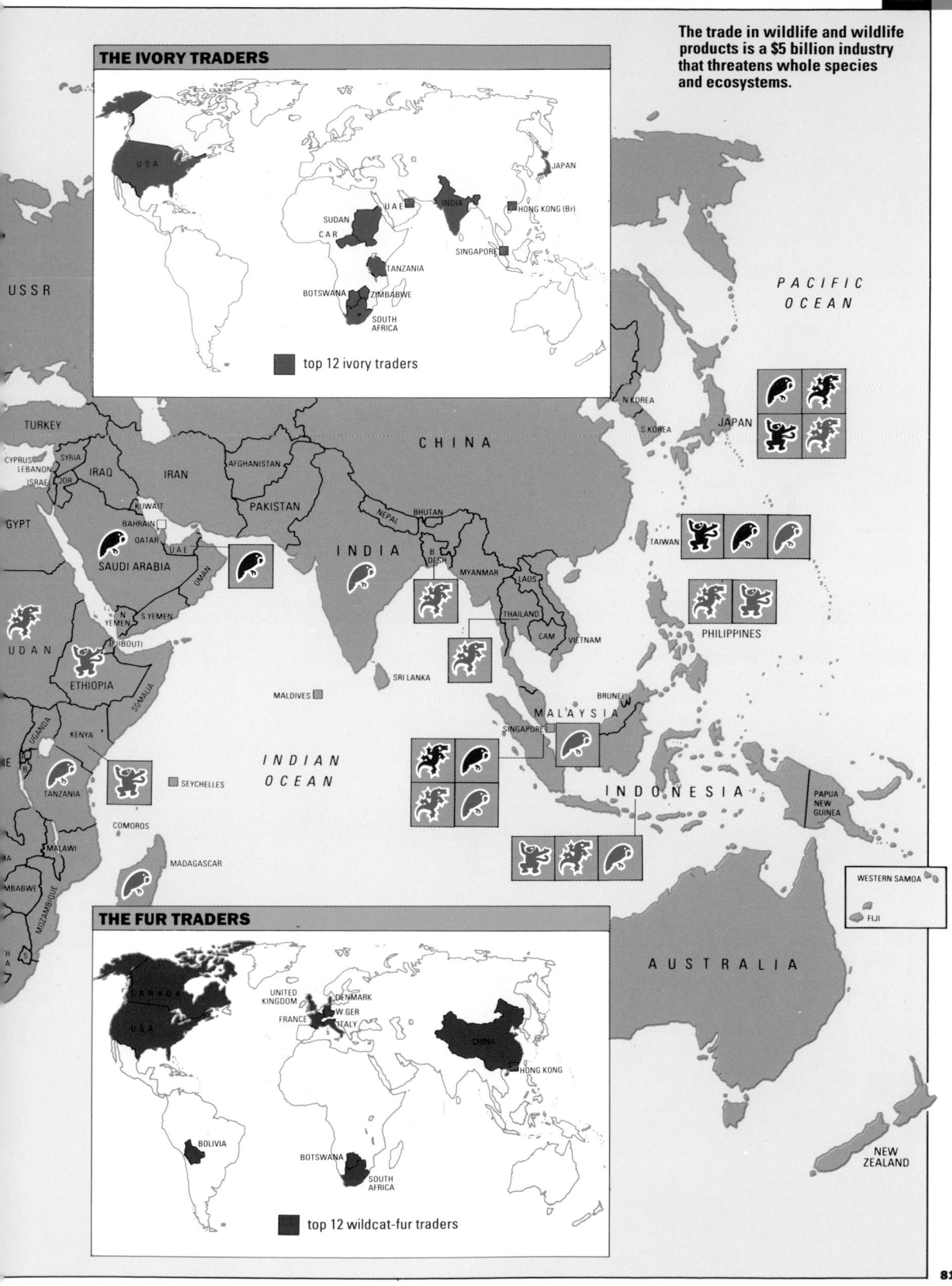

Copyright © Swanston Publishing Limited

Data compiled by Andy Crump Main sources: Burton & Pearson; Fitter (1986); Inskipp & Wells (1979); World Resources Institute (1987, 1988); OECD *Environmental Data Compendium* (1989); IUCN Monitoring Centre (1988).

Hunting for sport or profit is one of the greatest threats to wildlife and wilderness ecosystems.

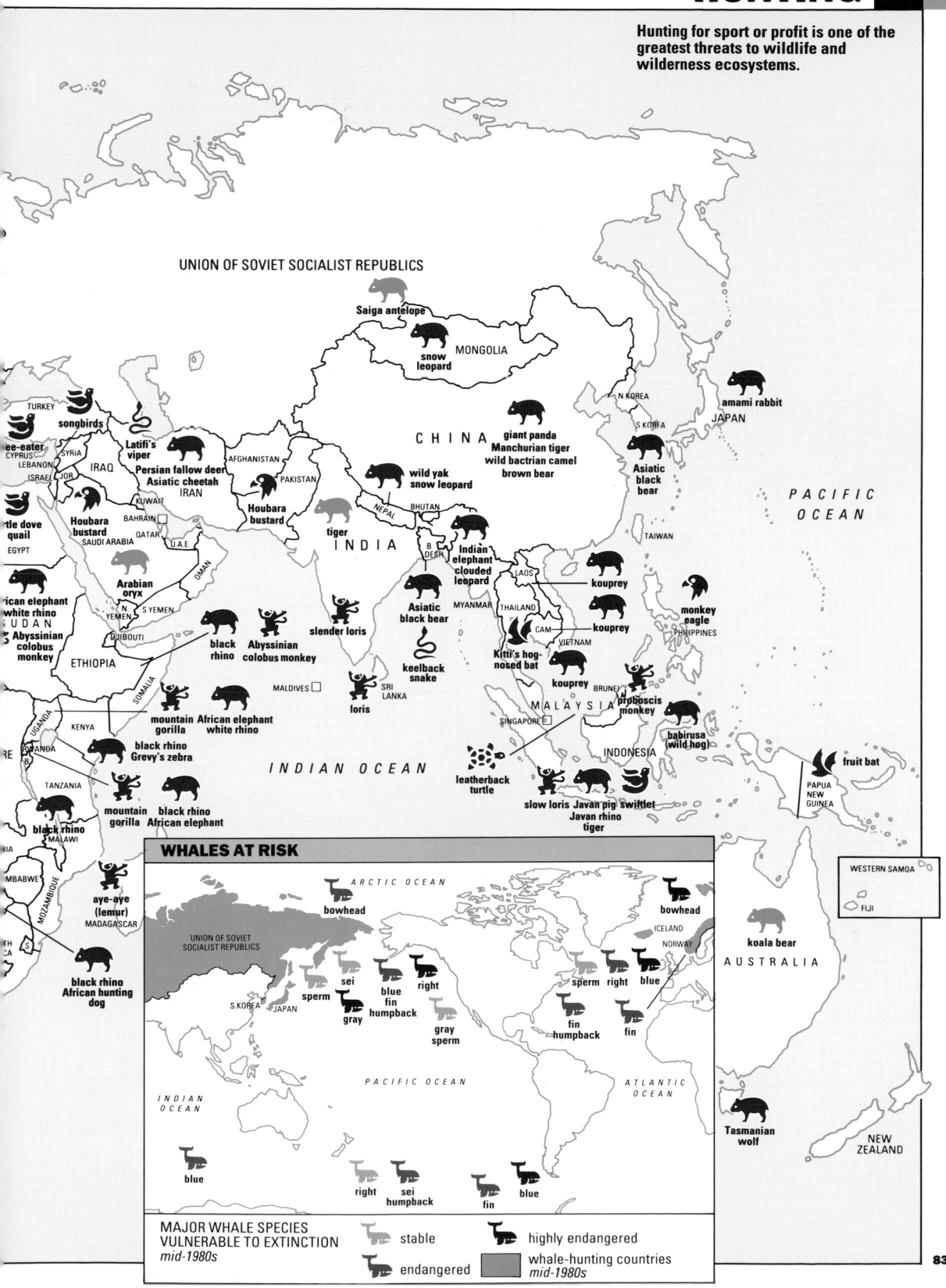

Copyright © Swanston Publishing Limited

Data compiled by Friends of the Earth/Jan McHarry Main sources: Nectoux & Dudley (1987); Myers & Houghton (1989).

THE TIMBER TRADE 35

Every year tropical timber worth more than US$8 billion is shipped from poor countries to rich, destroying 12 million acres of tropical forest.

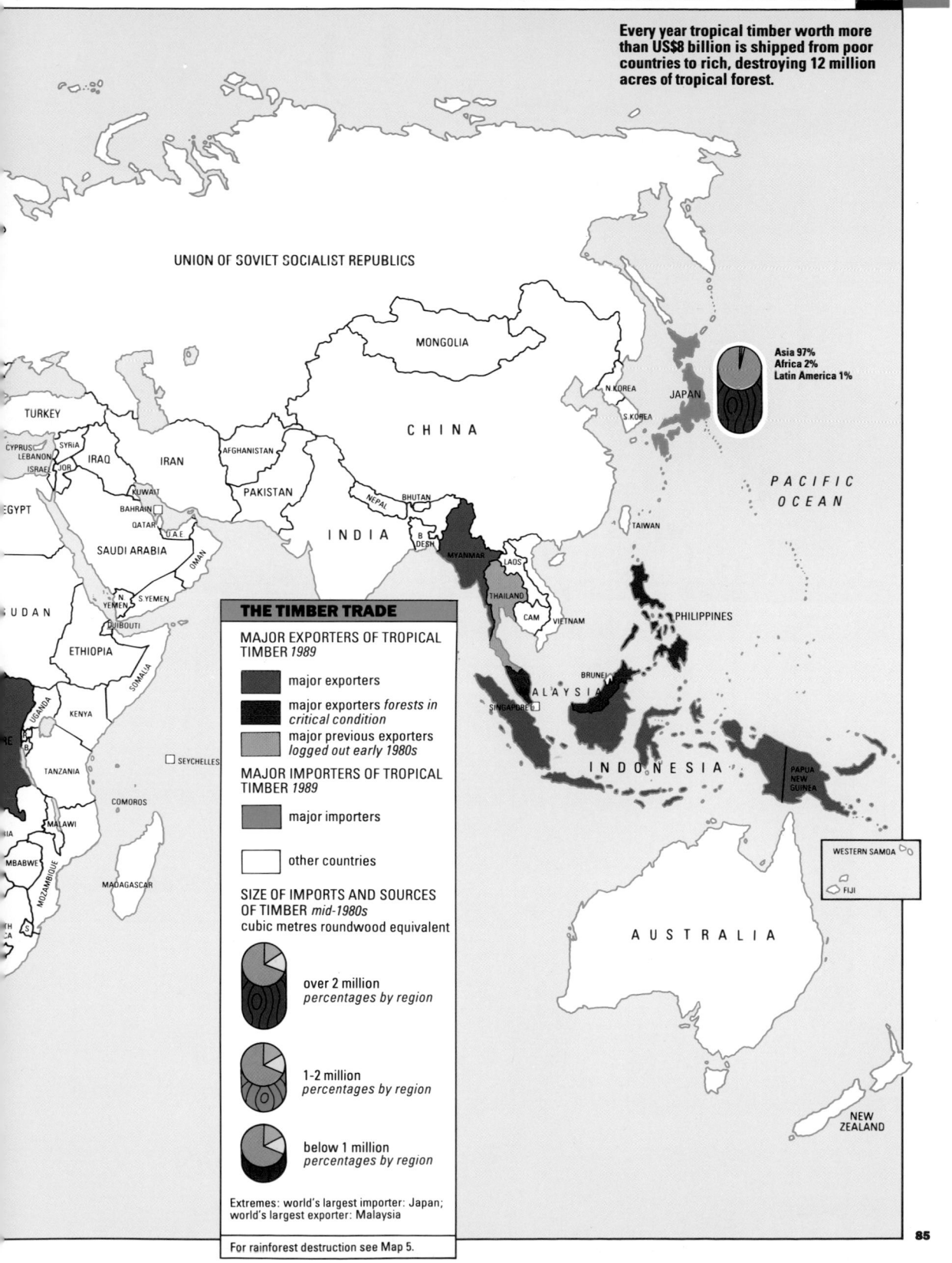

For rainforest destruction see Map 5.

Copyright © Swanston Publishing Limited

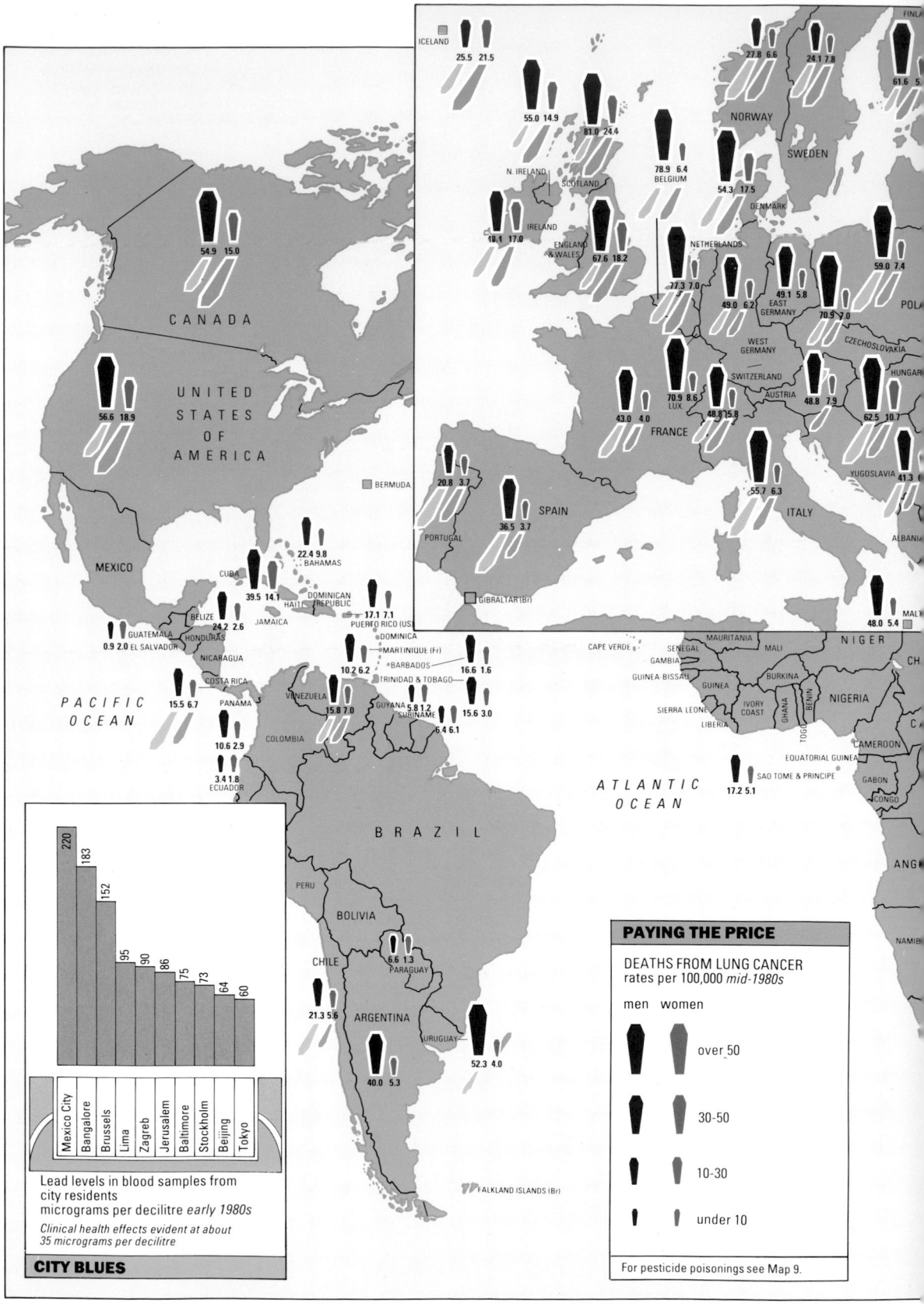

Data compiled by Jean MacRae Main sources: WHO, *World Health Statistics* (1988); Vater (1982).

The links between specific illnesses and environmental factors are difficult to prove. Nor can they be discounted. Smoking continues to be the most identifiable cause of lung cancer.

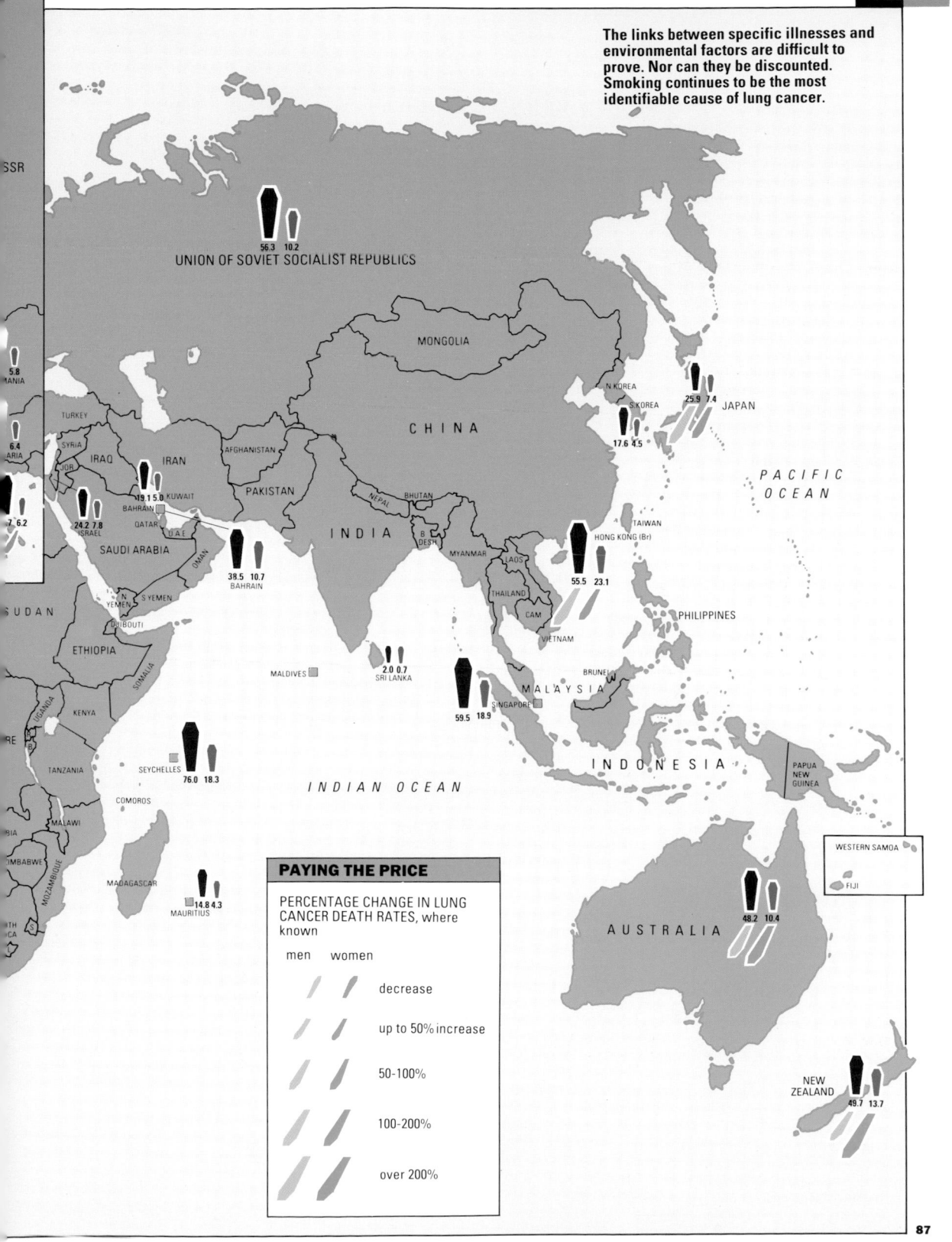

Copyright © Swanston Publishing Limited

Data compiled by Michael Renner Main sources: press reports.

Environmental issues are increasingly in the foreground of relations between citizens and their governments, and between states.

	1 **Population 1989** millions	2 **Population growth rate 1985-90** percentages	3 **Urban population 1985** percentages of total population	4 **Land area protected 1988** percentages of total land	5 **Carbon dioxid emissions 1987** million tonne
Afghanistan	20.2	4.83	18.5	00.2	3.996
Albania	3.3	2.10	34.0	2.0	9.458
Algeria	24.7	3.21	42.6	0.2	3.666
American Samoa (US)			48.2		
Angola	9.7	2.67	24.5	1.2	4.399
Antigua & Barbuda			30.8		0.367
Argentina	32.4	1.46	84.6	1.7	109.247
Australia	16.5	1.25	85.5	4.7	234.257
Austria	7.5	0.01	56.1	5.1	52.057
Bahamas			57.5		1.100
Bahrain	0.5	3.72	81.7	0.0	16.130
Bangladesh	112.3	2.61	11.9	0.7	12.464
Barbados	0.3	0.60	42.2	05.8	0.733
Belgium	9.9	0.09	96.3	0.4	94.949
Belize			50.0		0.183
Benin	4.6	3.12	35.2	7.6	0.367
Bermuda					0.733
Bhutan	1.5	2.03	4.5	18.6	0.0
Bolivia	7.1	2.76	47.8	4.5	4.033
Botswana	1.3	3.70	19.2	17.0	1.466
Brazil	147.4	2.07	72.7	1.4	184.400
Brunei			57.7		2.933
Bulgaria	9.2	0.38	66.5	1.0	120.611
Burkina	7.7	2.65	7.9	2.5	0.367
Burundi	5.3	2.84	5.6	0.0	0.0
Cambodia	8.1	2.48	10.8	0.0	0.367
Cameroon	11.0	2.80	42.4	3.6	5.866
Canada	26.5	1.01	75.9	2.5	400.694
Cape Verde	0.4	2.36	5.3		
Central African Republic	2.8	2.42	42.4	6.3	0.367
Chad	5.5	2.44	27.0	0.1	0.367
Chile	12.8	1.52	83.6	17.1	25.662
China	1110.8	1.18	20.6	0.2	2092.553
Colombia	31.2	2.05	67.4	4.7	48.025
Comoros	0.5	3.08	25.2		
Congo	1.9	2.73	39.5	4.0	1.833
Costa Rica	2.9	2.44	49.8	8.9	2.200
Cuba	10.47	0.98	71.8	2.6	31.894
Cyprus	0.7	1.01	49.5	0.0	3.666
Czechoslovakia	15.8	0.32	65.3	14.4	234.257
Denmark	5.1	0.01	88.9	3.0	60.856

Sources: Col. 1: UN *World Population Prospects* (1988); **Col. 2**: UN *World Population Prospects* (1988); **Col. 3**: UN *Prospects of World Urbanization* (1988); **Col. 4**: World Resources Institute (1988); **Col. 5**: Oak Ridge National Laboratory; **Col. 6**: FAO *Fertilizer Yearbook* (1988); **Col. 7**: *World Motor Vehicle Data* (198

INTERNATIONAL TABLE

6 **Artificial fertilizer use 1987** kgs per hectare	7 **Cars 1986-87** thousands	8 **CITES signatories as of Jan.1990**	9 **Montreal Protocol signatories as of Dec.1989** □ non-ratifying	10 **National Green Parties mid-1980s**	11 **Offices as of Jan.1990** Friends of the Earth Greenpeace W W F
9.7	33.0	●			
133.1					
38.0	589.0	●			
2.9	58.0				
	11.0				
4.5	4,060.0	●	□		G F
28.6	7,073.0	●	■		G F W
197.8	2,685.0	●	■	GP	G F W
50.0	68.0	●			
750.0	60.0				
77.0	45.0	●			F
93.9	35.0				
509.8	3,457.0	●	■	GP	G F W
81.8	0.5	●			
4.9	22.0	●			
	18.0				
1.0					
3.4	40.0	●			
<1.0	17.0	●			
53.2	10,827.0	●		GP	F
200.0	60.0				
180.4	1,100.0				
5.4	22.0		●		
2.0	7.5	●			
<1.0					
7.1	68.0	●	■		
48.1	11,500.0	●	■	GP	G F W
<1.0	43.0	●			
1.7	7.0	●			
52.3	591.0	●	□		
236.5	995.0	●			
94.8	579.0	●			
2.5	26.0	●	□		
180.6	114.0	●			G
197.0					
126.8	131.5	●			F
303.1	2,724.0				
233.5	1,588.0	●	■	GP	G F W

ol. 8: US State Department; **Col. 9:** US Environmental Protection Agency; **Col. 10:** Sara Parkin, *Green Parties: An International Guide*, London: Heretic ooks 1989; **Col. 11:** Friends of the Earth, London office; Greenpeace, Washington office; World Wildlife Fund, Washington office.

	1 **Population 1989** millions	2 **Population growth rate 1985-90** percentages	3 **Urban population 1985** percentages of total population	4 **Land area protected 1988** percentages of total land	5 **Carbon dioxid emissions 1987** million tonne
Djibouti	0.4	3.32	77.7	0.0	0.367
Dominica					0.0
Dominican Republic	6.8	2.21	55.7	11.8	6.599
Ecuador	10.5	2.79	52.3	38.4	13.931
Egypt	51.4	2.27	46.4	0.6	70.387
El Salvador	6.3	3.10	39.1	1.0	1.833
Equatorial Guinea	0.4	2.31	59.7	0.0	0.0
Ethiopia	48.7	2.79	11.6	1.6	2.566
Fiji	0.7	1.59	41.2	0.3	0.733
Finland	5.0	0.30	84.0	2.6	52.424
France	55.3	0.31	73.4	8.7	335.439
French Guiana			72.6		0.367
Gabon	1.2	2.01	40.9	6.8	5.132
Gambia	0.7	2.13	20.1	0.0	0.0
East Germany	16.9	0.15	77.0	0.7	324.074
West Germany	60.4	0.18	85.5	11.3	652.915
Ghana	15.5	3.36	31.5	5.1	2.933
Greece	10.0	0.41	60.1	1.1	52.424
Greenland (Den)			76.8		0.367
Guadeloupe (Fr)			45.7		0.733
Guatemala	8.9	2.88	40.0	0.9	2.566
Guinea	6.7	2.48	22.2	0.1	1.100
Guinea-Bissau	1.0	2.08	27.1	0.0	0.0
Guyana	1.0	1.74	32.2	0.1	1.100
Haiti	7.3	2.62	27.2	0.4	0.733
Honduras	5.0	3.10	40.0	3.2	1.466
Hong Kong (Br)			92.4		26.395
Hungary	10.7	0.07	56.2	4.8	74.420
Iceland	0.3	0.95	89.4	7.9	1.833
India	813.4	1.72	25.5	4.3	542.201
Indonesia	178.5	1.74	25.3	7.5	120.978
Iran	49.9	2.77	51.9	1.9	139.308
Iraq	18.2	3.31	70.6	0.0	42.892
Ireland	3.8	1.26	57.0	0.3	27.495
Israel	4.5	1.65	90.3	1.7	28.595
Italy	57.5	0.09	67.4	2.5	355.969
Ivory Coast	11.3	3.45	42.0	6.2	4.766
Jamaica	2.5	1.52	53.8	0.0	5.866
Japan	123.3	0.51	76.5	6.1	885.339
Jordan	4.1	3.99	64.4	0.4	8.798
Kenya	24.4	4.20	19.7	5.4	4.399

Sources: **Col. 1**: UN *World Population Prospects* (1988); **Col. 2**: UN *World Population Prospects* (1988); **Col. 3**: UN *Prospects of World Urbanization* (1988); **Col. 4**: World Resources Institute (1988); **Col. 5**: Oak Ridge National Laboratory; **Col. 6**: FAO *Fertilizer Yearbook* (1988); **Col. 7**: *World Motor Vehicle Data* (198

INTERNATIONAL TABLE

6 **Artificial fertilizer use 1987** kgs per hectare	7 **Cars 1986-87** thousands	8 **CITES signatories as of Jan.1990**	9 **Montreal Protocol signatories as of Dec.1989** □ non-ratifying	10 **National Green Parties mid-1980s**	11 **Offices as of Jan.1990** Friends of the Earth Greenpeace W W F
	15.0				
176.5	3.0				
55.6	103.0	●			
32.1	257.0	●			F
350.5	417.0	●	■		
126.2	73.0	●			
	4.5				
3.9	41.0	●			
89.6	31.0		■		
216.3	1,699.0	●	■	GP	G W
299.0	21,950.0	●	■	GP	G F W
166.7					
3.5	16.0	●			
15.3	5.0	●	■		
337.3	3,462.0	●	■	GP	G F
420.7	28,304.0	●	■	GP	G F W
3.8	60.0	●	■		F
170.6	1,433.0		■	GP	
142.9					
67.9	175.0	●	■		
<1.0	12.0	●			
<1.0	3.0				
26.9	33.0	●			
2.5	35.0				
23.1	41.0	●			
	184.0				F W
259.5	1,660.0	●	■		
2917.1	113.0		■	GP	
53.6	1,471.0	●			W
106.8	1,060.0	●	□		F
65.8	1,600.0	●			
39.7	376.0				
681.5	737.0		■	GP	G F
223.7	649.0	●	□		
190.1	22,800.0	●	■	GP	G F W
6.0	164.0				
91.4	93.0				
432.7	29,478.0	●	■	GP	G F W
34.8	136.0	●	■		
40.6	126.0	●	■		

ol. 8: US State Department; **Col. 9:** US Environmental Protection Agency; **Col. 10:** Sara Parkin, *Green Parties: An International Guide*, London: Heretic ooks, 1989; **Col. 11:** Friends of the Earth, London office; Greenpeace, Washington office; World Wildlife Fund, Washington office.

	1 **Population 1989** millions	2 **Population growth rate 1985-90** percentages	3 **Urban population 1985** percentages of total population	4 **Land area protected 1988** percentages of total land	5 **Carbon dioxid emissions 1987** million tonne
Kiribati			33.5		
North Korea	22.4	2.36	63.8	0.0	143.707
South Korea	44.1	1.89	65.3	5.7	162.770
Kuwait	2.1	4.15	93.5	0.0	32.994
Laos	4.5	2.43	15.9	0.0	0.0
Lebanon	2.9	2.13	80.1	0.0	8.065
Lesotho	1.7	2.61	16.7	0.2	
Liberia	2.5	3.25	39.5	1.4	0.733
Libya	4.2	3.67	64.5	0.1	24.929
Luxembourg	0.4	0.10	81.0	44.2	8.432
Madagascar	11.2	2.90	21.8	1.8	0.733
Malawi	7.9	3.32	12.0	11.3	0.367
Malaysia	17.0	2.12	38.2	4.9	40.326
Maldives			20.2		
Mali	9.1	2.94	18.0	0.7	0.367
Malta	0.4	0.66	85.3	0.0	0.0
Mauritania	2.1	3.08	34.6	1.4	3.299
Mauritius	1.1	1.65	42.4	2.0	1.100
Martinique (Fr)			71.1		0.733
Mexico	87.0	2.39	69.6	0.5	287.414
Mongolia	2.1	2.74	50.8	0.2	9.165
Morocco	24.1	2.30	44.8	0.7	18.330
Mozambique	15.5	2.69	19.4	0.0	0.733
Myanmar (Burma)	40.1	1.89	23.9	0.0	5.499
Namibia			51.3		
Nepal	18.1	2.28	7.7	7.1	131.976
Netherlands	14.7	0.34	88.4	4.4	0.733
New Zealand	3.4	0.86	83.7	11.4	20.896
Nicaragua	3.7	3.36	56.6	0.4	2.200
Niger	6.9	3.01	16.2	0.3	0.733
Nigeria	109.4	3.49	23.0	1.1	55.357
Norway	4.2	0.17	72.8	4.1	43.992
Oman	1.4	3.18	8.8	0.3	21.629
Pakistan	109.7	2.23	29.8	9.4	47.771
Panama	2.4	2.07	52.4	10.9	2.566
Papua New Guinea	3.9	2.38	14.3	0.4	2.200
Paraguay	4.1	2.78	44.4	2.8	1.833
Peru	21.8	2.51	67.4	4.2	22.363
Philippines	59.7	2.25	39.6	1.7	34.460
Poland	38.3	0.70	61.0	5.5	460.083
Portugal	10.5	0.64	31.2	4.2	27.862

Sources: Col. 1: UN *World Population Prospects* (1988); **Col. 2**: UN *World Population Prospects* (1988); **Col. 3**: UN *Prospects of World Urbanization* (1988); **Col. 4**: World Resources Institute (1988); **Col. 5**: Oak Ridge National Laboratory; **Col. 6**: FAO *Fertilizer Yearbook* (1988); **Col. 7**: *World Motor Vehicle Data* (198

INTERNATIONAL TABLE

6 **Artificial fertilizer use 1987** kgs per hectare	7 **Cars 1986-87** thousands	8 **CITES signatories as of Jan.1990**	9 **Montreal Protocol signatories as of Dec.1989** □ non-ratifying	10 **National Green Parties mid-1980s**	11 **Offices as of Jan.1990** Friends of the Earth Greenpeace W W F
311.7					
422.4	844.0				
82.0	435.0				
<1.0	10.0				
67.1					
12.5	6.0				
7.3		●			
28.8	404.0				
	162.0	●	■	GP	G
5.9	49.0	●			
20.4	16.0	●			
159.6	1,269.0	●	■		F W
			■		
13.9	21.0				
45.9		●	■		
5.0	15.0				
306.9	35.0	●			
1150.0					
75.3	5,403.0		■		
18.4					
35.7	565.0	●	□		
2.1	87.0	●			
15.4	35.0				
22.9		●			
687.9	5,118.0	●	■	GP	G F W
708.6	1,424.0	●	■	GP	G F W
43.3	32.0	●			F
<1.0	23.5	●			
9.9	774.0	●	■		
270.4	1,623.0	●	■	GP	G W
91.7	109.0				
82.9	273.0	●			F W
65.7	104.0	●	■		
38.1	17.0	●			F
4.4	88.5	●			
62.2	390.5	●			
65.0	359.0	●	□		
222.4	4,000.0				F
102.6	1,290.0	●	■		F

Col. 8: US State Department; **Col. 9:** US Environmental Protection Agency; **Col. 10:** Sara Parkin, *Green Parties: An International Guide*, London: Heretic Books 1989; **Col. 11:** Friends of the Earth, London office; Greenpeace, Washington office; World Wildlife Fund, Washington office.

	1 **Population 1989** millions	2 **Population growth rate 1985-90** percentages	3 **Urban population 1985** percentages of total population	4 **Land area protected 1988** percentages of total land	5 **Carbon dioxid emissions 1987** million tonne
Puerto Rico (US)			70.7		14.297
Qatar	0.4	5.44	88.0	0.0	11.365
Romania	23.7	0.68	49.0	0.6	205.663
Rwanda	6.9	3.36	6.2	10.5	0.367
Saudi Arabia	13.5	3.84	72.4	0.2	164.603
Senegal	7.2	2.71	36.4	11.3	1.833
Sierra Leone	3.9	1.93	28.3	1.4	0.733
Singapore	2.7	1.09	100.0	4.3	28.228
Solomon Islands	0.3	3.96	9.7	0.0	
Somalia	5.1	2.11	34.1	0.5	1.100
South Africa	35.8	2.53	55.9	4.7	278.249
Spain	39.5	0.62	75.8	3.4	161.304
Sri Lanka	17.2	1.48	21.1	10.6	3.666
Sudan	24.2	2.89	20.6	0.9	3.299
Suriname	0.4	1.46	45.7	4.6	1.100
Swaziland	0.7	3.14	26.3	2.3	0.367
Sweden	8.3	0.11	83.4	4.2	56.800
Switzerland	6.4	0.04	58.2	3.0	38.126
Syria	12.2	3.69	49.5	0.0	2.200
Taiwan					
Tanzania	26.1	3.65	22.3	12.0	25.662
Thailand	54.8	1.61	19.8	7.8	52.790
Togo	3.3	3.06	22.1	8.5	0.0
Trinidad & Tobago	1.3	1.59	63.9	3.1	17.597
Tunisia	7.7	2.17	56.8	0.4	9.898
Turkey	53.6	2.06	45.9	0.3	122.444
Uganda	17.8	3.49	9.5	6.7	0.733
United Arab Emirates	1.5	3.46	77.8	0.0	50.224
United Kingdom	56.2	0.02	91.5	6.4	569.696
USA	246.3	0.86	73.9	7.4	4457.123
USSR	289.3	0.93	65.6	0.0	3745.552
Uruguay	3.1	0.76	84.6	0.2	2.933
Venezuela	19.2	2.61	86.6	8.4	95.316
Vietnam	64.8	2.05	20.3	0.6	18.330
Western Sahara			52.9		0.367
South Yemen	2.4	3.01	39.9	1.3	2.933
North Yemen	7.7	2.92	20.0	0.8	5.499
Yugoslavia	23.8	0.63	46.3	1.3	120.611
Zaire	33.8	3.04	36.6	3.9	3.299
Zambia	7.6	3.43	49.5	8.6	2.200
Zimbabwe	10.1	3.61	24.6	7.1	15.397

Sources: Col. 1: UN *World Population Prospects* (1988); **Col. 2:** UN *World Population Prospects* (1988); **Col. 3:** UN *Prospects of World Urbanization* (1988); **Col. 4:** World Resources Institute (1988); **Col. 5:** Oak Ridge National Laboratory; **Col. 6:** FAO *Fertilizer Yearbook* (1988); **Col. 7:** *World Motor Vehicle Data* (198

INTERNATIONAL TABLE

6 **Artificial fertilizer use 1987** kgs per hectare	7 **Cars 1986-87** thousands	8 **CITES signatories as of Jan.1990**	9 **Montreal Protocol signatories as of Dec.1989** □ non-ratifying	10 **National Green Parties mid-1980s**	11 **Offices as of Jan.1990** Friends of the Earth Greenpeace W W F
	1,280.0				
172.5	78.0				
130.1	250.0				
2.0	7.0	●			
367.8	2,245.0				
4.0	78.0	●	□		
<1.0	23.0				F
1833.3	236.0	●	■		
4.0	17.0	●			
53.8	3,079.0	●			W
98.9	10,219.0	●	■		G F W
113.1	148.0	●			
2.5	34.0	●			
161.6	35.0	●			
39.6	21.0				
135.7	3,367.0	●	■	GP	G F W
430.6	2,733.0	●	■	GP	G F W
40.5	95.0		■		
	1,255.0				
8.9	42.0	●			F
29.3	572.0	●	■		
7.5	3.5	●	□		
52.5	264.0	●	■		
22.2	171.0	●	■		
61.8	193.0				
<1.0	32.0		■		
163.2	250.0	●			
355.5	20,097.0	●	■	GP	G F W
93.3	137,324.0	●	■		G F W
117.8	11,800.0	●	■		G F
42.7	164.0	●			F
158.0	1,601.0	●	■		
62.9					
12.1	12.0				
5.8	121.0				
132.8	3,040.0			GP	
<1.0	94.0	●			
18.4	98.0	●			
50.4	254.0	●			

ol. 8: US State Department; **Col. 9:** US Environmental Protection Agency; **Col. 10:** Sara Parkin, *Green Parties: An International Guide*, London: Heretic Books 1989; **Col. 11:** Friends of the Earth, London office; Greenpeace, Washington office; World Wildlife Fund, Washington office.

COMMENTARY

1 A GLOBAL GREENHOUSE

Certain gases, including carbon dioxide, methane, nitrogen oxides and chlorofluorocarbons (CFCs), are accumulating in the upper atmosphere at a faster rate than ever before. Proponents of the theory of global warming warn that this mixture is creating a layer that traps the earth's radiated heat, which will cause global temperatures to rise significantly. It is argued that this could lead to a rise in sea levels, higher tides and extraordinary storm surges; and the impact of these changes would mean salination of drinking water supplies, disruption of food crop and plant habitats, the expansion of deserts and the inundation of entire islands. Low-lying countries such as Bangladesh, the Netherlands, the Maldives and many small Pacific island states are especially vulnerable. Most of the world's major cities, including many capitals, are coastal and even a slight rise in sea-level would bring some threat of flooding. At a more extreme level, large scale changes to weather and agricultural patterns would wreak havoc with local livelihoods and national economies.

Environmentalists are mapping out strategies to stave off global warming. These focus on the need for cutbacks in the use of fossil fuels (see Maps 23 and 31) and CFCs (see Map 28), as well as the need to call a halt to further global deforestation (see Maps 5 and 35). Such an agenda has sweeping implications. It would require dramatic changes in the priorities of industrial economies and industrial lifestyles; more difficult still is its potential impact on the plans of poor countries for economic expansion. The enormity of the demands is paralysing political and economic agreements and creating an uproar in scientific circles. But business and governments have short-term vested interests which make it convenient to dispute the theory of global warming.

Sources for map and commentary:

Boyle, Stewart & John Ardill, *The Greenhouse Effect*, London: New English Library, 1989; Hansen, J. et al, 'Global Climate Changes as Forecast by the Goddard Institute for Space Studies'. *Journal of Geophysical Research*, vol. 93, 1988; *Climatic Change, Rising Sea Level and the British Coast*, Institute of Terrestrial Ecology, NERC, 1989; Stevens, William, 'Adapting to Global Greenhouse', *International Herald Tribune*, November 16, 1989; World Resources Institute/International Institute for Environment and Development, *World Resources 1988-89*, New York: Basic Books, 1988.

2 A POPULAR PLANET

In 1985, Africa and Europe were approximately the same size in population; by 2025, Africa's population will be three times larger than that of Europe. Nigeria alone will grow from being half the population size of the USA to being slightly larger. In the mid-1980s, the Middle East dominated the ranks of states with the highest population growth rates: Oman, Libya, UAE, Qatar, Saudi Arabia, Kuwait, Bahrain, and Iran were all in the top ten. Dramatic increases such as these, together with the shifting relationships within the global population balance, form the backdrop to many of the environmental themes in this atlas.

But the relationship between population and the environment is complex. Some would argue, including some environmentalists, that there is a direct correlation between the world's growing population and the world's growing environmental problems. The evidence does not bear this out. While population growth is now a Third World phenomenon, the large-scale global environmental crises we face are largely the product of the voracious resource appetites of industrial economies and lifestyles. In terms of how much we burden the atmosphere, one economist estimates that the 'cost' of one US citizen is 16 times that of a Third World person; of a West European, five times. The average person in the developed world consumes 10 times as much energy, 10 times as much steel, 15 times as much paper, and one-and-a-half times as much food as does the average person living in the Third World. If we check off the world's most pressing environmental problems – fossil fuel pollution (and the related threat of global warming), the use and production of ozone depleting chemicals, the resource use and pollution generated by oil dependency, acid rain emissions, production of household waste, municipal waste, toxic industrial waste, the luxury trade in exotic animal and bird species, and the stripping of the world's forests – it becomes clear that the biggest contributing cause of these problems is not the 'excessive' number of people in the poor countries of the world, but the excessive pressures exerted by the richer countries.

This is not to suggest that growing numbers of people do not burden natural ecosystems; they do. Destruction of wildlife habitats, forest cutback for subsistence agriculture and deterioration in the quality of urban water, to name but a few pressing environmental problems, stem in some measure from the sheer pressure of human need. Ultimately, though, most of these are problems of poverty and misdirected public priorities rather than problems of numbers. Military priorities are often the biggest stumbling block. For the cost of a single British Aerospace Hawk aircraft, for example, 1.5 million people in the Third World could have clean water for life; the annual cost of the proposed anti-desertification programme for Ethiopia is the equivalent of two months of Ethiopian military spending.

In turn, environmental problems themselves, in a world of social inequities, encourage high rates of population growth - in countries where infants die regularly from gastro-intestinal disease brought on by lack of clean water, for example, women have to bear higher numbers of children simply to meet perceived population replacement levels.

Population growth may well be a 'problem', but not in the ways that most of us are encouraged to believe. And the solution to environmental problems is not simply, or even primarily, through population controls; indeed, the reverse may well be true.

Sources for map and commentary:

Dankelman, Irene & Joan Davidson, *Women and Environment in the Third World*, London: IUCN/Earthscan, 1988; Greanville, Patrice, 'Who's Got the Answer to the Overpopulation Riddle?' *Animals' Agenda*, November 1988; United Nations, Department of International Economic and Social Affairs, *World Population Prospects, 1988*, 1989; World Commission on Environment and Development, *Our Common Future*, Oxford: Oxford University Press, 1987.

3 A SHRINKING WORLD

Overexploitation, loss of habitat (particularly through deforestation), hunting and the luxury trade in animals are the major causes of the spiralling scale of animal extinctions. By the year 2000, between 40,000 to 50,000 species will be lost annually.

Information about the world's animal communities is very uneven. As with plant species, more is generally known for richer, industrialized countries. Many others, including a number rich in both animal and plant species such as Brazil or Zaire, have little in the way of scientific monitoring services. The data is uneven in other important respects. More money is available to fund studies of large mammals and primates (perhaps because of perceived kinship and 'usefulness' to humans). Little attention is given to less attractive animals and birds and even less to fish or insects. There are only broad estimates for losses of fish and although many insect species are disappearing there is not even a 'best estimate' for the number becoming extinct.

Birds are especially vulnerable to extinction because they are migratory and range over a wide territory. There needs to be coordinated international action for the protection of birds but this will be difficult to achieve. For example, the annual hunting massacre of millions of songbirds along their migration paths in the Mediterranean has gained considerable notoriety and drawn protests from the EEC. It has not yet been halted. A third of Europe's birds are threatened with extinction, of which hunting is major cause, followed by habitat destruction. Hunters kill an estimated 900 million migrating birds each year. They justify this slaughter as a male ritual with links to cultural traditions that go back thousands of years.

Environmentalist Norman Myers comments wryly on the path down which we seem to be rushing: 'Unwittingly for the most part, but right around the world, we are eliminating the panoply of life. We elbow species off the planet, we deny room to entire communities of nature, we domesticate the Earth. With growing energy and ingenuity, we surpass ourselves time and again to exert dominion over fowl and fish ... Eventually we may achieve our aim, by eliminating every other competitor for living space on the crowded Earth. When the last creature is accounted for, we shall have made ourselves masters of all creation. We shall look around and we shall see nothing but each other. Alone at last.'

Sources for map and commentary:

Cocker, Mark, 'The Fall of Europe's Birds', *The Guardian* (London) July 25, 1989; IUCN Conservation Monitoring Centre, *Red List of Threatened Animals*, Cambridge: IUCN, 1988; Myers, Norman, ed., Gaia: *An Atlas of Planet Management*, London: Pan; New York: Doubleday, 1984; Organization for Economic Cooperation and Development (OECD), *OECD Environmental Data Compendium, 1989*, Paris: OECD, 1989; World Resources Institute/International Institute for Environment and Development, *World Resources 1988-89*, New York: Basic Books, 1988.

4 CUTTING OUR ROOTS

All life on the planet depends, directly or indirectly, on plants. And yet plants and plant species are being destroyed at an alarming rate. If present rates of habitat destruction continue, then some 40,000 - 60,000 vascular plants will face extinction within the next fifty years. In this map, we have included as much information as possible on small islands because they have distinctive biomes, tend to be rich in plant species and are suffering high rates of loss.

Beyond broad assessments, detailed information about plant extinctions is patchy. The Threatened Plants Unit of the International Union for Conservation of Nature (IUCN) in the UK collects the only available international database on plants, and publishes a floristic inventory in their Red Data Books. To date, Red Books have been compiled for 70 countries and islands. Most countries of the North, with predominantly temperate vegetation, are well covered by IUCN data, but there are few Red Books for countries of the South, where the vegetation is mostly tropical - and where most of the world's plants grow. There is almost no plant inventory or assessment for key areas such as Brazil, much of Central America and most of Africa. In the case of plant ecology, what we do not know is more problematic than what we do know. In general, it must be assumed that low rates of extinction reflect a lack of data more than they reflect the reality of plant losses.

The destruction of plants will threaten the world's food supplies and undermine medical advances. Wild plants are being lost which are needed to protect and maintain the world's major food crops. Eighty percent of our food comes from these crops and they are already suffering a dramatic decline in genetic diversity (see Map 10). Four-fifths of the world's population depends on natural plant sources for medicines. Even high-technology Western medicine uses a very high proportion of life-saving drugs that are initially derived from plant sources and then synthesized for large-scale production.

Sources for map and commentary:

Nature Conservancy Council, 'British Rare Plants: Threats and International Responsibilities', Data Support for Education, Sheet 60, 1989, Peterborough (UK) 1989; Davis, S.D., et al, *Plants in Danger: What do we Know?* Cambridge: IUCN, 1986; Fagan, Mary, 'Food Supply at Risk from Extinction of Plant Species', *The Independent* (London) December 16, 1989; World Resources Institute/International Institute for Environment and Development, *World Resources 1988-89*, New York: Basic Books, 1988.

5 RAINFOREST

Tropical forest originally covered about 16 million sq. kms. throughout the world; today, probably less than half remains. Although tropical forest (including rainforest) accounts for only a third of the world's total forest, it contains four-fifths of the world's vegetation: a single hectare of primary forest may support plant material weighing anywhere from 300 to 500 tonnes. More than that, it provides the habitat for about 50 percent of all animal and bird species. As tropical forest is destroyed, so other plant and animal life will disappear too. The recent recognition that tropical forests influence the global climate, and in particular may slow down the effects of global warming, has raised the stakes around tropical forest protection. However, to put an end to tropical deforestation will require strict regulation of multinational agricultural and logging industries. Although sustained international cooperation is essential, as well as a radical shift in the primary-resource economies of many countries, as of early 1990 there is still no international coordinating body.

The geography of rainforest has never been precise and reliable information on rates of deforestation does not exist. There are both practical and technical difficulties. One of these is the varying definitions of tropical forest, such as lowland, montane, dry, rain, swamp and so on. Further, when measuring deforestation, it is difficult to determine the difference between 'degraded' forest land and totally destroyed forest, especially since the one usually leads to the other. The term 'deforestation' itself means different things to different people. To commercial interests, deforestation means the loss of commercial timber stock. To environmentalists, deforestation is the destruction of an entire forest ecosystem, even though stands of trees may remain.

Whatever the definition, at the current rate of deforestation virtually all remaining tropical forests will disappear within 40 years. The tropical forests of the Ivory Coast, Nigeria, India, and Thailand are already severely depleted. By 2010, there will be very little forest left in Asia, and East and West Africa and almost none in Central America. Even in South America, the only large stands will remain in western Brazil and the highlands of Guyana.

Rainforest destruction has highlighted an important issue of social justice: the land rights of indigenous peoples. Large numbers of tribal people are each year losing their lands in the name of development and progress, and in the heart of Borneo, Brazil, the Philippines, and Malaysia, tribal peoples have been fighting a virtual life and death struggle to protect their rainforest homelands. Indigenous peoples and environmentalists are forming alliances to protect them.

There are many widely-accepted causes of rainforest loss: logging by commercial timber companies (see Map 35); migration of poor agricultural families into forests, often as part of government-promoted relocation schemes; conversion of forest land into commercial cash cropland, usually to grow beef or soya, and often to raise capital to pay off foreign debts; and firewood collection and the production of charcoal for energy (see Map 21).

Sources for map and commentary:

Campbell, David & David Hammond, *Floristic Inventory of Tropical Countries*, London: Friends of the Earth, 1989; Myers, Norman & Richard A. Houghton, 'Deforestation Rates in Tropical Forests, and Their Climatic Implications' (First Draft), London: Friends of the Earth, 1989; 'Paradise Lost?' London: EarthLife Foundation, 1986; World Resources Institute/International Institute for Environment and Development, *World Resources 1988-89*, New York: Basic Books, 1988.

6 DRINKING WATER

The World Health Organization defines reasonable access to safe drinking water in an urban area as 'access to piped water or a public standpipe within 200 metres of a dwelling'; for rural areas, the WHO definition of reasonable access is 'drinking water within 15 minutes walking distance'. Interpretation of these definitions, even in the definition of what is rural and what is urban, is clearly open to subjective judgement; variations in definition mean that comparisons between countries may be misleading. In general, much of the international data available on water provision must be accepted with scepticism.

In 1980, the United Nations launched the International Drinking Water Supply and Sanitation Decade in an effort to improve access to potable water and sanitation in developing countries. The mid-decade report showed promising signs for rural dwellers: worldwide, access to safe water had increased from 33 percent to 45 percent; the picture for the world's urban population had remained static: the worldwide average being about 75 percent. However, the report also noted that the per capita cost of providing water and sanitation services continued to increase despite the development of less expensive technologies, which suggests that governments may not be able to sustain improvements in water supply.

To support a reasonable quality of life requires approximately 80 litres of water per person per day. Around the world, average consumption ranges from 5.4 litres per day in Madagascar to more than 500 litres (approximately 160 US gallons) per day in the USA. Everywhere, demands on water are high, and growing fast. In the USA, it is estimated that household water consumption will quadruple between 1967 and 2000, and that the demands of industry will increase fivefold.

The main problems in relation to water supply vary between rich and poor countries, although sewage is polluting rivers everywhere (see Map 16). In poor countries, the greatest difficulty is the cost of bringing piped water to more people. In the rich world, there are growing problems of protecting water supplies from pollution. Groundwater and rivers are threatened by the use of pesticides and fertilizers in agriculture and by disposal methods for the increasing quantities of industrial and toxic waste produced by industry (see Maps 25 and 27). The UK Department of the Environment reported in 1988 that some drinking water sources had had to be 'abandoned because of pollution from landfill sites'. And in February 1990 the *Observer* reported that over 1300 landfill sites used for disposal of toxic waste were posing 'some risk' to water supplies.

Ideally, drinking water should come from unpolluted groundwater. However, this is an ideal in rapid retreat, and currently more than half the population of OECD countries and 70 percent of the US population drinks water that has been passed through waste water treatment plants. The danger in this is that not all waste can be removed in treatment, and the chemical agents used in treatment may themselves pose health risks.

Sources for maps and commentary:

Goldsmith, Edward & Nicholas Hildyard, eds., *The Earth Report*, London: Mitchell Beazley, 1988; Myers, Norman, ed., *Gaia: An Atlas of Planet Management*, London: Pan; New York: Doubleday, 1984; Lean, Geoffrey and Polly Ghazi, 'Britain's Buried Poison', *The Observer*, February 4, 1990; Organization for Economic Cooperation and Development (OECD), *OECD Environmental Data Compendium, 1989*, Paris: OECD, 1989; World Health Organization (WHO), International Drinking Supply and Sanitation Decade, *Review of National Progress 1983*, Geneva, 1986; WHO, *World Health Statistics Annual*, Geneva, 1986.

7 HUNGER AND PLENTY

The Hunger Report, an annual assessment of the state of hunger in the world, introduces the issue in this way: 'No one really knows how many hungry people there are in the world. No one knows the toll of hunger because hunger is difficult to define, because the statistical data are weak or nonexistent, and because efforts to improve data collection and analysis have been limited. But beyond these real difficulties, we may not know how many hungry people there are in the world because we may not want to know. To know how many hungry there are in a world of plenty is to measure the inadequacies of our economies to sustain all, of our societies to provide for all, and of our common humanity to care for all'.

It is by now commonplace to observe that there does exist more than enough food in the world to feed everyone adequately. Hunger reflects social derangement more than it reflects the capacity for food production.

Most international statistics on food and hunger measure the average availability of food supply, which is not the same as food consumption: because food is 'available' does not mean that everyone has access to it. Food consumption is mediated by class, gender, and age, among other variables. It is subject to serious disruption, most noticeably by war. Food supplies are often the intentional targets of armed conflict, which, not surprisingly, affects the poorest, hungriest, and most vulnerable in the population first, chief among whom are women and their dependent children.

The production and supply of food are obviously affected by environmental factors. Agendas for action on food and hunger have to tackle such issues as land erosion (see Map 11); increasing agro-chemical dependence (see Map 9); the need to conserve wild genes for the protection and maintenance of crops (see Map 10); and even the possibility of a changing world climate.

Sources for map and commentary:

Food and Agriculture Organization (FAO), *The State of Food and Agriculture*, 1989; FAO, *Production Statistics Yearbook*, Rome, 1987; Kates, Robert, et al, *The Hunger Report: 1988* and *Update: 1989*, Brown University: Alan Shawn Feinstein World Hunger Program, 1989.

8 LIVING OFF THE LAND

The proportion of people directly engaged in agriculture worldwide is dropping rapidly: in developing countries, from 70 percent in 1970 to 50 percent in 1990; in developed countries over the same period, from 16 percent to 8 percent. Meanwhile the number of people that each hectare of land must support is increasing dramatically. The amount of land available is relatively fixed, while the world's population is growing.

The race to obtain bigger crop yields out of a fixed agricultural base has been directed by large multinational chemical and agro-business enterprises. While all evidence shows that small farms are more efficient and productive than large farms, the worldwide trend is towards larger and larger consolidated agricultural holdings. Similarly, although food grown with heavy doses of chemicals is known to have a lower nutritional value, the 'drugging' of world agriculture continues (see Map 9). Finally, although land reform has proven to be the single most-effective means of increasing agricultural productivity, and despite recent revolutions waged on the promise of land reform, little is changing: in Peru, for example, 93% of all agricultural land is owned by the top 10% of landowners; in El Salvador, 78%; in Guatemala, 76%.

Much deforestation in Central and South America (see Map 5) is a direct consequence of distorted land tenure systems: huge areas of forest have single owners, who then assume the right to clear-cut forest to make way for large cattle-ranching enterprises. The cattle businesses themselves are often owned by foreign companies in conjunction with a country's largest landholders. Intervention in deforestation almost always brings environmentalists into direct conflict with the political and economic elite who own most of the land. In many countries, land reform and environmental reform must go hand in hand.

Sources for map and commentary:

Gramfors, Bo, *Concise Earth Atlas: The Book of Everything*, Stockholm: Esselte Map Service, 1989; Kurian, George, *The New Book of World Rankings*, New York: Facts on File, 1984; Food and Agriculture Organization (FAO), *Production Statistics Yearbook, 1988*, Rome: 1989.

9 CHEMICAL FIX

World agriculture is hooked on synthetic chemicals. The use of agro-chemicals has increased tenfold since World War II, and most crops are now grown with the assistance of artificial fertilizers and biocides. In 1988, for example, American farmers used almost 19 million tonnes of synthetic fertilizers and 255,000 tonnes of pesticides. The demand is for new and stronger chemicals, and for heavier doses. But chemical dependence is cyclical: fertilizers, which may appear to be the most benign of agro-chemicals, disrupt natural soil balance and crop ecology; this then encourages the use of herbicides, insecticides, and pesticides; these chemicals then strip soils of nutrients, which then necessitates heavier use of fertilizers.

Agricultural chemicals pose a grave pollution threat to entire ecosystems. Chemical runoff from croplands causes river eutrophication; insecticides and herbicides kill 'benign' animals and birds as well as 'pests'. DDT nearly wiped out dozens of domestic bird species on the eastern seaboard of the USA before its use was banned in the early 1970s; meanwhile in Thailand, DDT is now threatening drinking water supplies throughout the country; and over large regions of Central America, where pesticide use levels are among the highest in the world, wildlife is being decimated and the natural ecology is crumbling.

In addition to the indirect health threat of chemical residues remaining in food, agro-chemicals pose additional direct threats to human health. One person in the world dies from pesticide poisoning every two hours. In the USA, the Environmental Protection Agency estimates that at least 66 of the roughly 300 pesticide ingredients commonly used by farmers are 'probable carcinogens', and dozens more are known to cause birth defects, nervous system disorders, and other chronic illnesses. Accidents in the manufacture and storage of agro-chemicals have killed thousands of people worldwide and caused grave environmental damage. Many of the major industrial accidents over the past twenty years have involved agro-chemical production facilities: among the most prominent of these have been the accidents at Bhopal and Seveso plus the Basle chemical spill into the River Rhine (see Map 26).

Although agricultural chemicals are a known threat to the environment and to human health, the agro-chemical industry is very big business and the chemical lobby is powerful enough to evade or defeat most regulatory efforts. One favoured tactic of the industry is to shift production and markets when domestic regulation threatens chemical production. Current estimates suggest that 75 per cent of the pesticides used in the Third World would not be allowed in the USA, and many of the chemicals used by farmers in poorer countries are actually banned in first world markets, but produced by American and West European firms for overseas use. The USA exports more than 18 million kgs of DDT annually, but a clear example of the shift from home consumption to export is offered by British export figures for DDT. In 1980, British exports were 1840 kgs, yet in 1984, after the pesticide was banned for domestic use, exports rose to 125,503 kgs.

Fertilizer use is monitored closely by the United Nations' Food and Agriculture Organization (FAO). There is no comparable record of international pesticide manufacture and use; the best monitoring of this side of the chemical industry comes from independent environmental and consumer groups.

Sources for map and commentary:

Food and Agriculture Organization (FAO), *Fertilizer Yearbook 1988*, Rome, 1989; FAO, *Production Statistics Yearbook 1987*, Rome 1988; FAO, *Trade Statistics Yearbook 1988*, Rome 1989; Goldsmith, Edward & Nicholas Hildyard, eds., *The Earth Report*, London: Mitchell Beazley, 1988; Mercier, Michel & Morrell Draper, 'Chemical Safety: The International Outlook', *World Health*, August/Sept., 1984; Schneider, Keith, 'Pesticide Regulation: Slow and Unsteady,' *New York Times*, March 19, 1989; Weir, David & Mark Schapiro, *Circle of Poison*, Berkeley, CA: Institute for Food and Development Policy, 1981.

10 SHRINKING GENES

Genetic diversity is essential for the maintenance of ecological stability. Food plants that people have 'domesticated' do not endure on their own, isolated as they are from cross-fertilization with other genetically diverse plants. Most of the world's food now derives from about 20 plant species. Yet food crops must always be reinforced with infusions of genes from wild species. These wild relatives possess genes, for example, that protect against pests and disease, improve tolerance to drought and even improve nutritional values.

A number of cultivated crops have wild gene relatives found only in rainforest, which is being rapidly destroyed (see Map 5). The loss of this and other important plant habitat is one primary problem. So also is the spread of monoculture practised by large-scale agro-business, especially in industrial countries. This reliance on monoculture is itself destroying important wild plant genetic material. One observer has noted: 'The products of agro-technology are displacing the source upon which the technology is based. It is analogous to taking stones from the foundation to repair the roof.' The foundation of plant genetic diversity in the world is on the point of collapse.

Genetic material, or germplasm, can be collected and stored as seeds, plants, cuttings, pollen and/or tissue culture, depending on the species. Most of the critical areas for collection of wild genetic material so far identified are in the 'Third World'. However there are many less valuable sources that also need urgent attention and preservation. The identification of the genetic origins of plants is a herculean task, and one barely begun.

There is no such thing as self-sufficiency in plant resources. The International Board for Plant Genetic Resources (IBPGR) is supported by the United Nations and has taken global responsibility for the coordination of germplasm collection and storage. Most species now being collected and preserved by the IBPGR as priorities are cultivated crops. A number of international, mostly private, agencies are also engaged in collecting and preserving genetic material in gene banks.

Genetic engineering involves the deliberate manipulation of an organism's nucleic acid, or genes, to give it new properties. Genetic engineering has great potential for improving food production.

increasing resistance to disease and replacing 'defective genes'. However, it is possible for a genetically-engineered organism to escape the confines of a controlled experiment and become an opportunistic organism that could cause widespread disease and ecological disruption. The deliberate release of genetically-engineered organisms in field trials has been vigorously opposed, but releases are occurring at an increasing rate. Four releases of engineered organisms have occurred in countries other than those identified on the map.

Sources for map and commentary:
UK Department of the Environment, personal communication; Myers, Norman, ed., *Gaia: An Atlas of Planet Management*, London: Pan; New York: Doubleday, 1984; Prescott-Allen, R & C. Prescott-Allen, *Genes from the Wild*, London: Earthscan, 1988.

11 LOSING GROUND

Desertification was a big media issue of the 1970s and early 1980s. Described as a problem of over-exploitation of marginal lands in arid climates (especially in the Sahel area of Africa), the term conjured up images of 'deserts on the march'. Desertification has now taken on a low profile, replaced by newer global concerns such as ozone depletion and the greenhouse effect, and the concept itself has come under much critical review.

Nonetheless, soil loss - whether technically described as desertification or not - is still a pressing global concern. Soil loss is threatening agricultural viability on all six continents. In Australia, six tonnes of topsoil are eroded for every tonne of produce grown; in the USA, a third of all cropland is affected by erosion; over much of Asia, 40 percent of the land is at high risk of erosion or desertification.

Erosion - the removal of soil by wind or water - is a natural and ongoing process, but one that is dramatically aggravated and advanced by human activity, particularly the removal of vegetation. When forests are cut down or land is cleared for agriculture or animal grazing, there is nothing left to stabilize the soil, and rapid soil loss follows. In the late 1980s, the deadly landslides and floods that have plagued many Himalayan states, Bangladesh in particular, are largely attributed to the linked problems of deforestation and erosion.

Traditional peasant farming systems are often blamed for erosion problems. In fact, the greater problem is the spread of mechanized farming, the development of cash crops for export, and the introduction of vast livestock ranges that have led to overgrazing and unsustainably intensive agriculture.

Sources for map and commentary:
Goldsmith, Edward & Nicholas Hildyard, eds., *The Earth Report*, London: Mitchell Beazley, 1988; Myers, Norman, ed., *Gaia: An Atlas of Planet Management*, London: Pan; New York: Doubleday, 1984; United Nations Environment Programme (UNEP) *World Conservation Strategy*, 1980; World Resources Institute/Institute for Environment and Development, *World Resources 1988-89*, New York: Basic Books, 1988.

12 FISHING FOR FOOD

Fish is a major source of food for many in the world - fisheries supply 23 percent of the world's protein - and fishing provides a livelihood for millions of people. Since 1950, global yields of fish (both marine and fresh-water) have risen over fourfold, from 20 million tonnes to more than 85 million tonnes.

However, world fish stocks are now threatened by many factors, including over-exploitation, pollution, (see, for example, Map 22) and wetlands destruction (see Map 14). After some years of increasing yields, the stocks of many fisheries are declining precipitously. According to a mid-1980s survey by the United Nations' Food and Agriculture Organization (FAO), 11 major ocean fishing grounds, including some newly exploited grounds, are now overfished to the point of collapse. Given the greater dependence on fish for food in Third World countries, it is the poor who will be suffering first and most as fisheries decline.

Statistics monitoring the state of fisheries are often contradictory, and usually considerably out of date. Estimates of catches are highly unreliable and even the most reliable figures, from FAO, must be treated with some caution. In most statistical summaries, 'artisanal' fishing and small coastal independent fishing enterprises are often overlooked, although these supply much of the demand for fish in poorer countries.

Sources for map and commentary:

Food and Agriculture Organization (FAO), *World Food Report*, Rome, 1985; FAO, *Fishery Statistics*, 1986, 1987; Myers, Norman, ed., *Gaia: An Atlas of Planet Management*, London: Pan; New York: Doubleday, 1984.

13 CITY SPRAWL

Cities have always acted as focal points in the development of nation-states, and as symbols of opportunity in the popular imagination. They remain symbolically powerful, but the reality of urbanization is rapidly changing. Some cities remain small in scale and functionally intact. But as other cities — the 'hotspots' on this map, as well as others unnamed — grow into vast conglomerations, they are both uncontrollable and unsustainable. Governments cannot afford to provide the vast infrastructure that is needed to accommodate adequately the huge numbers of people drawn to city life.

In consequence, the social structure of 'mega-cities' around the world is increasingly bifurcated into a small, powerful, and often extremely wealthy elite class, and a huge underclass that is ill-housed or homeless, ill-fed, and unserved by even basic municipal services. There is no poverty more squalid than urban poverty, and in the rapidly urbanizing centres of the world, city life and poverty seem synonymous. Most of the people migrating to the largest and fastest-growing cities in the world today will end up living in shanty-towns, slums or 'cardboard cities' on the outskirts, with no running water, sanitation services or health services. Many will end up with work as street vendors, as exploitatively-paid piece-workers or, especially many young women, as prostitutes or domestic servants for the wealthy.

Many of today's new urban arrivals are unwilling migrants, people displaced from their rural landholdings by war, famine, massive 'development' schemes such as large dams (see Map 20), and agricultural 'modernization'. For others, willing migrants, the attractions of the city are not diminished by the reality of urban poverty: cities still offer the possibility of economic opportunities not found elsewhere, the hope of greater social, political or religious freedom, and amenities not possible in rural settings.

The locus of global urbanization is shifting. In 1960, six out of ten of the world's largest cities were in industrialized countries: New York, Los Angeles, London, the Rhine/Ruhr conglomeration, Paris, and Moscow. By the year 2000, only two cities in the industrial world, New York and Tokyo, will remain in the top ten ranking. Mexico City, ranked 15 in size in 1960, will be the world's largest city by the year 2000.

As cities grow, in absolute size and proportional importance, they play a larger part in shaping the global environment. Under the pressure of urban sprawl, agricultural land is paved over, wetlands are drained, natural habitats are destroyed, rivers are diverted, and wildlife habitats are pushed further and further into the margins. The internal ecology of cities also changes: pollutants of all kinds are concentrated in urban centres, and many cities have become highly hazardous places to live. Environmental action must acknowledge the global nature of the urban problem. Efforts must be made to make cities more humane places to live - and more environmentally benign.

Sources for map and commentary:

Atlas de Carreteras Mexico, Mexico City, Guia Roji, 1987; McDowell, Bert, 'Mexico City: An Alarming Giant', *National Geographic*, August 1984; United Nations, Department of International Economic and Social Affairs, *The Prospects of World Urbanization*, 1987; United Nations, *Compendium of Human Settlement Statistics*, 1983.

14 COASTAL CRISIS

Wetlands fringe most coastlines of the world, as mangroves in the tropics and subtropics, and as salt marshes in the temperate zones. They mediate between the ecosystems of land and sea, serving as huge reservoirs of species diversity, providing rich wildlife habitats for birds, animals, and fish. They provide the spawning grounds for most of the world's commercial fisheries, they act as natural buffers that temper the effects of extreme flooding and drought, they filter pollutants out of maritime systems, they recharge groundwater drinking supplies, and they stabilize coastal erosion. They stabilize and support the health of the planet.

Wetlands are under extreme threat almost everywhere in the world. Clear-cutting is perhaps the greatest single threat, but pollution and urban development rank close behind. Urban development alone has claimed almost half the wetlands in the USA, and in California and Iowa, more than 90 percent. South-East Asia has the largest mangrove ecosystem in the world, but it is rapidly being clear-cut by commercial logging operations, especially in Malaysia, Indonesia, and Bangladesh.

Like many other environmental problems, but especially so, the world's wetlands need international cooperation for their protection. The significance of wetlands, and the consequences of their loss, cannot be contained by national borders. The migrating birds of Western Europe, for example, depend on wetlands in northern Africa for refuge on their journey; the drainage of wetlands in Louisiana threatens the fisheries of the entire Gulf of Mexico.

Since 1971, some measure of international wetlands protection has been offered through the Convention on Wetlands of International Significance (also known as the 'Ramsar Convention'), but this convention is ratified by only 43 countries, and while 77,000 square miles of wetlands have fallen under its statutory protection, this represents less than 2 percent of the world's wetland areas.

Sources for map and commentary:

Chapman, V.J., *Ecosystems of the World and Wet Coastal Ecosystems*, New York: Elsevier, 1977; Conservation Foundation, *State of the Environment: A View Toward the Nineties*, Washington DC, 1987; Houck, Oliver, 'America's Mad Dash to the Sea,' *The Amicus Journal*, Summer 1988; 'Mangroves: An Ecosystem in Danger', *Ambio*, vol. 9, 1980; Saenger, P., E.J. Hegerl & J.D.S. Davie, *Global Status of Mangrove Ecosystems*, IUCN (Cambridge) Commission on Ecology Papers no. 3, 1983.

15 WASTE

International information on levels of municipal and household waste generation, most experts agree, is little more than an educated guess, although some general points are clear: worldwide generation of waste appears to amount to about one billion tonnes per year, and is growing rapidly; the biggest waste producers are rich countries and, within poor countries, rich people. Affluence produces effluence, literally.

There is also a significant difference in the kind of garbage thrown away by rich and poor: in rich countries, glass, paper, metals and other durables constitute a larger share of garbage than in poor countries, where more of the waste is organic material. This difference has important implications for waste disposal: organic garbage can be composted, which is the safest method of waste disposal, whereas other materials are less easily disposed of. Plastics are the least disposable of any garbage, yet the proportion of plastics in garbage is increasing dramatically. In 1987, the USA alone produced 26 billion kgs. of plastics; by volume, plastics now represent about 30 percent of the US waste stream.

At the beginning of the 1990s, most garbage in most places in the world is dumped in landfills. But cities and countries everywhere are running out of landfill space. Given the landfill crisis, attention is turning to incineration (optimistically called, by those in the industry, 'waste to energy' disposal). Incineration is a high-cost means of waste treatment that generates air pollution and leaves a highly toxic residue that itself then needs disposal. A number of countries, including Belgium, France, West Germany, and the UK, burn some of their waste at sea on incinerator ships, although the international community is moving closer to banning this highly polluting and very dangerous practice. Other countries simply dump their municipal garbage at sea. Although this practice, too, is being phased out, we will live with its legacy for years to come, in the form of increasing epidemics of marine mammal illnesses, and increasing incidents, some of which are already recorded in Western Europe and the USA, of deep-sea trash washing up on beaches.

Recycling, which is a cheap, revenue-generating, and low-technology solution, is slowly gaining favour in most industrialized countries, but still faces heavy competition from incineration. In poor countries, recycling has always ranked high in waste reduction, and whole communities of people in most Third World cities support themselves as dump-scavengers and recyclers.

The waste crisis has sparked interest among rich countries in the possibilities of an international waste trade. With no room in their own backyards, states and industries in the developed world are scanning the globe for countries poor enough to want to accept municipal trash for (usually low) dumping fees. (See Map 27 for a parallel trade in toxic waste). In 1989, an American waste disposal firm closed a deal to dump thousands of tonnes of US household waste on a Pacific atoll in the Marshall Islands. It is a great irony that one of the selling points for the deal was that the garbage could provide landfill for the low-lying Marshalls, which would otherwise be vulnerable to flooding if sea levels rise as a result of global warming.

Sources for map and commentary:

Cointreau, Sandra, *Solid Waste Recycling: Case Studies in Developing Countries*, Washington DC: World Bank, 1987; Levenson, Howard, Office of Technology Assessment, US Congress, personal communication; Organization for Economic Cooperation and Development (OECD), *OECD Environmental Data Compendium, 1989*, Paris: OECD, 1989; World Resources Institute/Institute for Environment and Development, *World Resources 1988-89*, New York: Basic Books, 1988; World Action on Recycling Materials for Energy from Rubbish (WARMER), Tunbridge Wells, personal communication; Worldwatch Institute, *State of the World: 1989*, New York: Norton, 1989.

16 SEWAGE

In heavily populated areas, especially the rapidly-growing urban conglomerations of poorer countries, sewage pollution is a primary cause of the worldwide trend in deterioration of water quality. In developing countries, most municipal sewage receives little or no treatment, and separation of drinking water from sewage disposal is inadequate; sewage contamination of drinking water is a major factor in the high rates of infant mortality and morbidity recorded in many poorer countries, much of which is caused by gastro-intestinal infections.

In older industrial areas, municipal water and sewage facilities, many built in the last century, are overwhelmed by population pressures, and a decline in investment in sewage disposal in the late 1970s and early 1980s has resulted in the downgrading of river water quality in most urban areas. Until recently, sewage in most industrialized countries was dumped directly into the nearest body of water: for example, until the mid-1960s, American and Canadian cities pumped untreated sewage directly into the Great Lakes, contributing to its reputation as one of the most polluted bodies of water in the world. In most cases, it was not municipal farsightedness but agitation by independent environmental groups that led to pressure for sewage treatment and an end to direct dumping. Efforts to clean up urban waterways, now underway in many industrialized cities, are estimated to cost billions of dollars.

The accuracy of statistics that measure the provision of sanitation facilities is widely suspect. International compendiums typically provide dramatically different figures: for example, while the World Health Organization reports adequate sanitation provisions for 40 percent of Uganda's urban population in the mid-1980s, an independent development agency reports only 20 percent coverage. In some cases, statistics may be manipulated to serve political agendas that might be undercut by reports of low levels of public health services provision. These statistical variations, often dramatic or confusing, suggest the difficulties inherent in attempts to monitor public and environmental wellbeing on a global basis.

Sources for map and commentary:
Organization for Economic Cooperation and Development (OECD), *OECD Environmental Data Compendium, 1989*, Paris: OECD, 1989; United Nations Environment Programme (UNEP), *Environmental Data Report*, 2nd ed. 1989-90, Oxford: Blackwell, 1989; World Health Organization (WHO), *World Health Statistics Annual*, 1986; World Resources Institute/Institute for Environment and Development, *World Resources 1988-89*, New York: Basic Books, 1988.

17 AIR QUALITY

This map depicts urban levels of three major air pollutants - sulphur dioxides, nitrogen oxides, and particulates ('dust and dirt'). Ninety percent of anthropogenic sulphur dioxide emissions are from the burning of certain fossil fuels; nitrogen oxides come primarily from car and truck emissions; and particulates from both cars and fossil fuel combustion. All three contribute to a range of respiratory illnesses, including bronchitis, pneumonia, asthma and lung cancer, although the health effects vary with the intensity and duration of exposures. Both sulphur dioxide and nitrogen oxides are major components of acid rain and nitrogen oxides are also a minor greenhouse gas.

Measuring air quality is a precise science that must, by its nature, be carried out under imprecise and unpredictable conditions. Standardized international measurements are only available for a scattering of cities, and drawing comparisons from city data is difficult because of wide variations in place, time and the frequency of air monitoring samples. Sometimes, indeed, monitoring is only carried out at sites where there is a known severe problem. This leads to a bias towards sampling cities with higher concentrations of pollutants. Despite these caveats, though, it is still possible to make certain generalizations about air quality problems in the world's cities.

The air in most cities is in fact a chemical soup of dozens of pollutants. There are a number of others beyond the three pollutants illustrated on the map. Carbon monoxide, largely the product of car emissions, is one of the mostly widely distributed urban air pollutants, but there is no available international data set measuring its levels. Similarly, ozone, also known as 'photochemical smog', is a serious air quality concern in many cities, but again there are no worldwide statistics. Los Angeles is still the city with the greatest ozone problem in the world. Ozone was originally believed to be a problem peculiar to Los Angeles, because of its special topography and high density of cars, but photochemical smog is now known to occur in and downwind of most major cities in the world. Dublin also has a serious smog problem - but in this case, the smog is from the 350,000 tonnes of coal burned in the city's households each year.

Most urban air pollutant levels are increasing, largely because of increases in the numbers of cars and trucks (see Map 31). There are some broad estimates of the costs involved in reducing air pollutant levels: that to cut sulphur dioxide emissions in half in the USA would cost an estimated US$5 billion a year; to halve sulphur emissions in the EEC would cost from US$5 billion to US$7 billion per year. It is even more difficult to quantify the real costs of existing air pollution, but one EEC estimate gives US$13 billion for loss of fisheries, crops, forests, and health.

Sources for map and commentary:
Global Environment Monitoring System (GEMS), *Assessment of Urban Air Quality*, Nairobi: UNEP/WHO, 1988; 'Monitoring the Global Environment: An Assessment of Urban Air Quality,' Special Issue report, *Environment*, October 1989; Organization for Economic Cooperation and Development (OECD), *OECD Environmental Data Compendium*, 1989, Paris: OECD, 1989; World Health Organization (WHO), *Air Quality Guidelines for Europe*, Copenhagen: 1987; World Commission on Environment and Development, *Our Common Future*, Oxford: Oxford University Press, 1987; World Resources Institute/International Institute for Environment and Development, *World Resources 1988-89*, New York: Basic Books, 1988.

18 ENERGY BUDGETS

Energy production and consumption are closely monitored, both by government agencies and private industry, and statistics on international use are widely available, if sometimes highly technical. As always, information on commercially-traded commodities, such as oil or coal, is much more reliable than is information on fuels of local reliance, such as firewood and small-scale hydropower. Firewood, the largest biomass energy source, and other biomass fuels together provide approximately 14 percent of the world's energy.

The USA is by far the largest consumer of commercial energy, but a number of other countries in Western Europe have comparable per capita consumption levels. Current global energy consumption rates are increasing on an average of 3 percent per year, the largest share of which is in the industrialized world. Overall, it would appear that the pace of growth in consumption is somewhat lessening, but consumption rates often fluctuate considerably over the short term.

Energy consumption provides a measure of our impact on ecological systems. The production, extraction and use of coal, oil, gas, and nuclear power, which power much of the world, all have destructive environmental consequences (see Maps 17, 22 and 23). The renewable energy sources most widely used, hydro power and firewood, are more environmentally benign, but are not unproblematic (see Maps 20 and 21). Firewood is in increasingly short supply, and even though it provides the sole energy source for many 'third world' households, it may not continue to be a viable energy source far into the next century.

Given this array of poor choices, energy conservation is crucial to the long-term viability of the planet. After the oil crisis of 1973, systematic efforts were made throughout the industrial world to increase energy efficiency, with impressive results: in the USA, cars will now travel 29 percent farther on a gallon of gasoline than they did in 1973; Denmark was able to reduce its total use of direct fuels by 20 percent between 1976 and 1980. The reasons to reduce energy consumption are now different but they are even more compelling.

Some would argue that conservation is necessary but not sufficient, and that we must radically alter our industries and economies to incorporate large-scale use of solar, geothermal, and wind energy sources, which hold the promise of being both renewable and non-polluting. Others see them as introducing environmental problems of their own. As yet, however, these technologies have received little support or interest, nor have they made much of a dent in traditional energy budgets.

Sources for map and commentary:

Conservation Foundation, *State of the Environment: A View Toward the Nineties*, Washington DC, 1987; Goldsmith, Edward & Nicholas Hildyard, eds., *The Earth Report*, London: Mitchell Beazley, 1988; United Nations, *Energy Statistics Yearbook 1987*, 1989; US Department of Energy, Energy Information Administration (EIA), *International Energy Annual, 1988*, Washington DC: DOE, 1989.

19 THE NUCLEAR FAMILY

Electricity generation by nuclear power began in 1955 with a small reactor in the Soviet Union. Since then, the growth of the industry has been dramatic. There are currently 421 operating nuclear power plants in the world, and another 144 reactors planned or under construction. In addition to the 32 countries with operating power plants, another 27 have some form of nuclear facility. Though the industry is widely perceived to have fundamental problems, there are actually few signs of its demise.

The USA is the world's largest exporter of nuclear technology, followed by the USSR; it is not coincidental that these two countries are also the world's largest military powers, and the world's largest military exporters. Military nuclear agendas and commercial nuclear programmes are closely intertwined. Any nuclear power reactor can be used to produce plutonium for bombs. Some, like 'fast breeder' reactors, are designed specifically to produce plutonium; others produce it as a by-product; many reactors are used for both weapons and energy production. Whether governments choose to acknowledge the interconnectedness of the military and civilian uses of nuclear programmes depends largely on domestic politics and international approbation.

The link between civilian nuclear power and military nuclear capability is made through the nuclear fuel cycle. To be able to make a nuclear weapon, a country has to have access to all five stages of the nuclear cycle, from uranium production through fuel reprocessing. Thus, South Korea, which is technically striving for independence in its nuclear power capabilities, has no enrichment or reprocessing facilities; on the other hand, Argentina, which does not produce much power through nuclear facilities, has completed the fuel cycle. The fuel cycle also brings countries into the nuclear family even if they are not producing nuclear energy: Iraq, for example, has a nuclear fuel fabrication plant and Gabon mines uranium.

Spokespeople for the nuclear industry are quick to point out that nuclear power plants emit none of the greenhouse gases produced by oil and coal. This, however, is a dubious virtue, given that the operation of nuclear plants represents an ongoing public safety and health threat, and given the large volumes of highly toxic waste generated by the nuclear industry. Over the next 30 years, more than 25,000 cubic metres of high level waste will be generated by the top ten nuclear countries alone. There is literally no place to safely dispose of radioactive waste, and there are fewer and fewer places to store it. Until 1983, Belgium, the Netherlands, Switzerland and the UK dumped low-level radioactive waste at sea. This practice was halted by an international moratorium under the London Dumping Convention, an agreement consistently opposed by the British government. With the ban on ocean disposal, there is also no place, any more, to dispose of low-level radioactive waste. Most nuclear states are building up huge stockpiles of nuclear waste that no one wants and no one knows how to get rid of.

The nuclear accident at Chernobyl in 1986 provided powerful evidence that nuclear disasters transcend state borders and undermined support for nuclear power throughout Europe. Polls showed that opposition to nuclear power in the UK jumped frpm 70% before Chernobyl, to 85% after the accident; in Austria, opposition increased from 50% to 75%; in France, from 40% to 50%. In a national referendum in 1987, Italians voted to shut down permanently their nuclear power plants, although as of early 1990, it appeared that one plant was still operating.

Sources for map and commentary:

Commission of the European Communities, *The State of the Environment in the European Community, 1986*, Brussels, 1988; International Atomic Energy Agency *Annual Report for 1988*, Vienna: IAEA, 1989; 'The World's Nuclear Fuel Cycle Facilities', *Nuclear Engineering International*, December 1987; 'World List of Nuclear Power Plants', *Nuclear News*, August 1989.

20 HYDRO POWER

In 1950, there were about 5000 large dams in the world; thirty years later, by the early 1980s, there were 35,000 large dams, 53 percent of which were in China. The frenzy of dam construction appears to have now slowed worldwide, and in China in particular - in large measure because of environmental concerns.

Hydro power (which accounts for about 6 percent of worldwide energy use) is in itself a relatively cheap, renewable and non-polluting energy source. However the dams built to produce it present a number of serious environmental problems. The reservoirs for large dams are created by flooding vast swathes of land, often inundating valuable forest area, wildlife habitat or wetlands - often entire ecological communities. In warm climates, reservoirs can pose health hazards, increasing the incidence of waterborne disease, such as schistosomiasis, and 'river blindness'. The quality of water from dams often deteriorates, due to a build-up of salts and chemicals, posing threate to irrigated crops and drinking water supplies.

The construction of a large dam is a huge undertaking. Many of the largest dam projects in the world are funded with assistance from international aid agencies, most notably the World Bank. The twin Sadar Sarovar and Narmada Sagar dam projects in India, for example, estimated to displace 70,000 people by submerging 438 villages, was started with a US$450 million loan from the World Bank; it has become one of their most controversial projects. If the World Bank honours its recent commitment to phase out support for environmentally destructive projects, many of the largest dam projects now planned around the world will be halted. Local environmental pressure is also halting work on some large dams (see Map 37). Plans for a major dam on the Danube at Nagymaros, Hungary, were scrapped in 1988. In 1990, French environmentalists are fighting proposals for four large dams on the Loire, France's longest river. They have had some success. Two dams have already been cancelled and the battle continues.

The definition of 'large' dams, as agreed by international engineering associations, includes dams from 15 metres in height to 'mega' dams over 200 metres high. Statistics on hydro power, and on dams, are readily available from 'pro-dam' sources, mainly detailed records of dam characteristics and construction, and from 'anti-dam' groups who monitor the environmental and social costs of dams.

Sources for map and commentary:

International Commission on Large Dams, *World Register of Dams*, Paris: 1984; International Rivers Network, *World Rivers Review*, July/August, 1989; Mermel, T.W., 'The World's Major Dams and Hydro Plants', *International Water Power and Dam Construction*, vol. 41, 1989; Parcels, S. & T.B. Stoel, 'The Large Dam Controversy', Unpublished draft for the World Bank, 1989; Probe International, 'Water Projects With World Bank Involvement', *World Rivers Review*, September/October 1989; Simons, M., 'Brazil Wants its Dams, But at What Cost?' *New York Times*, March 12, 1989.

21 FIREWOOD

Firewood is a local, self-reliant energy source. Since most statistical information is collected on a national or even international level, information on the supply and use of firewood is partial, inconsistent, and often based on very small samples. Official reports also invariably underestimate rural fuelwood use.

Within a single country there is often considerable variation in firewood provision – variations lost in national summaries. Information on the amount of time spent collecting firewood – always women's work – must be treated with a good deal of caution. The data we provide on this subject is based on a small sample of communities and cannot be assumed to represent a general or national average.

Nonetheless, the general situation in relation to firewood is clear. Many people in many 'third world' countries rely entirely on firewood for energy, cooking, and warmth. About 70 - 95 percent of all firewood is used for rural domestic purposes, and the remainder is used in cottage industries and small-scale commercial enterprises. Almost everywhere in the world, firewood is becoming scarce, and the effort to collect it is taking a larger and larger share of the working day. Many women in rural areas report that they are now spending so much time collecting firewood that they have little time for other activities, such as growing and cooking food. With less time to prepare food, simpler diets are being adopted – in the Sahel, for example, many women have shifted from cooking millet to rice. Nutrition suffers even before a full firewood crisis arises.

The firewood shortage has been precipitated by a number of converging factors. Everywhere in the world, deforestation for commercial logging or agriculture is the primary cause of local firewood scarcity. In addition, though, urban demand is putting pressure on rural resources. Firewood for Delhi, for example, comes from Madhya Pradesh, 700 kilometres away, and requires clear-felling of 6 hectares of forest a day. Whereas fuelwood for rural uses is often twigs and fallen branches, commercial users will cut down an entire tree – representing the difference between sustainable tree use and deforestation.

Sources for map and commentary:

Agarwal, Bina, *Cold Hearths and Barren Slopes: The Fuelwood Crisis in the Third World*, Riverdale, MD: Riverdale Press, 1986; Food and Agriculture Organization (FAO), *Map of the Fuelwood Situation in the Developing Countries*, Rome: FAO, 1981; FAO, *Yearbook of Forest Products, 1982, 1984*; Richard Hosier, University of Pennsylvania, personal communication; Smil, V. & W.E. Knowland, eds., *Energy in the Developing World: The Real Energy Crisis*, Oxford: Oxford University Press, 1980; United Nations Environment Programme (UNEP), *Environmental Data Report*, 2nd ed. 1989-90, Oxford: Blackwell, 1989; United Nations Statistical Office, *Energy Statistics Yearbook 1985,1987* and *Energy Statistics Yearbook 1986*, 1988.

22 OIL POLLUTION

The economy – and lifestyle – of the industrialized world is entirely dependent on oil. Oil is big business, both for private and public enterprise and state revenue: Exxon, the world's largest oil company made a net profit of US$5 billion in 1987; 55 states depend essentially on a single product for their export income – for 24 of them, that product is oil and gas. The oil industry seems larger than life; so, unfortunately, is the pollution it causes. The extraction and transport of oil are among the highest-risk industrial activities, causing long-lasting ecological disruption and widespread pollution.

More than 6 million metric tonnes of oil are released into the world's oceans each year; roughly 1 tonne is spilled for every 1000 tonnes extracted. Marine tanker accidents are not the largest source of oil pollution, but they are often the most dangerous, releasing large amounts of oil in a short period of time, often close to shore. The threat posed by single acute oil spills has increased over the past twenty years, as oil companies have switched to larger and larger vessels in an effort to cut costs. Today's supertankers average twice the size and carry ten times the amount of oil as tankers that worked the oil routes twenty years ago.

The chronic release of oil from maritime shipping operations represents an even greater environmental problem than acute spills. On oil supply routes, for example, oil tankers routinely flush out their tanks with sea water on the return trip, in so doing releasing thousands of tonnes of oil annually. Oily trails around the world mark the major shipping routes.

When accidental maritime oil spills do happen, as they do on an average of three a day worldwide, legal and financial responsibility for the ensuing pollution is often difficult to assign. Many oil companies register their ships under 'flags of convenience' in such countries as Liberia, the Bahamas, Cyprus or Panama. These 'open registries' allow companies to run ships with lower-cost, non-union crews, to evade certain corporation taxes, and to avoid some national and international regulations. Registries of convenience also obscure the trail of corporate responsibility for accidents and spills.

In mapping the distribution of oil spills, our original intention had been to allocate responsibility to individual oil companies. This proved to be impossible. Despite the volumes of data kept by tanker associations, oil associations, and maritime associations, no one, it appears, monitors oil spills by company – or, if such records do exist, they are not open to public scrutiny. This gap reinforces the sense that oil accidents 'just happen', somehow without human agency. It is even difficult to establish, in the first place, the occurrence of spills. Unless they are spectacular accidents, most domestic media coverage ignores spills that occur elsewhere in the world, and most small spills in domestic waters are not newsworthy. The data used here is a compilation from dozens of sources, and yet we know the information to be still incomplete.

A primary argument against increased use of renewable energy sources, such as solar power, is its cost. It is argued that conventional sources of energy, such as oil, are much cheaper. However, the true cost of oil is mostly hidden. The real tally of the cost of our oil dependency should include the cost of environmental damage and clean-ups. It should also include expenditure on military forces used to 'secure' oil supply routes and oil production regions; oil company subsidies and tax allowances, and the cost of the trade deficits that most oil-dependent nations now face.

Sources for map and commentary:

Couper, A., ed., *The Times Atlas of the Oceans*, London: Times Books; New York: Van Nostrand, 1983; International Tanker Owners' Pollution Federation (ITOPF), 'Spills over 5000 barrels,' mimeograph document; Levy, Eric, 'Oil Pollution in the World's Oceans,' *Ambio*, vol. 13, no. 4, 1984; McKenzie, Arthur, *Guide to the Selection of Tankers*, New York: Tanker Advisory Center, 1989; other Tanker Advisory Center publications; National Academy of Sciences (NAS), *Oil in the Sea: Inputs, Fates and Effects*, Washington DC: NAS, 1985; Organization for Economic Cooperation and Development (OECD), *OECD Environmental Data Compendium, 1989*, Paris: OECD, 1989; Starr, Gary & Susan Bryer Starr, 'The True Cost of Oil,' *Earth Island Journal*, Summer 1988.

23 FOSSIL FUEL POLLUTION

Fossil fuels are oil, gas and coal. Most industrial economies are entirely fossil-fuel dependent. The price of this dependency is severe pollution and, looming, the possible onset of global warming. The burning of fossil fuels produces a number of pollutants, including sulphur dioxide, nitrogen oxides, particulates (dirt and dust) and carbon monoxide.

The most serious fossil fuel pollutant is carbon dioxide. This is not in itself toxic, but in conjunction with other gases is the primary greenhouse gas (see Map 1). Most carbon dioxide in the atmosphere stems from burning fossil fuels. Worldwide releases from carbon dioxide from fossil fuel combustion currently amount to 22 billion tonnes per year. Other human activities that produce carbon dioxide include tropical forest destruction (see Map 5), cement production and natural gas burn-off flares. Smaller quantities are produced from natural sources, such as volcanoes and animal respiration.

Most fossil fuel pollution comes from a handful of rich, industrial countries. Canada and the USA produce, between them, 33 million tonnes of carbon dioxide a year. Carbon dioxide pollution is a pollution of privilege; but as is often the case in environmental concerns, the consequences and costs are borne globally.

Attempts to curb the problem are being thwarted by the very countries most responsible. In autumn 1989, 65 countries sponsored an international resolution to cut carbon dioxide emissions in industrial countries. It was defeated by objections from Japan, the USA and the USSR. The US and Japanese governments urged postponing action for 'further study', while USSR and other East European representatives opposed pollution limits claiming they could not afford them. In the countries creating most pollution, the adoption of carbon dioxide limits would probably require more fuel-efficient cars, more fuel-efficient electricity and extensive tree planting.

The other pollutants included on this map, sulphur dioxide and nitrogen oxides, are both major contributors to acid rain (see Map 24). Again, the primary sources of these pollutants are in the industrialized world and acid rain is a particular problem for Western Europe. Most West European governments, the UK being a notable exception, have joined together to form a '30% Club'. This commits them to reducing sulphur dioxide emissions by 30 percent by 1993 – not just by cutting back on fossil fuel use, but by persuading industry to devise less polluting techniques.

Sources for map and commentary:

Eliasson, Anton, et al, *Estimates of Airborne Transboundary Transport of Sulphur and Nitrogen over Europe*, Norwegian Meteorological Institute, 1988; Global Environment Monitoring System (GEMS), *Assessment of Urban Air Quality*, Nairobi: UNEP/WHO, 1988; Goldsmith, Edward & Nicholas Hildyard, eds., *The Earth Report*, London: Mitchell Beazley, 1988; Montgomery, Paul, 'US, Japan and Soviets Prevent Accord to Limit Carbon Dioxide', *New York Times*, November 8, 1989; Oak Ridge National Laboratory, *Estimates of CO2 Emissions from Fossil Fuel Burning and Cement Manufacturing*, Environmental Sciences Division Publication no. 3176, 1989.

24 ACID RAIN

The term 'acid rain' includes both the wet deposition of acidic sleet, snow, fog or rain and the dry deposition of nitrates and sulphates as they settle. Since the industrial revolution the chemical balance of the atmosphere has changed and acidification is being increased. This is mainly through the release of a very large additional burden of sulphur dioxide and nitrogen oxides from burning fossil fuels, notably coal in power stations and oil in motor vehicles (see Maps 23 and 31).

The acidity of a solution is measured in terms of 'pH'; pH1 is strongly acid, pH14 strongly alkaline, and pH7 is neutral. Weak acids such as lemon juice or vinegar have a pH of 3 to 4. Natural rainfall is usually slightly acid and has a pH of 6 to 7. On the map, 'high' acid rain pollution corresponds to an average rainfall pH of 4.9 to 5.1, 'very high' to pH4.5 – 4.7, and 'extremely high' to pH4.2 – 4.3.

Acid rain spares little. It erodes railway tracks; it corrodes the masonry of historic buildings and public statues. It causes natural ecosystems to crumble, destroying forests, crops and fish life in lakes. To date, acid rain is doing the greatest damage in Europe. In southern Norway, 80 percent of the lakes and streams are technically 'dead'; 64 percent of UK forest is showing signs of acid rain damage; in central Switzerland, more than 40 per cent of conifer forest is dead or severely damaged.

Acid rain is, by definition, a trans-national problem – it shows no regard for state boundaries. Acid deposition has been a contentious issue between Canada and the USA for years; most acid deposition in Scandinavia is from other countries, coming downwind from Europe's major industrial centres.

Solutions to the acid rain problem are energy conservation, a shift to less polluting forms of transport, and the fitting of special equipment to reduce acid gas emissions: 'flue gas desulphurization' at power stations and three-way catalytic converters on motor vehicles. In 1985, 19 countries agreed to reduce sulphur emissions by a further 30 percent, but scientists estimate that the reduction must be very much higher if the lakes and forests of Scandinavia are to be saved from further damage.

Sources for map and commentary:

Goldsmith, Edward & Nicholas Hildyard, eds., *The Earth Report*, London, Mitchell Beazley, 1988; McCormick, John, *Acid Earth*, London: Earthscan, 1989; United Nations Environment Programme (UNEP), *Forest Damage and Air Pollution*, 1988; World Resources Institute/International Institute for Environment and Development, *World Resources 1988-89*, New York: Basic Books, 1988.

25 INDUSTRIAL WASTE

Industrial activity generates millions of tonnes of waste annually, much of it extremely toxic. Nowhere in the world are there effective constraints or regulations to control this practice, and the decision-makers in industry seem largely unwilling to police themselves. Industry likes to conduct 'business as usual' and the typical response is to fight tooth and nail against the demands of clean air legislation, chemical regulation, water quality standards, automobile emission standards, workplace health regulations, and any other legislation designed to protect our environment. In state-controlled economies, where the state and industry are one, there are even fewer opportunities for independent monitoring or control of industrial pollution.

Some 350 million tonnes of hazardous industrial wastes are generated worldwide each year, about 90 percent of which comes from industrial countries. The US Environmental Protection Agency has identified a top-priority national list of over 5000 hazardous sites ('Superfund sites') left behind by industry, which, together will cost billions of dollars to clean up. As the curtain of secrecy lifts from Eastern Europe, tales of dead rivers, unbreathable air, villages abandoned because of extreme pollution, and other industrial horrors are being revealed daily.

There are no good ways of getting rid of hazardous waste. In the UK, 82 percent of hazardous industrial waste is dumped in landfills (see commentary to Map 6). At the beginning of the 1990s, the UK was still dumping 8 percent of its hazardous waste at sea. Protests from other EEC countries and from environmentalists mean that this practice is to be phased out. In the USA, incineration is increasingly favoured by industry, but this creates other forms of pollution.

Detailed information on the extent, nature, and origin of industrial pollution is patchy: there are powerful forces at work to ensure that much of it remains unidentified. The 'blighted zones' identified on this map represent the most extreme cases of industrial pollution; literally thousands more zones of local blight scar every industrial country.

Sources for map and commentary:

Bellini, James, *High Tech Holocaust*, San Francisco: Sierra Club Books, 1986; National Wildlife Federation, *The Toxic 500*, 1987, New York: NWF, 1989; press reports; United Nations Environment Programme (UNEP), *Environmental Data Report*, 2nd ed. 1989-90, Oxford: Blackwell, 1989.

26 DEADLY INDUSTRY

This map identifies the major accidents of the past twenty years that have occurred during the manufacture and transport of hazardous industrial products. It does not include accidents that occur in their end-use and application. There are several biases in the data. More is known about accidents in the 'developed' world and, by definition, the focus is on acute events rather than chronic releases (see Map 25). Then there is a general absence of accidents involving weapons factories, military research laboratories and other military installations because of a dearth of information.

Industrial accidents involving the release of hazardous substances are a daily occurrence. But the record-keeping of these releases is entirely inadequate. Only large and spectacular accidents, such as the explosion of gas tanks in Mexico City in 1984, attract international attention, and most smaller-scale accidents do not even attract notice from a national press. In the USA, several quasi-official groups attempt to monitor accidents – the Acute Hazardous Events Data Base (AHE/DB) and the National Response Center of the Department of Transportation among them – but few other countries have systems for tracking industrial accidents.

What we do know about industrial accidents is that they are no accident. They have come to be accepted adjuncts of an industrial culture that, using materials of ever-greater toxicity, is extending its reach around the world.

Sources for map and commentary:

Gittus, J.H., et al, *The Chernobyl Accident and Its Consequences*, London: UKAEA, 1988; Kasperson, Roger, et al, *Corporate Management of Health and Safety Hazards: A Comparison of Current Practice*, Boulder, CO: Westview Press, 1988; Kleindorfer, Paul & Howard Kunreuther, *Insuring and Managing Hazardous Risks: From Seveso to Bhopal and Beyond*, Berlin: Springer, 1987; Lagadec, Patrick, *Major Technological Risk: An Assessment of Industrial Disasters*, Oxford: Pergamon Press, 1982; Organization for Economic Cooperation and Development (OECD), *OECD Environmental Data Compendium, 1989*, Paris: OECD, 1989; press reports, 1988-90; United Nations Environment Programme (UNEP), *Environmental Data Report* 2nd ed. 1989-90, Oxford: Blackwell, 1989.

27 TOXIC TRADE

Industrialized countries produce over 300 million tonnes of hazardous waste each year. These wastes pose a threat to human and animal health and any number of towns and ecosystems around the world have been poisoned by improper disposal of toxins. The dilemma of toxic waste is that there is really no 'proper' or safe way to dispose of it; if dumped in landfills or storage pits, poisons almost inevitably leak out into drinking water and residential areas; if burned, it leaves toxic residue; if dumped at sea (now banned by most countries), it threatens marine mammal and fish life. In lieu of solving the waste problem, many governments and private firms have chosen simply to ship the problem away – out of sight, out of mind. Poor countries are targeted to be recipients of the rich world's industrial waste – they need the revenue that dumping contracts can provide, and they often do not have the resources independently to assess the potential health and pollution effects of the waste they accept.

Between 1986 and 1988, over three million tonnes of waste were known to be shipped from rich to poor countries. This figure represents the tip of the iceberg; much of the trade is illicit or illegal, and its actual extent is difficult to determine. The international waste disposal business is a shady one: in many cases toxic shipments have been illegally dumped on the shores of poor countries; in other cases, governments of Third World countries are deliberately misled about the nature of proposed shipments.

The toxic trade has roused Third World anger – such countries have no interest in being the rich world's dumping ground – and almost 40 countries, mostly in the Third World, have now banned toxic waste shipments.

In addition to the Third World dumping trade, many industrialized countries exchange waste, although the flow of trade still reflects power imbalances between exporters and importers. Canada receives a large share of US toxic waste; East Germany, Hungary and the UK are major repositories for European waste; China accepts waste from the USA and from Europe. This trade may be more consensual than Third World dumping, but it is no less dangerous.

Sources for map and commentary:
Organization for Economic Cooperation and Development (OECD), *OECD Environmental Data Compendium, 1989*, Paris: OECD, 1989; Vallette, Jim, *The International Trade in Wastes: A Greenpeace Inventory*, Washington DC: Greenpeace, 1989.

28 HOLES IN THE SKY

A thin layer of ozone, high in the stratosphere, acts as a shield against harmful solar ultraviolet radiation. A reduction in ozone allows more ultraviolet radiation to reach the earth. This is likely to result in long-term increases in skin cancers and damage to the human immune system. It will also lead to disruption of agriculture, reductions in crop yields, and possible large-scale alterations in a number of ecosystems. Ozone depletion is already a considerable and growing problem; the rate of destruction is so extensive that 'holes' in the ozone layer – varying in size, depending on the time of year - have formed over and close to the polar regions.

Since the mid-1970s, scientists have known that chlorine from synthetic compounds called CFCs (chlorofluorocarbons), and to a lesser extent a number of other chemicals, destroy ozone in the stratosphere. CFCs are entirely artificial compounds – they were developed in the 1930s and since then have been the basis of very powerful and profitable chemical industries. For many years, these industries, as well as governments in CFC-producing countries, dismissed theories of ozone depletion and resisted increasingly urgent calls from the scientific community for curbs in the production of CFCs and other ozone-depleting chemicals. The connection is now accepted, however, and the weight of opinion has finally shifted.

Agreement on the most appropriate and rapid solution is more difficult to achieve. The Montreal Protocol represents a first step. It was first signed in 1987 by 24 countries; by the end of 1989 it had been signed by 48 countries and agreed to in principle by another nine non-ratifying states (although ratification usually follows quickly, it cannot be assumed). Ratifying countries in the industrialized world agree to freeze CFC production at 1986 levels, with allowances for continued growth in the Third World for ten more years. While this agreement is a major step forward, environmentalists consider that it falls far short of what is necessary. The Montreal Protocol does not stop CFC production and ozone depletion – it merely slows down the pace of acceleration.

The US Environmental Protection Agency estimates that each 2.5 percent increase in CFCs causes an additional one million skin cancers, which will result in 20,000 additional deaths over the lifetime of the existing US population. Since the 1960s, CFC production has increased at an average 5 percent per year. In the mid-1980s, worldwide CFC production was over one million tonnes per year. The USA is the world's largest producer (and consumer).; in Europe, the UK is the largest producer. The uses of CFCs vary; in Europe aerosols account for 37 percent of CFC use; in the USA, 39 percent of all CFCs are used in motor vehicle air-conditioning and refrigeration. Globally, aerosols are the largest source of CFC emissions.

Sources for map and commentary:
US Environmental Protection Agency, *Effects of Changes in Stratospheric Ozone and Global Climate*, Washington DC: 1986; Hammit, J., *Product Uses and Market Trends for Potential Ozone-Depleting Substances, 1985-2000*, Santa Monica, CA: Rand Corporation, 1986; ozone hole graphics from the NASA Ozone Trends Panel, 1989, courtesy John Gille, National Center for Atmospheric Research, Boulder, CO; Shea, Cynthia Pollock, 'Protecting the Ozone Layer' in Worldwatch Institute, *State of the World: 1989*, New York: Norton, 1989; United Nations Environment Programme, *The Ozone Layer*, Nairobi: UNEP, 1987.

29 WAR-WASTED LANDS

Despite an encouraging number of ceasefires, peace talks and arms control talks, warfare was still widespread in 1989, affecting nearly a fifth of the world's states. Since 1945, most warfare has taken place in the 'Third World', and most wars raging in the late 1980s were civil wars. There is no universally accepted definition of war. This map includes wars defined politically – armed unrest involving quasi-military structures, as in Northern Ireland – as well as wars defined by high death tolls.

Wars are acutely destructive to the environment. Often, as in Vietnam in the 1960s and 1970s and in Central America in the 1980s, the natural environment is itself a military target. In Nicaragua, the US-backed contras made targets not only of the environment, but of environmentalists. Between 1982 and 1989, contras are known to have killed 30 environmental workers and kidnapped 70 more, forcing the closure of several national parks and halting several water pollution control projects. The largest contiguous area of unspoiled rainforest in Central America is to be found in Guatemala; by the late 1980s, one-third of Guatemala had been sprayed with defoliants as part of the government's anti-insurgency campaign, and also as part of the US-initiated 'war against drugs'. In the Vietnam war, US herbicide teams dumped millions of gallons of herbicides and defoliants (chief among them the now-notorious Agent Orange) over half the forests in the country; more than 50 per cent of the coastal mangrove swamps in the south were destroyed by bombs, defoliants, napalm, and bulldozers, and most will never regenerate. In the Iran-Iraq war, major wetlands were destroyed by bombing, chemical exposure and deliberately-set fires.

Even when the environment is not a designated target, it inevitably suffers. Agricultural areas become unworkable as villages are destroyed, farming families are killed or forced to flee, crops and livestock are seized or destroyed. And as in Afghanistan, large tracts of land are strewn with mines or with unexploded bombs and shells.

The environmental effects of war are rarely documented systematically, and thus this map can only suggest the nature and extent of the problem.

Sources for map and commentary:

Environmental Project on Central America (EPOCA), Green Paper Series, 1985 to present, Earth Island Institute, California; Stockholm International Peace Research Institute (SIPRI), *World Armaments and Disarmament: SIPRI Yearbook*, 1987, 1988, 1989, Oxford, OUP; Sivard, Ruth Leger, *World Military and Social Expenditures 1989*, Washington DC: World Priorities Inc., 1989; Wallensteen, Peter, ed., *States in Armed Conflict 1988*, Uppsala University: Department of Peace and Conflict Research, Report no. 30, July 1989.

30 NUCLEAR BLIGHT

In the late 1980s, the world nuclear weapons stockpile was approximately 50,000 warheads, about 16,000 of which are deployed at sea. Only five states acknowledge possession of nuclear weapons, although Israel and South Africa are also widely believed to be nuclear states. A number of other states allied with the USA and the USSR have nuclear weapons based on their territories, willingly or not. The development, production, storage, transport and deployment of nuclear weapons requires an extensive support network of bases and facilities, each one of which poses a permanent environmental hazard.

Recent revelations in the US media underscore the chronic nuclear pollution and heavy environmental damage caused by military nuclear facilities. Leaks of radioactive materials from the Rocky Flats facility threaten the drinking water supply of Denver; the Fernald materials production plant in Ohio has released more than 300 tonnes of uranium dust into the surrounding air and water; the agricultural land around Hanford, Washington, shows high levels of radiation.

In addition to chronic nuclear pollution, there are dozens of accidents each year involving military storage and transport of nuclear weapons or material. In this map, we focus on the most serious, known, nuclear accidents at sea – in which either nuclear reactors and/or nuclear weapons have been lost. Many more accidents may have happened but been kept secret. There are currently about 50 nuclear weapons and seven nuclear reactors known to be resting on the ocean floor.

There would be even more nuclear material dumped at sea without strong international opposition. As recently as 1989, the British government was proposing to dump its nuclear submarines on the sea-bed once they are obsolete. The US government has officially rejected sea dumping as an option for getting rid of old nuclear military equipment, but the current administration is known to be reconsidering this possibility. France, the UK and the USA oppose a permanent ban on dumping although non-nuclear states are almost universally in favour.

The Pacific Islands have borne the greatest brunt of nuclear might and nuclear blight. Long used as nuclear testing grounds by France, the UK and the USA, whole island chains in the Pacific have been 'vaporised', while others are so radioactive as to be uninhabitable for thousands of years. The populations of many Pacific territories have become nuclear refugees. The Pacific nuclear-free movement, largely a women's movement, is now one of the most active grassroots anti-nuclear campaigns in the world.

Sources for map and commentary:

Arkin, William & Joshua Handler, *Naval Accidents 1945-1988*, Neptune Papers no. 3, Washington DC: Greenpeace/ Institute for Policy Studies, 1989; Arkin, William & Richard W. Fieldhouse, *Nuclear Battlefields*, Cambridge, MA: Ballinger, 1985; Kidron, Michael & Dan Smith, *The War Atlas*, London: Pan; New York: Simon & Schuster, 1983; Radioactive Waste Campaign, *Deadly Defense*, New York: RWC, 1988; Stockholm International Peace Research Institute (SIPRI), *World Armaments and Disarmament: SIPRI Yearbook*, 1968/69, 1974, 1975, 1985, 1989, London: Taylor & Francis; Oxford, OUP.

31 AUTO CULTURE

In much of the world, most people still rely on bicycles, public buses and trains, animal-drawn carts and their own feet for transport. But the global trend is clearly towards automobile-centred transport.

The costs are high. Private automobiles clog the streets of most world cities bringing urban services to a standstill; expanding road networks gobble up scarce space and degrade agricultural land, especially in developments on the outskirts of cities; the fuel demands of private transport deplete fossil fuel resources. Worldwide, at least a third of an average city's land is devoted to roads, parking, and other car-related infrastructures. One of the most serious consequences is that cars play a prominent role in generating virtually all the major air pollutants (see Maps 17 and 23). In OECD countries, for example, 75% of carbon monoxide emissions, 48% of nitrogen oxides and 13% of atmospheric particulates (dirt and dust) are produced by cars and trucks; in the USA, motor vehicles are responsible for about 70% of total carbon monoxide emissions, 40% of nitrogen oxides, and 20% of particulates. Lead pollution, a serious health problem in most cities, is largely attributable to motor vehicle emissions.

The growing emphasis on private car ownership usually comes at the cost of public transport. Governments often assign priority to private motorized travel in traffic planning, budget decisions, and urban design. As the emphasis on private transport increases, funding and planning for public transit declines proportionally. This has the effect of further marginalizing people on the economic and social fringes of society – the poor, the elderly and, especially, women of all classes and ages. Women everywhere in the world are much more dependent on public transport since they are less likely than men to own private automobiles. A survey taken in London in the mid-1980s, for example, established that men drive cars twice as often as women, only a third of British women have a driving licence and 70 percent do not have a car. Automobile ownership both reflects and reinforces social inequities. The social structures that promote and reward car ownership will need to change if we are to be serious about environmental protection.

The global growth in private automobile production and ownership is fueled by automobile manufacturers who have a vested interest in the continuous expansion of their markets. As rich countries become saturated with automobiles, the Third World beckons as the next promising market. Car culture already has a firm grip on the large cities of Mexico, Brazil, and India, and is making strong inroads almost everywhere else in the developing world.

This map includes only information on cars. In some countries, such as China, the number of trucks and buses exceeds the number of cars and these, too, must be considered as major contributors to urban clog and air pollution.

Sources for map and commentary:
Mick Hamer, 'Men have Wheels While Women have Feet', *New Statesman*, May 24, 1985; Stan Luger, 'Stagnant Politics, Dirty Air', *In These Times*, December 13-19, 1989; Motor Vehicle Manufacturers' Association, *World Motor Vehicle Data: 1989*, New York, 1989; Michael Renner, 'Rethinking Transportation', Worldwatch Institute, *State of the World: 1989*, New York: Norton, 1989.

32 TOURIST TRAPS

By the mid-1980s, the global tourism business employed more people than the global oil industry; by the end of this century, tourism will be the world's largest economic activity. Tourism is increasingly the largest single revenue source for poor countries, and most governments actively promote the development of tourist trade. Without tourism, the economies of many of the Caribbean nations, for example, would collapse, as would the economies of many Mediterranean coastal towns.

The ratio of tourists to residents is a guide to the strain which tourists place on their host environment. High rates of tourism can overwhelm water supply, sewage treatment and municipal refuse facilities. St. Maartens, a small island in the Netherlands Antilles, receives the equivalent of its own population in tourists every 10 days. Tourist traffic and its related infrastructure can be a serious threat to fragile environments and often wipes out natural habitats entirely. To serve the tourist trade, many governments have embarked on ambitious programmes of road, airport, and hotel construction, often without serious regard for the environmental consequences of these developments. The wildlife trade, which threatens many rare species (see Map 33) often flourishes with tourism: rare and exotic birds and animals are hunted to sell to tourists – either alive, or as ivory trinkets, tortoise-shell combs, stuffed-toys made of animal fur, brilliantly-coloured corals, and the like.

The figures on tourism, collected by the World Tourism Office, monitor visitor arrivals. These include arrivals by guest workers or multiple border crossings by the same person or family. A few countries, Hungary for example, thereby appear to receive more tourists than they do in reality.

Another niche in the market has been spotted and tourism is now being heralded as a potential force for environmental good. The development of national parks and game reserves in many countries, most noticeably in Costa Rica and a number of African countries, is spurred on by the lure of tourist revenue. But present evidence suggests at best an uneasy coexistence of 'eco-tourism' and environmental protection.

Sources for map and commentary:
Commission of the European Communities, *Quality of Bathing Water: 1987*, Luxembourg: 1989; Enloe, Cynthia, *Bananas, Beaches and Bases: Making Feminist Sense of International Politics*, London: Pandora Press, 1989; World Tourism Organization, *Yearbook of Tourist Statistics: 1988*, Geneva, 1989.

33 WILD TRADE

Statistics on the extent of the traffic in wildlife are, at best, unreliable. An international body, the Convention on International Trade in Endangered Species (CITES) monitors the trade, and imposes restraints on the trade in certain animals designated for protection. Currently, trade is officially banned for about 675 species (identified as 'Appendix I' species), and regulated for at least 27,000 more ('Appendix II' species). CITES figures are the best available, but are known to be underestimates. Although CITES does make estimates of the scope of illegal trade, it is almost impossible to verify these figures; the information presented on this map refers to both legal and illegal trade, although it must be assumed that most illegal trade is not reported. The representation of CITES statistics on this map includes the secondary trade in processed animal products and the re-export traffic – thus some countries are identified as both major exporters and importers of the same animals.

For the two inset maps, on the top 12 ivory and wildcat fur trading countries, we have used total trade by volume, both import and export, for the mid-1980s.

The trade in wildlife is almost entirely a luxury trade: the demand comes from rich countries, the supply from poor countries. The trade rests on a triad of commodification, greed, and desperation. To the brokers in wealthier countries, animals are mere commodities, exotic 'things' to be traded as expensive baubles. It is difficult to interpret the selling of wildlife, often pursued to the brink of extinction, as anything other than a sign of desperation. The closest parallel is perhaps prostitution; in extreme poverty, all the sellers have left to sell is themselves. In many poor countries, wildlife is what there is left to sell.

The traffic in animals is also a male enterprise. It is mostly men who poach the animals in poor countries; or men who organize expensive hunting safaris from rich countries; it is men who act as brokers of the international trade; and it is men who purchase the animals and their by-products: rhinos for aphrodisiacs, for example; or elephants, for ivory-handled daggers.

The traffic in wildlife is big business. The annual legal trade is worth about US$5 billion annually, and illegal trade is estimated at another $2 billion. In one year alone, 1985, the known trade included 43,000 primates, almost 9 million reptile skins, and 720 tonnes of ivory. While animal counts are imprecise, it appears that the trade in wildlife, dead and alive, has reduced the number of snow leopards left in the world to about 500, reduced tiger populations in India from about 40,000 to less than 3000, precipitated a decline in world rhino numbers of 70 percent since 1970, and reduced the herds of African elephants to about 625,000 out of an original population of over two million. It is widely thought that the only hope for preventing extinction of the elephant may be an absolute ban on ivory production and consumption. In 1989, the CITES countries (see pages 90-97) voted to do just this, but some African countries, such as South Africa and Zimbabwe, claim that their managed herds offer greater protection. CITES has been unable to persuade Hong Kong from selling its vast stockpile of imported ivory, though this is known to encourage illegal poaching.

Sources for map and commentary:

IUCN Conservation Monitoring Centre, *Red List of Threatened Animals*, Cambridge: IUCN, 1988; United Nations Environment Programme (UNEP), *UNEP News*, December 1989; World Resources Institute/International Institute for Environment and Development, *World Resources 1988-89*, New York: Basic Books, 1988.

34 HUNTING

Comparatively few human populations meet their food and clothing needs by hunting any more; and among those that do, their subsistence hunting leaves relatively little mark on the ecosystem. This map focuses on recreational hunting, whether for 'sport' alone or to supply the luxury trade in wildlife (see Map 33).

The primary source of information on animal extinctions is the IUCN's *Red List of Threatened Animals* which is published every two years. Species extinctions are often caused by a number of stress factors, such as habitat loss combined with over-hunting. The species identified on this map are those for whom the primary threat appears to be luxury or sport hunting.

Recreational hunters often defend their sport by saying that it is a celebration of nature, but the record speaks otherwise. Around the world recreational hunting has pushed hundreds of species to the brink of extinction and, over recent history, hundreds more have been hunted out of existence. Some species, shown on the map as endangered, are virtually extinct already. For example, by 1990 over much of eastern Africa, there were only 55 remaining Java rhino, about 800 Kemp's ridley turtles and fewer than a thousand black rhinos.

Despite repeated calls by the international community for an end to whaling, five countries still hunt whales. Whaling is conducted by these countries under the pretext of 'gathering scientific information' on whale populations, but in fact whaling is still the basis of a small but thriving commercial enterprise.

Hunting is big business. Apart from the fantastic sums of money sometimes paid for trophy hunting of rare animals (or merely parts, such as gorilla's paw or rhino horn), the ordinary business of hunting generates considerable revenues. Hunters in the USA spend around US$16 billion a year on fees and equipment. In poorer countries, hunting is often a major source of external revenue earned from rich foreigners. In 1983, Zimbabwe for example, earned US$6.2 million in fees and licenses from hunting for sport. Yet given the damage they do and the revenue that is generated, surprisingly few people hunt: in the USA, 7%; in Western Europe, 2%, in the USSR, 1%. Everywhere hunting is primarily a men's activity, and may often be construed as a rite of passage into manhood.

Sources for map and commentary:

Burton, J.A. and B. Pearson, *Rare Mammals of the World*, New York: Collins, 1987; Fitter, R., *Wildlife for Man*, New York: Collins, 1986; Inskipp, T. & S. Wells, *International Trade in Wildlife*, London: Earthscan, 1979; IUCN Conservation Monitoring Centre, *Red List of Threatened Animals*, Cambridge: IUCN, 1988; Organization for Economic Cooperation and Development (OECD), *OECD Environmental Data Compendium, 1989*, Paris: OECD, 1989; World Resources Institute/International Institute for Environment and Development, *World Resources 1988-89*, New York: Basic Books, 1988.

35 THE TIMBER TRADE

The tropical forests of the world are rich in highly-prized, 'luxury' woods such as teak, mahogany and balsa, among dozens of others. Extracting this timber is a high- profit, fast-moving big business. Most commercial logging operations in the tropics are monopolized by a handful of multinational timber conglomerates based in France, West Germany, the UK and Japan. They follow in the footsteps of the colonial traders in tropical timber, and in many ways replicate patterns of colonial exploitation – marked by utter disregard for the environment of Third World countries, perceived primarily as suppliers of raw materials to meet the 'refined tastes of the 'developed' world.

Uncontrolled logging has left many tropical forests in critical condition. Deforestation has already become a major problem in some of the earliest centres of commercial logging. Thailand, for example, once a major exporter, became a net importer of wood in 1980. Nigeria is virtually logged out. Many forests in Southeast Asia and West Africa are in a critical condition. Of the 56 timber-exporting countries, 23 are now net importers.

Timber is a valuable commodity of wide commercial interest - so valuable that the statistics are considered to be privileged commercial intelligence and are not widely available to the public. Independent environmental groups, particularly the UK-based Friends of the Earth, appear to have the most comprehensive accessible data on both the timber trade and the state of tropical forests. The International Tropical Timber Organization, formed in 1987 and based in Japan, is currently the only international body with oversight of the timber trade, but this organization's close ties with industry make suspect its effectiveness as an independent monitoring agency.

Sources for map and commentary:

Myers, Norman & Richard A. Houghton, *Deforestation Rates in Tropical Forests, and Their Climatic Implications*, London: Friends of the Earth, 1989; Nectoux, F. & Nigel Dudley, *The Hardwood Story*, London: Friends of the Earth / WWF 1987.

36 PAYING THE PRICE

In the course of an ordinary day, which many us live in a fog of pollution, we encounter a barrage of harmful chemicals, most of them invisible and many of them unknown – in our workplaces, on the streets, in our food and in our homes. In much of the world, air and water quality are, at best, suspect. That environmental derangement on this scale brings with it severe health repercussions cannot be doubted. As environmental damage escalates, so, too, will problems of health. However, specific and definitive links are often difficult to establish. As yet, only a few environmental problems are known to have identifiable health consequences - such as the depletion of the ozone layer (see Map 28) causing rising rates of skin cancer. However, the hazards of urban living are clearly illustrated by increased lead levels found in the blood of most inhabitants of most large cities.

Exposure to carcinogenic chemicals and low-level radiation are the two principal causes of cancer and there has been little action to limit either. It is thus not surprising that, worldwide, cancer rates are rising – the World Health Organization reports six milion new cancer cases each year.

Lung cancer, the most common cancer in the developed world, is known to be caused by a number of factors, including occupational hazards and chemical exposures, but its primary cause is smoking. Tobacco fuels an extremely profitable and commercially aggressive industry. As rates of smoking decline in many industrial countries, tobacco firms are now exerting heavy pressure on Third World consumers, especially women, to take up smoking. Trends in lung cancer follow trends in smoking habits. As the lifestyles and environmental problems of the industrial world spread around the globe, so does lung cancer.

The increasing use of tobacco in many parts of the world has important implications for the environment. As a lucrative cash crop, tobacco is replacing traditional and subsistence crops in many Third World countries. Tobacco depletes soil nutrients and encourages heavy use of fertilizers and herbicides. Further, the World Health Organization estimates that one tree in six is cut for use in curing tobacco.

Health statistics are fairly complete for the industrial world, and unavailable or inconsistently available for most of the rest of the world. In any case, internationally available health statistics are not presented in conjunction with any discussion or evidence of contributing causes. Environmental causality, which must be superimposed on the raw health data, is usually best illustrated on the level of very specific and very closely-analysed case studies, not on a national or global level.

Sources for map and commentary:

Vahter, Marie, *Assessment of Human Exposure to Lead and Cadmium through Biological Monitoring*, Stockholm: UNEP, 1982; World Health Organization (WHO), *World Health Statistics*, 1988.

37 A CLASH OF INTERESTS

The global environment is a commons, shared by all countries. Increasingly, countries also share in its deterioration. Most pollution and degradation of the environment cannot be contained within national borders. Acid rain from the rest of Europe is devastating Sweden's forests and lakes; water diversion plans for irrigation in Ethiopia will diminish Egypt's water supplies; deforestation in Nepal, China, Bhutan and India has increased the frequency and extent of destructive flooding in Bangladesh. An estimated 40 percent of the world's population depends, for drinking water, irrigation or hydro power, on major river systems shared by two or more countries; in some cases, waterways are shared by as many as five or more countries.

In most cases, this share-out of environmental problems is inevitable. Occasionally, though, governments and private industries take active measures to 'ship' their pollution abroad. They may build smokestacks tall enough to disperse airborne pollutants, for example, or export unwanted and hazardous waste to poorer countries.

Increasingly, relations between governments are mediated by environmental issues. As certain resources are diminished and transboundary pollution increases, the environment is moving closer to the centre of international relations. Similarly, as individuals become more informed about environmental issues, national governments are judged on the efficacy of their environmental programmes. 'Green consciousness' poses a challenge to traditional notions of national sovereignty and international diplomacy, and to established forms of governance.

Sources for map and commentary:

Press reports; Renner, Michael, *National Security: The Economic and Environmental Dimensions*, Washington DC: Worldwatch Paper no. 89, May 1989.

INDEX

Acid rain, 62-63; 115-116
disputes over, 88-89

Agriculture, 30-31; 104; 106
chemicals, 32-33; 104-105
soil suitability, 30-31; 36-37
water use, 26-27

Air quality, 48-49; 110

Amazon Basin
dam construction, 54-55
rainforest loss, 24-25

Animals *see* Wildlife

Automobiles *see* Cars

Beaches, 78-79

Birds
extinction threats, 20-21; 100
hunting, 82-83, 100
trade in, 80-81
wetlands loss, 42-43

Cancer
lung cancer rates, 86-87; 124
carcinogen releases, 64-65

Carbon dioxide
emission levels, 60-61, 115
global warming, 16-17; 99

Cars
pollution caused by, 48-49; 120
manufacturers, 76-77
number of, 76-77; 90-98 (table); 120

Central America
environmental destruction from war, 72-73

CFCs (chlorofluorocarbons)
and greenhouse effect, 16-17
consumption, 70-71
ozone depletion, 70-71; 118

C.I.T.E.S., 90-98 (table)

Cities, 40-41; 107
air quality, 48-49
lead levels in blood of residents, 86-87

Coal
share of global energy, 50-51

Dams, 54-55; 113

Deforestation, 24-25; 84-85; 104

Desertification, 36-37; 106

Dirt and dust, 48-49

Driftnet fishing, 38-39
disputes over, 88-89

Drinking water *see* Water quality

Drought, 28-29

Endangered species
regulation of, *see* C.I.T.E.S.
see also Extinctions

Electricity
nuclear power, 52-53
hydro power, 54-55

Energy
consumption, 50-51; 110-111
pollution, 60-61
sources of, 50-51
see also Firewood; Hydro power; Nuclear power; Oil

Erosion, 36-37; 106

Extinctions
caused by hunting, 82-83; 122
of animals, 20-21; 100
of birds, 20-21; 100
of plants, 22-23; 101

Famine, 28-29

Fertilizers
artificial, 32-33; 104-105

Firewood, 56-57; 113
share of global energy, 50-51

Fish
supplies, 38-39; 106-107

Fishing
environmental disputes, 88-89
major fishing grounds, 38-39

Food
availability, 28-29; 103
fish supplies, 38-39
genetic resources, 34-35; 101; 105
major crops, 34-35
see also Agriculture

Forests
acid rain damage, 62-63
and environmental disputes, 88-89
rainforest loss, 24-25; 101-102
timber trade, 84-85; 123

Fossil fuels, 60-61; 115

Friends of the Earth
worldwide offices, 90-98 (table)

Fuelwood *see* Firewood

Fur trade, 80-81

Genetic engineering, 34-35; 105-106

Genetic resources, 34-35, 105-106

Global warming, 16-17; 99
and fossil fuels, 60-61

Green parties, 90-98 (table)

Greenhouse effect, 16-17; 99

Greenhouse gases, 16-17; 99

Greenpeace
worldwide offices, 90-98 (table)

Habitat loss, 24-25
wetlands, 42-43

Health, 86-87; 123-124
uninhabitable zones, 64-65
waterborne diseases, 26-27

Hunger *see* Food

Hunting, 82-83; 100

Hydro power, 54-55; 113
shares of global energy, 50-51

Industry
CFC production, 70-71
industrial accidents, 58-59; 66-67; 105; 114; 117
industrial waste, 64-65
water use, 26-27
see also Cars; Oil

Ivory trade, 80-81; 122

Land
agricultural, 30-31; 36-37; 106
erosion, 36-37; 106
Mexico City, 40-41

Logging *see* Forests; Deforestation

Mammals *see* Wildlife

Mangrove wetlands *see* Wetlands

Men
and hunting, 100, 122
and the wildlife trade, 121-122

Mexico City, 40-41

Militaries
and environmental disputes, 88-89
see also Central America; Nuclear issues; Wars

Montreal Protocol, 70-71; 90-98 (table)

Nepal
tourism in, 78-79

Nitrogen oxides
air pollution, 48-49

Nuclear issues
nuclear power, 50-51; 111-112
disputes over, 88-89
nuclear fuel cycle, 52-53
military accidents, 74-75; 119-120
military/civilian link, 111-112
military facilities, 74-75; 119-120
share of global energy, 50-51
nuclear testing, 74-75
nuclear waste, 112
nuclear weapons, 74-75

Oceans
environmental disputes, 88-89
fishing grounds, 38-39
industrial waste dumping, 64-65
oil pollution, 58-59; 114
sea-level rise, 16-17; 99
sewage dumping, 46-47

Oil
pollution, 58-59; 114
share of global energy, 50-51

Ozone depletion, 70-71; 118

Pesticides, 32-33; 104-105

Plants
number of species, 22-23
extinction threats, 22-23; 101

Plastics
in waste stream, 108

Pollution
disputes over, 88-89
from agricultural chemicals, 104
from fossil fuels, 60-61; 115
from industry, 64-65
from oil, 58-59
from sewage, 46-47
of air, 48-49, 110
of beaches, 78-79
of fishing grounds, 38-39
of wetlands, 42-43

Populations
and environmental pressures, 99-100
growth rates, 18-19
projected, 18-19
size of, 18-19
urban, 40-41

Protected areas, 90-98 (table)

Protests, 88-89

Rainforests *see* Forests

Recycling, 44-45

Relocations of people, 54-55; 113

Reptiles
hunting, 82-83
skins, 80-81

Sewage, 46-47; 109

Smoking, 86-87; 124

Soil loss, 36-37; 106

Sulphur dioxide
acid rain, 62-63
air pollution, 48-49
emissions, 60-61

Timber trade, 84-85; 123

Tourism, 78-79; 121

Toxic chemicals
releases, 64-65

Toxic waste
exports, 68-69; 117-118

Tropical rainforests *see* Forests

Uranium, 52-53

Urban issues
air quality, 48-49
lead levels in blood of city residents, 86-87
migrants, 107
population, 40-41

War, 28-29; 72-73; 119

Waste
exports of, 68-69; 117-118
household, 44-45; 108-109
industrial waste, 64-65; 116
ocean dumping, 46-47; 64-65
sewage, 46-47

Water quality
beach pollution, 78-79
drinking water, 26-27; 102
sewage pollution, 46-47; 109

Water supply, 26-27; 102
disputes over, 88-89

Water use, 26-27; 102-103

Wetlands, 42-43; 108

Whales, 82-83; 122-123

Wildlife
extinctions, 20-21; 82-83
habitat loss, 24-25
hunting, 82-83; 122-123
number of species, 20-21
and tourism, 121
trade in, 80-81; 122
see also Wetlands; Birds

Women
as collectors of firewood, 86-87
as urban migrants, 107
and transport, 120

Worldwide Fund for Nature (WWF), 90-98 (table)

Other Pluto Projects available from Touchstone Books

WOMEN IN THE WORLD: AN INTERNATIONAL ATLAS

by Joni Seager and Ann Olson

With vivid maps and graphs, the global status of women is detailed in economic, political, social, and educational terms—an indispensable reference source for all those concerned with women's issues.

0-671-63070-9, paper, $12.95

*"**WOMEN IN THE WORLD: AN INTERNATIONAL ATLAS** is wonderful! It focuses on the right areas, asks the right questions, and the answers to those questions are instantly available because of the format."*

—Marilyn French

THE NEW STATE OF THE WORLD ATLAS

by Michael Kidron and Ronald Segal

An up-to-date view of a constantly changing, often confusing world. This, the first Pluto Project, has sold more than 400,000 copies and been published in 13 languages. The third edition was published in 1987. The fourth edition, comprehensively revised, will appear in 1991.

Third edition 0-671-64555-2, paper, $13.95

"... an essential book for personal and reference libraries."

—New Internationalist

"... belongs in every school and Oval office."

—The New York Times

Coming from Touchstone Books in spring 1991:

THE NEW WAR AND PEACE ATLAS

by Michael Kidron and Dan Smith

A graphic depiction of war—its consequences and the preparations for it—and of outbreaks of peace, both stable and tenuous.

First published as **The War Atlas**, the updated second edition will be published in Spring 1991.

First edition 0-671-47253-4, paper, $9.95

*"**THE WAR ATLAS** deserves this year's Nobel prize for data presentation ... this book comes with a flavor of originality hard to find in publishing today."*

—The New Scientist

Simon and Schuster/Touchstone, Simon & Schuster Building,
1230 Avenue of the Americas, New York, NY 10020.